Palgrave Macmillan Studies in Banking and Financial Institutions

Series Editor: **Professor Philip Molyneux**

The Palgrave Macmillan Studies in Banking and Financial Institutions are international in orientation and include studies of banking within particular countries or regions, and studies of particular themes such as Corporate Banking, Risk Management, Mergers, and Acquisitions, etc. The books' focus is on research and practice, and they include up-to-date and innovative studies on contemporary topics in banking that will have global impact and influence.

Titles include:

Steffen E. Andersen
THE EVOLUTION OF NORDIC FINANCE

Seth Apati
THE NIGERIAN BANKING SECTOR REFORMS
Power and Politics

Caner Bakir
BANK BEHAVIOUR AND RESILIENCE
The Effect of Structures, Institutions and Agents

Dimitris N. Chorafas
BASEL III, THE DEVIL AND GLOBAL BANKING

Dimitris N. Chorafas
SOVEREIGN DEBT CRISIS
The New Normal and the Newly Poor

Stefano Cosma and Elisabetta Gualandri (*editors*)
THE ITALIAN BANKING SYSTEM
Impact of the Crisis and Future Perspectives

Violaine Cousin
BANKING IN CHINA

Peter Falush and Robert L. Carter OBE
THE BRITISH INSURANCE INDUSTRY SINCE 1900
The Era of Transformation

Juan Fernández de Guevara Radoselovics and José Pastor Monsálvez (*editors*)
CRISIS, RISK AND STABILITY IN FINANCIAL MARKETS

Juan Fernández de Guevara Radoselovics and José Pastor Monsálvez (*editors*)
MODERN BANK BEHAVIOUR

Franco Fiordelisi and Ornella Ricci (*editors*)
BANCASSURANCE IN EUROPE
Past, Present and Future

Franco Fiordelisi, Philip Molyneux and Daniele Previati (*editors*)
NEW ISSUES IN FINANCIAL AND CREDIT MARKETS

Franco Fiordelisi, Philip Molyneux and Daniele Previati (*editors*)
NEW ISSUES IN FINANCIAL INSTITUTIONS MANAGEMENT

Kim Hawtrey
AFFORDABLE HOUSING FINANCE

Jill M. Hendrickson
FINANCIAL CRISIS
The United States in the Early Twenty-First Century

Jill M. Hendrickson
REGULATION AND INSTABILITY IN U.S. COMMERCIAL BANKING
A History of Crises

Paola Leone and Gianfranco A. Vento (*editors*)
CREDIT GUARANTEE INSTITUTIONS AND SME FINANCE

Caterina Lucarelli and Gianni Brighetti (*editors*)
RISK TOLERANCE IN FINANCIAL DECISION MAKING

Roman Matousek (*editor*)
MONEY, BANKING AND FINANCIAL MARKETS IN CENTRAL AND EASTERN EUROPE
20 Years of Transition

Gianluca Mattarocci and Alessandro Carretta (*editors*)
ASSET PRICING, REAL ESTATE AND PUBLIC FINANCE OVER THE CRISIS.

Philip Molyneux (*editor*)
BANK PERFORMANCE, RISK AND FIRM FINANCING

Philip Molyneux (*editor*)
BANK STRATEGY, GOVERNANCE AND RATINGS

Imad A. Moosa
THE MYTH OF TOO BIG TO FAIL

Simon Mouatt and Carl Adams (*editors*)
CORPORATE AND SOCIAL TRANSFORMATION OF MONEY AND BANKING
Breaking the Serfdom

Victor Murinde (*editor*)
BANK REGULATORY REFORMS IN AFRICA

Bernardo Nicoletti
CLOUD COMPUTING IN FINANCIAL SERVICES

Anders Ögren (*editor*)
THE SWEDISH FINANCIAL REVOLUTION

Özlem Olgu
EUROPEAN BANKING
Enlargement, Structural Changes and Recent Developments

Fotios Pasiouras
GREEK BANKING
From the Pre-Euro Reforms to the Financial Crisis and Beyond

Daniela Pîrvu
CORPORATE INCOME TAX HARMONIZATION IN THE EUROPEAN UNION

Ramkishen S. Rajan
EMERGING ASIA
Essays on Crises, Capital Flows, FDI and Exchange Rate

Allesandro Roselli
FINANCIAL STRUCTURES AND REGULATION: A COMPARISON OF CRISES IN THE
UK, USA AND ITALY

Yasushi Suzuki
JAPAN'S FINANCIAL SLUMP
Collapse of the Monitoring System under Institutional and Transition Failures

Ruth Wandhöfer
EU PAYMENTS INTEGRATION
The Tale of SEPA, PSD and Other Milestones Along the Road

The full list of titles available is on the website:
www.palgrave.com/finance/sbfi.asp

Palgrave Macmillan Studies in Banking and Financial Institutions
Series Standing Order ISBN 978–1–4039–4872–4

You can receive future titles in this series as they are published by placing a standing order.
Please contact your bookseller or, in case of difficulty, write to us at the address below with your
name and address, the title of the series and the ISBN quoted above.

Customer Services Department, Macmillan Distribution Ltd, Houndmills, Basingstoke,
Hampshire RG21 6XS, England

Cloud Computing in Financial Services

Bernardo Nicoletti
University of Rome 'Tor Vergata', Italy

First published 2013 by
PALGRAVE MACMILLAN

Palgrave Macmillan in the UK is an imprint of Macmillan Publishers Limited,
registered in England, company number 785998, of Houndmills, Basingstoke,
Hampshire RG21 6XS.

Palgrave Macmillan in the US is a division of St Martin's Press LLC,
175 Fifth Avenue, New York, NY 10010.

Palgrave Macmillan is the global academic imprint of the above companies
and has companies and representatives throughout the world.

Palgrave® and Macmillan® are registered trademarks in the United States,
the United Kingdom, Europe and other countries

ISBN: 978–1–137–27363–5

This book is printed on paper suitable for recycling and made from fully
managed and sustained forest sources. Logging, pulping and manufacturing
processes are expected to conform to the environmental regulations of the
country of origin.

A catalogue record for this book is available from the British Library.

A catalog record for this book is available from the Library of Congress.

10 9 8 7 6 5 4 3 2 1
22 21 20 19 18 17 16 15 14 13

Printed and bound in the United States of America

Contents

List of Illustrations

Figures

Tables

Foreword

Financial institutions need to take important decisions in order to provide value for their customers. Simplification will be important and technology will play its part in reviewing both the banking model and the way that banking is conducted. *Cloud Computing in Financial Services* is a welcome contribution to the current literature in a situation where information is very often distributed by vendors, and rarely with a systems approach. My views on the cloud, as the author well knows, are provocative. One of my basic questions is: are we talking about a cloud or a fog?

According to predictions by the IT company Gartner, cloud computing is one of the aspects most relevant for information and communications technology (ICT) in the near future. This is certainly true, but only if we consider the cloud in broader terms than the merely technological. As we know, for decades a number of organizations have outsourced part or all of their ICT. Cloud computing is based on traditional as well as new technologies. It certainly requires technology as a base – but it is not only technological in its focus. For me the real cloud is the cloud of services.

If you take this view, cloud computing can certainly help in terms of increasing efficiency. It could do much more. If it were only a matter of efficiency, there are situations where the cloud would be of limited application. Take the case of the banking group where I work, Gruppo Intesa Sanpaolo, which services roughly 30 different legal entities from its data centres. With such a huge volume of transactions, we have obtained improvements in efficiency thanks to the steps we have taken, including server consolidation, virtualization and the creation of a catalogue of services.

Beyond efficiency, cloud computing can support financial services in a much more interesting way. A bank is essentially a network and thus has the ability to provide integrated services. What is interesting is this potential combination of infrastructure (be it domestic or international) and the supply of services.

Certainly, the technology behind the cloud is still evolving, and it is essential to take into account at least two factors: data protection and security. The latter is particularly important, as we well know. The private cloud offers security in this respect. We can expect that a sectorial cloud with vertical applications might be of interest in the near future.

The cloud can also support organizational change. At Gruppo Intesa Sanpaolo we have created two new units, the first dedicated to operations and the second to innovation. The former should create economies which will be re-invested in the latter, creating new business models for more interesting customer sectors, innovative products in areas such as payments systems and consumer credit, and creative ways of integrating small and medium size enterprises and corporate banking. The main task of the unit is to create a network with suppliers, partners, universities and other institutions, which will have competences aimed at creating and implementing knowledge.

In all of these activities, the bank will be connected with the rest of the country and with systems and organizations elsewhere in Europe. Moreover, in uncertain times, it is essential to be as flexible as possible. The cloud potentially represents flexibility and variable costs. All of these aspects are discussed and exemplified in this book.

Pier Luigi Curcuruto
Direttore Generale, Intesa Sanpaolo Group Services

Acknowledgements

This volume has gone through a long process. It summarizes my working experience, reading and thinking over a long period. In a similar fashion to any project, it could not have been completed without the contribution of many people. In particular, I thank Steven Lanzi, who worked with me on a thesis on this subject. He helped me systematize my experiences and thoughts. Some sections of the book originated in this thesis. Thanks go to Professors Gustavo Piga and Corrado Cerruti at "Tor Vergata" in Rome, and all the people I have worked with or interviewed during my activities as a professor and business consultant. They contributed to the development of the project with their knowledge and experience. Special thanks go to Pier Luigi Curcuruto, who wrote the Foreword.

Lastly, I wish to thank my family, who suffered from my absence during the long hours spent in front of my computer, in addition to my daily ordinary working duties, in order to synthesize and summarize my experiences. This book has been written with the aim of encouraging the use of cloud computing in financial services so that as many organizations as possible can benefit from it.

List of Abbreviations

ABI	Associazione Bancaria Italiana
AICPA	American Institute of Certified Public Accountants
AWS	Amazon Web Services
B2B	Business to Business
BI	business intelligence
BIAN	Banking Industry Architecture Network
BPaaS	Business Process as a Service
BPM	Business Process Management
BPO	Business Process Outsourcing or also Business Process Optimization
BPR	Business Process Re-engineering
BSC	Balanced Score Card
CaaS	Cloud as a Service
CAAT	Computer-Assisted Audit Techniques
Capex	Capital Expenditure
CCTV	Closed Circuit Television
CIPA	Convenzione Interbancaria per i Problemi dell'Automazione
Cloud Arcs	Cloud Architectures
CM	Configuration Management
COBIT	Control Objectives for Information and related Technology
CRM	Customer Relationship Management
CSA	Cloud Service Architecture or Cloud Security Alliance
DaaS	Data as a Service
EC2	Elastic Compute Cloud
ECM	Enterprise Content Management
EMEA	Europe, Middle East, and Africa
ERP	Enterprise Resource Planning
ETS	European Treaty Series
EU	European Union
FedRAMP	Federal Risk and Authorization Management Program
FISMA	The Federal Information Security Management Act
FY	Fiscal Year
GDP	Gross Domestic Product
GL	General Ledger
HR	Human Resources
IaaS	Infrastructure as a Service
ICT	Information and Telecommunication Technology
IP	Internet Protocol

IPO	Initial Public Offering
IPsec	Internet Protocol Security
ISO	International Standard Organization
ITIL	Information Technology Infrastructure Library
ITSM	ICT Service Management
KPI	Key Performance (or Process) Indicators
KPO	Knowledge Process Outsourcing
KRI	Key Risk Indicators
KYC	Know Your Customer
MIPS	Microprocessor without Interlocked Pipeline Stages
MSA	Master Service Agreement
NIST	National Institute of Standards and Technology
Opex	Operating Expenditures
OS	Operating System
OTP	One-Time Password
PaaS	Platform as a Service
PC	Personal Computer
PDCA	Plan-Do-Check-Act
PIN	Personal Identification Number
POC	Proof of Concept
PSD	Payment Service Directive
QoS	Quality of Service
RAD	Rapid Application Development
RMD	Risk Management Department
ROI	Return on Investment
RSS	Simple Syndication
SaaS	Software as a Service
SDLC	System Development Life Cycle
SLA	Service Level Agreement
SME	Small- and Medium-Size Enterprises
SOA	Service-Oriented Architecture
SOX	Sarbanes Oxley Act
SSAE	Statements on Standards for Attestation Engagements
STP	Straight-Through Processing
SWIFT	Society for Worldwide Interbank Financial Telecommunications
TP	Transaction Processing
UCC	Unified Collaboration and Communication
UK	United Kingdom
US	United States of America
VM	Virtual Machine
VoIP	Voice over IP
VPC	Virtual Private Cloud
WAN	Wide Area Network

Introduction

The world is in the middle of a financial crisis. It started in 2008 – but when it will end is still unclear. Financial institutions need to dramatically improve the financial ratios in their equity, but on the other hand they need to take decisive actions to improve their position in the market. They must become better at coping with the dynamics of the markets and the changing socio-economic factors, which implies increasing their revenues and reducing their investments and costs.

There is only one way for them to progress in this direction: to become more agile. This means becoming leaner and using more digitization. Methods and technology are powerful aids for them to achieve this if used in the right way.

Information and Communication Technology (ICT) plays an important role as a strategic lever for innovation and improvement, and an example of this is the emergence of an organizational model of "virtual banks" and "virtual insurances". In this model, technologies become predominant in the organization. They can support innovation in products, services, and ways to relate to markets.

The impact of the financial turmoil on ICT has been immediate and widespread. The result has been a general reduction in investment and, above all, a clear change in the priorities and needs that ICT has to support.

For a business to recover its profitability, ICT needs to support its processes of change and streamlining. On the other hand, the ICT departments are increasingly hard pressed by the conflicting demands of cost reduction set against the requirement for an improved proactiveness and more rapid response times to the demands of the business.

Cloud computing is one of the most interesting ways to cope with these challenges, and the interest in it is growing. Many events have addressed this subject, and many vendors have made announcements to support cloud computing for the business world and for governments. These parties are increasingly turning to this new paradigm in order to find new solutions for improving their mission.

The most currently prominent, theoretical and accepted definition of cloud computing is provided by the National Institute of Standards and Technology (NIST), the American Standards Body[1]:

> Cloud computing is a model for enabling ubiquitous, convenient, on-demand network access to a shared pool of configurable computing resources (for instance, networks, servers, storage, applications, and services) that can be rapidly provisioned and released with minimal management effort or service vendor interaction[2].

This definition underlines the fact that cloud computing is not merely a technology; it is a model to support the transformation of organizations. In this respect, people should talk about cloud services or the cloud model. This book analyzes the implications and the applications of cloud services to the world of financial institutions, with precisely this view in mind. It starts by analyzing the development of financial institutions, and later it explores in depth the model of cloud computing and its status. Its most important contribution is the analysis of the future developments and the possible use of the model of cloud services to help innovation in financial institutions in domestic, and potentially global, markets.

Cloud services can change the paradigm of the financial institutions. The word "bank" comes from the Italian word *banco*, indicating the desk on which the 14th-century Italian institutions started to do business by lending money and collecting deposits. Our thesis is that the new banco, the new desk, is the cloud, so the 21st-century financial institutions will have to use the cloud computing model to achieve the necessary transformation to this new paradigm. In the following pages, we describe in detail what cloud services can do in terms of introduction of new products/services and the re-engineering of processes in financial institutions.

This book aims to help promote an understanding of the concrete benefits for the financial institutions when adopting the cloud computing model, also of the remediation of possible risks, and relationships with vendors.

This book provides evidence in support of the following thesis:

- Financial institutions must become more agile and flexible in the conduct of their business in order to increase revenues and decrease investments and costs. The adoption of new paradigms, ICT infrastructural framework and models based on cloud computing, can lead to the achievement of specific objectives: investment savings, cost efficiency and control but especially increased pace of innovation and business agility.

This book moves from the vision of the future financial institutions to a possible strategy. We leave to the practitioners the next steps: to select the way to progress in a specific institution and define a plan to achieve it. The method defined as "Lean and Digitize"[3] can help in this direction.

Primary and Secondary data were collected to support the thesis.

Quantitative and qualitative research methods were employed in order to gather the necessary data and information to achieve the overall aim of the book. They were selected based on the objectives of the study.

Primary data was collected by means of different data-gathering tools:

- Electronic Survey: a quantitative research method was launched under the sponsorship of the Master in Procurement at the University of Rome Tor Vergata, along with the research company Everest. Questionnaires were submitted via email to the company offices, mostly the ICT departments, of the financial institutions. At the same time, we contacted the companies directly by phone and email for soliciting responses to the questionnaires;
- Financial institution documentation: Some financial institutions provided documents relating to their first-hand experiences of cloud services; and
- Phone interviews and personal conversations.

Secondary data was collected in two ways:

- A literature review, in order to build the theoretical framework of the study. The web was the primary source due to the poor existing literature on the subject of cloud computing; and
- Notes and material collected at events, conferences, and meetings with other experts and practitioners on the subject.

The book is organized in chapters covering the relevant topics:

- Chapter 1 presents the current transformation and challenges of financial institutions and the support provided by ICT;
- Chapter 2 defines the model of cloud computing and its characteristics;
- Chapter 3 discusses how financial institutions use cloud computing now;
- Chapter 4 explores in depth the way to govern the use of cloud computing and the vendors;
- Chapter 5 shows how cloud computing can help in a disruptive innovation[4] of services and processes in financial institutions; and
- Chapter 6 presents the case of Gruppo Banca Intesa Sanpaolo moving to a private cloud.

This volume also includes:

- A list of abbreviations;
- A glossary of the most important definitions;

- A bibliography; and
- A sitography indicating some interesting websites and blogs related to cloud computing.

We recommend a sequential reading of all the chapters of this book. An equally valid option, however, is to start with Chapter 2 for an overview of the model and then read the chapters closer to your specific interests.

1
Financial Institutions and Information and Communication Technology

1.1 Introduction

This chapter examines the fundamental transformation of financial institutions in recent decades and points out the changes in the norms, regulations, and organizations. The last part of the chapter addresses the ways in which Information and Telecommunication Technology (ICT) can support this transformation.

1.2 Financial institutions

1.2.1 Classification of financial institutions

Financial institutions are private or public organizations that act as a channel between savers and borrowers of funds. These institutions focus on dealing with financial transactions, such as investments, loans, deposits, and insurance. Financial institutions include organizations such as banks, trusts, insurance companies, and investment dealers. Anything from depositing money to taking out loans and exchanging currencies is normally done through financial institutions. In the context of the modern financial services system, finance is "the science of funds management." Hence, the main role of financial institutions is to act as financial intermediaries. Financial institutions fulfill the task of collecting and channeling funds from those who have surplus, the fund providers, to those who do not have enough means to undertake their economic or personal activities, the users of funds[1].

There are three major types of financial institution[2]:

1. Deposit-taking institutions, which accept and manage deposits and provide credit. These institutions include banks, building societies, credit unions, trust companies and mortgage, and credit companies;

2. Insurance companies and pension funds, which help to protect individuals and companies by providing an insurance policy against any adverse events. They are divided into Life and Annuity Insurance and Non-Life Insurance; and
3. Brokers, promoters, underwriters, and investment funds.

This diversity has arisen as a result of historical reasons, market demands, and the continuous striving of financial institutions to supply services they perceive as desired or marketable.

The most widespread type of financial institution is known as a bank. This term encompasses a broad spectrum of institutions and services, some of which might be far from the original concept and purpose for which they were established in the first place[3]. A short classification of the set of business activities operated by financial institutions is the following[4]:

- Retail banking: deals directly with individuals and Small- and Medium-Size Enterprises (SME). This category includes the following types of banks: Retail banks, Community banks, Community development banks, Credit Unions, Postal Saving banks, Savings banks, Ethical banks, Direct or Online only banks. Typical products are current accounts and savings, cards, and consumer loans.
- Commercial and Business banking: provides services to larger domestic and multinational commercial clients. They support payments and cash management, trade services, and liquidity management. A slight variation is corporate banking. It is directed at very large business entities;
- Investment banking: provides funding to corporations, to other financial institutions, and public and local administrations via capital markets. Additional offerings include trading and investment services;
- Private banking: has as its main customers high net worth individuals and families, supporting them with wealth management. Typical products are portfolio management and investment services as well as financial planning and advice;
- Islamic banking: is different since its banking activities do not include interest, as the Islamic religion does not permit this type of charge. These banks earn profits (mark-up) and fees from the financial services that they charge to their customers along the course of their relationship;
- Conglomerates or universal banks (as in the traditional continental European model): are firms active in more than one sector of banking;
- Financial services: are normally corporate entities that provide credit and insurance services; and
- Central banks: are banks that issue money and have some governance, regulatory, supervisory, and inspection responsibilities.

The Consolidated Law on Banking and Credit System[5] defines a banking activity as the collection of deposits from the public and the exercise of credit. This activity is purely business, and legally can be exercised only by banks. It is carried out through the joint exercise of the acquisition of funds and disbursement of loans. There is an obligation to repay in the form of deposit or in another form.

1.2.2   New norms and new characteristics of the market

The financial economic crisis of the last decades led to a process of convergence among all financial intermediaries. There has been a blurring of the previous sharp distinctions between the traditional sectors of the financial system. The areas where they overlap among them have grown[6]. The Second European Banking Directive of 1989 introduced a broader definition of credit institutions. They, together with insurance companies and other financial institutions, are allowed to hold each other's unlimited shares[7]. During the 1980s, the banking system, which for a long time had been overseen by a set of protectionist style regulations, clashed in many countries with the need to increase competition. There was substantial financial innovation:

• New products were introduced; and
• New intermediaries entered the market because of the opening of the banking systems of other European Union (EU) countries.

The EU Banking Coordination Directive was a big push towards the reform of the banking systems in many European countries[8]. This regulation introduced more transparent regulation governing the authorization to access the banking markets. The introduction of this regulation brought about an important change of reference; the strong supervisory structure that had characterized the sector gave way to a new supervisory model based on objective and transparent parameters. Freedom to access the financial markets for new operators became subject only to their being in possession of objective requirements related to the capital base and the respectability and professionalism conditions of corporate banking officers.

The second EU directive regarding banking was introduced in the EU Member States from 1989[9]. One of its basic principles is "mutual recognition." Based on this principle, credit institutions may engage with any other EU Member State, either through the establishment of new subsidiaries or directly from the original location. There they are entitled to exercise all activities as in the country of origin and included in the list of the same directive.

Two fundamental processes occurred within the entire banking system:

• Gradual de-specialization; and
• Disintermediation.

These changes in turn brought the need for greater competitiveness within the banking industry. Banking innovation coupled with the de-regulation process. This led the banks, and in particular the credit institutions, into a gradual expansion of services and products offered. There developed, therefore, a reduction in operational differences between the various types of financial institutions (de-specialization). New intermediaries appeared on the market, and they generated a contraction in the volume of intermediation of the banking sector to the benefit of the new non-banking sector (disintermediation). The boundaries of the banking world with those of the securities market and the insurance sector became blurred. This made it necessary to redesign the organization of these sectors according to the new evolutionary processes.

The current structure of the banking and financial systems in many EU Member States is the result of a complex process The sector has transformed over a few years, with the aim of boosting integration within the European market. The main stages of this process, which began in the early 1990s, were:

- The reform of the sector's regulations. In Italy, for instance, this resulted in the passing of the "Consolidated Law on Banks and Finance"[10]. It defined clearly the purposes of the supervisory activity;
- The wave of privatizations that began at the end of 1993. This led to the transformation of state-controlled financial institutions into public limited companies; and
- A strong market consolidation trend and the gradual opening to the international system.

1.2.3 Services required from the banks

In terms of services offered by banks, it is interesting to distinguish between:

- Wholesale Banking Services; and
- Retail Banking Services.

1.2.3.1 Wholesale banking services

For large organizations, the demand for cash management services and working capital services largely derives from:

- The need to know in real time the liquidity and working capital position; and
- The awareness that liquidity in excess involves opportunity costs in terms of lost interest.

Among the services provided by wholesale banks aimed at improving efficiency for corporate customers managing their financial positions, are:

- Controlled disbursement accounts: thanks to this accounting feature, almost all payments made at a certain date can be known. The bank must notify the customer of the total amount of funds needed for the payments, and the customer can issue the bank transfer for the exact amount requested. In this way, the organization can instantly get a report of its net cash position;
- Account reconciliation: this accounting feature records which organization checks have been paid by the bank. Reconciliation is used to ensure that the money leaving an account matches the actual money spent;
- Lockbox: a centralized service for the collection and processing of organization payments, aimed at reducing the amount of time related to the collection of payments. The bank establishes a lockbox on behalf of the customer that is outside the territory. Local customers send payments by correspondence to the lockbox rather than to the organization's headquarters;
- Fund concentration: a service through which funds are redirected from accounts of a large number of different banks and subsidiaries to a few accounts at one bank, where they are balanced;
- Check deposit services: include the encoding, endorsement and microfilm of the customer's treatment of checks;
- Treasury management services: allow the efficient management of different currencies and securities portfolios for trading investments. The aim is to maximize the organization's liquidity while reducing operational and financial costs and risks;
- Electronic Fund Transfers (EFT): the automated transmission of payment messages through the domestic interbank network or through Society for Worldwide Interbank Financial Telecommunications (SWIFT), an international electronic messaging service owned and used by most international banks to transfer money orders;
- Electronic Data Interchange (EDI): structured transmission of data. It automatically transfers electronic documents or commercial invoices, purchase orders, or delivery notes;
- Electronic billing: for the presentment and collection of bills. This service is of interest to organizations that submit large volumes of bills on a frequent basis. Banks can send invoices by email or messages together with their automated payment services, through the interbank payment networks;
- Identification technology: the financial institution, by using an encrypt system, certifies the identity of its account holders and pretends to be an intermediary through which its customers can verify the identity of account holders from other banks; and

- Assistance offered to small organizations for setting up infrastructure for working with e-commerce[11].

1.2.3.2   Retail banking services

Retail customers seek efficiency and flexibility in their financial transactions. For these customers, the simple use of checks or the possession of liquidity in a bank account can often be less convenient and possibly more expensive, in terms of both time and cost, than the use of payment technology by electronic means and, increasingly, via the Internet. Below is a list of some of the most important innovative retail banking services:

- Automatic Teller Machine (ATM): Customers can access their bank account round the clock. They can withdraw cash and also pay their bills, make cash or check deposits, print checks, and so on. In addition to all these transactions, if the bank's ATM falls within a banking network, the retail depositors can benefit from the possibility of accessing their bank accounts throughout the national territory, and in many cases internationally, so can withdraw money via other banks' ATMs;
- Point-Of-Sale (POS) debit, credit, or prepaid cards: This system allows customers who make a purchase and choose not to pay by cash, check, or card, to make payments by using a card terminal via the Internet. In the case of debit cards, the merchant avoids any compensation delay generated by credit card payments, since the bank that offers the service pays the funds directly from the customer's account to the merchant's account at the time the card is used;
- Home Banking: This is the customer's direct link with his or her own accounts and brokerage. It allows the use of services such as online trading of securities and payment of bills via computers, telephones, or mobile devices;
- Debit and Credit Pre-Authorized Transfer: This service includes direct deposit of salaries in bank accounts and direct payments of mortgages or bills issued by third parties;
- Payment of bills via telephone:This is a service for the direct transfer of money from customers' bank accounts to external service providers via the voice commands function, touch tones or human operators; and
- Billing by email: This allows customers to receive payments and pay bills via the Internet, and thus save time and costs such as postage, printing etc.

1.3   Transformation of financial institutions

In the last two decades, the world financial markets have been shaken by structural changes and financial crises. The strong discontinuity generated by these international crises has transformed the system, with significant impacts on strategic business decisions and on the organizations themselves. More will follow in the coming few years.

In a recent chapter, Marco Onado has described the situation of the banks in the light of Basel III[12] Similar changes relating to insurance companies will be introduced with Solvency II[13]. Onado's main argument is that the new capital requirements imply substantial cuts in operating costs; he draws attention to the difficulties of the banks in the coming months/years caused by changing expectations and the need to satisfy what we call the four Cs[14]:

- Compliance, such as the requirement by the authorities to have more equity and a better quality of service (QoS);
- Customers, who expect better and fair products and services (in particular in terms of amount of credit granted);
- Co-workers, namely employees who aspire to stable and well remunerated jobs; and
- Co-investors, such as shareholders, who are asked to make available funds and who require adequate returns.

Marco Onado suggests responding to these challenges in two possible ways:

- Reduce the need for capital through the sale of assets; and
- Take a broad-based action at the heart of processes of production and the operating costs arising therefrom.

Financial institutions have started to take the first approach, but it does not appear that there is much more to squeeze. On the second approach, the operating costs of financial institutions in the last three years have not gone down; indeed, the ratio of operating costs on the margin (the so-called cost–income ratio, a simple indicator of efficiency) in 2008 was still at 1984 levels.

This book will concentrate on the second approach. It will describe a solution, cloud computing, which appears to provide the base infrastructure that can solve several problems in terms of effectiveness, efficiency, and economics of the financial institutions.

1.4 Lean and digitize approach to financial institution transformation

It may be of interest to examine which method the financial institutions could use to try to improve value to their customers and reduce their costs. A recent book describes a method, "Lean and Digitize," to tackle this kind of situation[15]. Many of the practical cases mentioned in that text refer to what can be done by the financial services companies. In the current climate, any organization will be struggling to meet its customers' quality and price requirements in terms of products and services, while reducing the costs of production and related services. To achieve these objectives, it is vital to focus on improvements in processes. The most effective methods for driving process improvement are Six Sigma and Lean Thinking. However, these methods are not always able to respond to a number of important questions:

- Is there is a consistent approach to cover both the methods of Lean Thinking and Six Sigma and the automation of management processes?
- How can Information Technology and Telecommunications support these projects, rather than hinder them?

The Lean Thinking and Six Sigma methods consider the analysis of physical flows and organization first, and then their optimization. But they ignore management automation and interactions between information systems and telecommunications networks with physical and organizational activities. The consequent risk is that the desired automation of the physical and organizational improvements might clash with the management of the processes required for the constraints imposed by such systems. So automation projects must be examined at the same time as the analysis in terms of organizational and physical flows; in this way, it will be possible to slash all sources of waste connected with the processes. Automation should add value for the customer through a reduction in Human Resources (HR); a rule of thumb says that 50 percent of processes can be improved independently of automation and that the remaining 50 percent of processes can be improved by using information systems and networks. These percentages are changing, however, with automation taking on a greater importance. The achievement of the maximum competitive advantage generated by process improvements is important, especially for financial institutions. In recent decades, they have not improved productivity, hence, the importance of a holistic approach that aims to optimize and improve processes from all points of view. This approach should:

- Be complete and operational;
- Be structured (through the use of Six Sigma method);
- Be driven by customer demand (in accordance with the approach of Lean Thinking);
- Not be limited to a specific sector but consider end-to-end activities in the processes; and
- Enhance the benefits of Lean Six Sigma with a rational use of information systems and telecommunications.

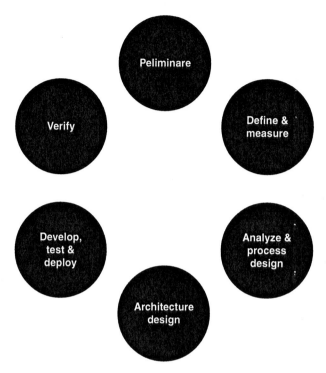

Figure 1.1   The lean and digitize method[16]

Lean and Digitize is a method that helps achieve these aims. It is based on various macro phases (see Figure 1.1):

- Preparation;
- Definition and measurement;
- Analysis and design of the process;
- Development of architecture of the solution;
- Development, test, and use; and finally
- Verification.

It is essential to apply this method and its tools in close collaboration with the sectors involved in the organization, quality management, and support functions (such as the middle and back office, the finance or operations). In this way, improvement projects should not start from a "problem" or a "challenge"; they must be rooted within the culture of the organization[17].

1.4.1   Transformation of organizations

Financial institutions can take two routes towards becoming leaner and more digitized:

- To achieve more integration; and
- To be more customercentric.

The following pages will examine both approaches.

1.4.1.1   Integration within and between financial institutions

The integration of the financial system has changed considerably in the last two decades, thanks to a complex set of factors, including:

- The easing of regulatory barriers between different sectors of financial intermediation;
- Changes in the organizational models and the distribution of businesses, made possible by new technologies;
- Changes in the asset allocation choices made by customers; and
- The growing importance of social security aspects.

To take into account all these factors, the Lean and Digitize method would suggest focusing on strategic developments[18]. Some possible approaches are:

- New organizational structures, which could consolidate homogeneous "functions" such as ICT services, call centers, collections, investment management, and back office; and
- The convergence between banking industry, insurance, and securities services, which is of particular relevance (the so-called bankassurance)[19]. This trend started in the mid-1980s with greater presence in some European countries, especially France[20]. The areas of integration first identified were commercial opportunities such as the distribution of insurance products through the financial institution networks.

The trends mentioned above have helped grow integration and stabilization; however it is not possible to trace with any certainty the evolutionary course via which a "final" model might emerge[21]. Rather, different models of integration will coexist. A variety of phenomena influences them, not only in connection with external regulations:

- On the demand side, a factor that can influence convergence between financial players is "one-stop shopping." Customers tend to want a single commercial space as a repository for their financial and insurance needs; and

- Mergers, acquisitions, and alliances, which influence the introduction of new operational procedures and service models. They bring fundamental changes and transformation. In order to cope with them, there has been a strong push towards cost cutting and increasing efficiency, especially through the implementation of concrete actions aimed at getting tangible results with rapid returns (not exceeding six months)[22].

1.4.1.2   Changing internal to customer centric orientation

A Lean and Digitize approach focuses on the relationship between customers and the financial institutions. In the last few years, this relationship has changed significantly, in that the financial institutions have moved from an internal focus to a customercentric one[23].

A customercentric financial institution does not squeeze its customers into one-size-fits-all products and services. It starts by considering the customer, and constructs the relationship to reflect his/her unique needs and the means through which s/he will use the institution's services.

The first step in achieving a customercentric approach is to understand how each business process of the organization exists to satisfy the customers; each activity in the process should provide added value for the customer.

A financial institution makes its front line customercentric when it is able to deliver to its customers:

- The ability and the authority for real-time decisions;
- A 360-degree understanding of the customer; and
- What the financial institution can do to improve value.

The way ahead for a financial institution should be the change of its business culture from productcentric to customercentric, perhaps by relying on a network of organizations: a federation. Given the fact that financial institutions today still appear to be vertical and heavily structured organizations, a fundamental transformation is required in their business logic. This implies a complex organizational change.

When following a customer-oriented strategy, a financial institution will no longer be creating a product and then looking for a customer to sell it to. The value chain will be the converse; it is the customer whose business strategy counts. She or he will become the "main actor," the person who the financial institution must please and satisfy.

Knowing how to manage a relationship with the customer becomes an essential factor in determining the success of the financial institutions. They must be capable of understanding the explicit and implicit needs of their customers in order to create a product or service that can easily find wide acceptance on the market. Therefore, financial institutions now require a high capacity for innovation, and they must be willing to take new and different types of risk. They must be run only with a sustainable knowledge-based organizational structure whose competitiveness relies on the ability to receive, disseminate, share, and create knowledge within itself for a dynamic interchange with the external environment.

Traditional financial institutions are internally oriented, whereas the customer-driven financial institution is externally oriented. It does not set policies and standards based on its capacity, costs, or competence, but on the actual needs, expectations, and convenience of its customers. First, it has to recognize and accept its customers' needs. It should invest in improvements or designs of products and processes that will meet its customers' needs as closely as possible. All activities in any process need to add value for the customer. As a corollary, the financial institution should hire, train, motivate and/or equip the right people with the task of running the processes and selling the products/services.

Customizing its services becomes important. A financial institution should direct a considerable effort into the improvement of customer experience and customer satisfaction through:

• Redefinition of typical banking functions; and
• The re-engineering of the business processes more oriented towards the end customer, and assuring a mutual exchange of information.

For instance, this means that depending on the nature of the information exchanged the remote device will display a message to the customer specifically related to the type of transactions that they are conducting. It is now possible to display news and promotions related to a customer's profile and activities, and these being more likely to be of interest to them assists the marketing initiatives of the institution.

1.4.2   Transformation of the ICT support

ICT has always supported financial institutions. This support has become more and more important, especially in connection with the current transformation of financial institutions. Some new technologies are particularly interesting, and have started to spread rapidly.

A customercentric approach has consequences for the organization and for automation. A major factor that will determine the future performance of the financial institutions is the extent to which its business operators decide on the adoption of the latest technology – social networking, mobiles, and the cloud.

The following sections describe some of the changes in the support of ICT to financial institutions in the last decades to support their transformation.

1.4.2.1   Multichannel access

One of the first developments in this roadmap for customercentricity is a move to a multichannel strategy.

In the past, branches and agencies were the only channel of communication between financial institutions and their customers. This was not a random choice, but arose because of the desire of supervisory authorities to protect financial activity from transformations that could complicate control over financial flows. A visible symbol of this was the initial prohibition – with very few exceptions – on locating ATMs outside branches. By doing this, the supervisory authorities intended to reaffirm the principle that the ATM was merely a machine, not a sales channel.

The increase in the number of delivery channels by the financial institutions is a trend that has been growing during the last decades, as a result of several influences:

- Increased competition;
- The fall in intermediation margins;
- Technological innovation;
- Mobility demand; and
- The possibility to use the services 24/7.

There is a close connection between the first two factors: financial institutions are now facing additional competition from the so-called non-banks. The latter are organizations which fall within the financial sector (such as brokerage firms) or may gravitate around it, such as telecommunication businesses and retail stores that provide payment cards with the aim of increasing customer loyalty. The entry of new players offering favorable prices and better service has caused great competitive pressure, especially as some organizations entering the financial sector have more streamlined structures than those of established credit institutions. An example is given by those organizations operating exclusively online; they can offer better conditions thanks to reduced structural costs.

So multichannel operation provides a real opportunity for:

- The financial institutions' customers, who can operate in a delocalized manner (remotely linked); and
- The financial institutions themselves.

A multichannel strategy can reduce the resources needed to work on traditional counter activities. At the same time, a financial institution can profile its customer base more thoroughly in order to offer ever more targeted and customized services.

Financial institutions now consider multichannel as a value, a competitive advantage obtainable through the use of information and telecommunication systems. Today, banks facilitate customer access to their services by making available to them an integrated set of multiple ICT-driven channels, including:

- Virtual Corners;
- Evolved ATMs;
- Phone Banking;
- Internet or Online Banking;
- Corporate Banking;
- SMS Banking; and
- Mobile Banking.

The innovation introduced by these multimedia components makes communication and the exchange of data between the financial institution and its customer faster, easier, and more effective. A certain number of financial institutions have tested fully automated branches without any onsite personnel; call center operators assist customers when necessary, via a multimedia connection.

The phone banking service uses a group of skilled operators to deliver information and support services to the bank's customers. This solution is increasingly integrated with the multichannel platform, giving the operator a comprehensive real-time view of the operations performed by the customer through other channels as well.

Solutions for online banking, or phone banking, consist of advanced platforms and interfaces developed specifically for intuitive and easy usability, integrated with all online functionalities present in the financial institution's information systems. The goal of financial institutions offering such a service is:

- To make available to its customers a seamless "user experience" in the transition between the various channels; and
- To enable customization of the services it provides, based on customer behavior.

There are several benefits of online banking perceived by the customer:

- Comfort and additional services are the main elements that encourage customers to make financial transactions online. Customers using the online banking do not need to travel to a branch, because they can carry out financial transactions from home, office or anywhere else they choose;
- Besides its ease of use, the availability of online banking is far superior to that afforded by conventional branches. Online banking is normally available to customers 24 hours a day, 365 days a year. Increased accessibility to banking services is a competitive advantage of online banking over traditional banking; and

- Online banks may offer some additional services. Some financial institutions may offer higher interest rates than the market average to their online customers, or high remuneration on their accounts or lower prices for insurance. This is possible also as a result of the savings provided by online banking.

An interesting study conducted in Italy by ABI, the Italian Bankers' Association, in 2010 shows that almost 20 million customers visit their banks via the Internet; one in three customers. The numbers have been growing steadily. In five years, they almost tripled, from 12 percent in 2005 to 34 percent in 2010. Based on this study, approximately 10 million Italians use home banking while continuing visiting their branch offices for advice (80 percent of cases). The branches are visited less often than a few years ago (in 2010, 1.5 times per month and in 2005 approximately 2) and mainly for more complex financial decisions. The approach of the nearly 30 million Italian bank customers has changed over time. The number of multichannel customers – that is, those using both the Internet and the branches depending on their needs – more than doubled in five years, reaching 8 million in 2010. Technologically well informed customers, who make payments and other operations only through ATMs or their computers, reached 2 million. Finally, traditional customers – those that in 2010 still used only branches or ATMs – were in the majority (17 million); the expectation is, however, that this number will decrease.

Moreover, banks offer now the possibility of accessing services through mobile banking. Today, supported by the growing presence of advanced phones and smartphones, easy to operate interactively, the ability to activate most home banking features via the mobile phone is evolving rapidly. However, although new generations use the phone as an extension of their operational life, a massive spread of mobile banking will take time; it will gradually increase as banking customers overcome their mistrust related to security concerns.

The use of mobile, smartphones and tablets (such as iPad, iPhones, and devices based on Android and Windows technologies) allow for an increasing number of online banking functionalities. The user can do such things as making payments, getting credit, or locating the nearest ATM through a geo-localization tool.

The integration of the bank's system architecture is a strategy that allows for greater simplification of access to delivery channels and banking services dedicated to the customer. Online banking enables customers to gain access into many services via the website, including bank accounts, deposits, credit cards, prepaid services, and so on.

It is worth while mentioning also the One-Time Password (OTP), a temporary authentication tool; this system provides a password allowing the customer to access all their multichannel options just once. This procedure minimizes the risk of fraud or of unauthorized access by third parties linked to of the customer's multiple access channels.

1.4.2.2   *Virtual financial institutions*

In addition to the development of online banking as a complement to the traditional services offered by financial institutions, a new segment of the industry has emerged. It is represented by financial institutions that operate solely via the Internet (online only banks), or banks with no physical location. ATM networks and online banking can potentially lower such a financial institution's operating costs relative to the traditional branch network.

A new type of customer service is becoming increasingly necessary: customers, in conducting their financial activities online, require fast and efficient advice and support for functional or technical issues. Financial institutions need to address the operational characteristics of the new types of customers or of their interaction with online banking. These customers typically do not visit the branch often. They operate online, while also having to deal with the materiality of certain banking operations such as a request for a checkbook or the withdrawal of a significant amount of cash. The financial institution can also perform such operations through virtual channels. The customer can make a remote request, launching an information flow, enabling authorizations to be processed by the helpdesk or the back or middle office; the result will be the physical delivery of the customer's request by the financial institution through one of the channels.

One of the biggest recent revolutions in the banking industry is the virtual bank. This relies on a range of systems for providing services, such as mobiles, tablets, and personal computers (PC), which are the most popular technologies. There are also other interface devices, such as interactive terminals, multimedia connections, and smartphones[24]. The virtual financial institution maintains direct contact with the customer, and there is no need for:

- Face-to-face relationships with customers;
- Branch offices;
- Tellers;
- Printed material; or
- Resources to be committed to other activities that are not directly productive.

The institutions' expanded and increased financial distribution channels are a consolidated trend in all countries[25]. In fact, where emerging countries do not have good infrastructure, online banking might have an advantage over traditional branches for both customers and the institutions themselves.

In order to gain an insight into how the relationship between financial institutions and customers has changed in recent years, it is important to take into account two factors:

- The emergence of a new type of customers who are increasingly well informed about digitization; and
- The changing role of the branch operator.

As a result of such an analysis, it is possible to understand how much weight a financial institution should accord to a multichannel strategy. There is a new generation of financial institution users showing increasing familiarity with technological tools. Financial institutions have progressively directed their customers towards self-management tools for the more traditional operations such as bank account consultations and credit transfers via online banking and phone banking. This, *inter alia*, allows banks to redefine the role of their branches. The role of the counter teller becomes more advisory; freed from the burden of handling many of the routine front office procedures, the operator can become the interface for customers to turn to for advice on their more complex choices (this might also be more profitable for the financial institution). The branch, having introduced multiple communication channels with the customer, possesses tools enabling the collection of more information in order to provide them with new and better advice and services. Driven by the market, all major operators have moved towards virtual channels for these reasons:

- The traditional financial institutions have added online channels to defend themselves against the threat of new financial institutions poaching their customer base; and
- The new virtual financial institutions have set themselves the goal of acquiring market share, and they embody new business models that go beyond the services provided by the traditional financial institution and their traditional territories.

The comparison is no longer made between financial institutions that have or do not have online channels or those which charge a lower fee; the comparison is among financial institutions whose traditional services are better presented and operated. Just as one compares, say, a loan by looking at the price, timing and delivery of services (for instance, insurance, reimbursement arrangements, and so on), the same happens with the services offered via virtual channels. Competition between financial institutions takes place in three different dimensions:

- Price;
- Variety of product/service offered; and
- Quality.

Differentiation based on price could represent an achievable goal for financial institutions that have successfully achieved efficiency. The strong presence of technological components within the new range of offerings would allow more user-friendly operators to emerge and displace competitors. Whether or not this is considered unfortunate, it is a strategy that in the medium term is rather risky, as competition based on price usually leads to the destruction of value.

Differentiation based on the scale of the portfolio of services offered – that is the number and range of services made available to customers across all channels – is based on the assumption that it is possible to achieve economies in the distribution system by moving customers onto lower-cost channels. In abstract terms, this path seems fine. The catch is that in the medium term it is easily attainable by all competitors.

Differentiation based on the quality of service results from the fact that the offer available online is easily comparable. Hence, the operators active in the online markets are very active in the development and sophistication of the services they offer, and the help they provide for them. Their offering is often both attractive and excellent. In this case, the challenges lie first in what the customers perceive as quality, and second in the presence of a market sufficiently large and rich to support the cost of excellence. In conclusion, coming up with a suitable offer on virtual channels, different from the competitors, is not easy.

Online banking is a system whose customers can use the retail banking and investment services provided through the Internet or their mobile. However, the computer's inability to respond in a flexible way to customers' demands and requests is no incentive to pursue the complete delegation of financial services operations to the information and telecommunication systems.

Customers in many cases feel the need to interact with a human to perform certain operations, for example requesting a loan or a mortgage to buy a property. So notwithstanding the deployment of new technologies, financial institutions certainly cannot lose their focus on the provision of convenient and quality services. In fact, despite the existence of large banks with branches all over the world and large insurance companies, the survival of small financial institutions, could be partially explained by the customers' belief that their overall quality of services is greater. In these institutions, the presence of human operators often encourages the establishment of a more personal relationship, as opposed to large financial institutions that make a greater use of online banking.

The conclusion is that financial institutions need to carefully manage a multichannel strategy and continuously upgrade it.

1.4.2.3 Mobile payments

With the increasing popularity of mobile phones and smartphones, payments by mobile will expand in the coming years[26]. Some global estimates are highly optimistic; the turnover forecast for 2015 is around US$670 billion.

Payment by mobile can be part of a business process that runs entirely on the mobile channel (mobile commerce), or be part of a multichannel business process: in this latter case, one can distinguish between:

- Mobile Remote Payment – when the phone lets the customer make payments using the cellular network; and
- Mobile Proximity Payment, enabling mobile proximity payments using short-range transmission technology (for instance using a mobile equipped with Near Field Communication (NFC) technology at a contactless POS).

The Mobile Payments system has a patchy distribution around the world. Payment via mobile digital content (such as the purchase of music, ring tones, or an App – the so-called mobile content) is quite common. Mobile commerce in goods and services is expanding.

There are several interesting Mobile Proximity Payment projects. Their diffusion is still limited – with the exception of some countries like Japan and South Korea. Europe is also interested in these developments for a variety of socioeconomic reasons, and for some legislation such as the Single Euro Payment Area (SEPA)[27].

The status of electronic payments via the mobile sees Italy with a particular placement. It is one of the first countries in the world in terms of penetration of mobile devices – in 2010 there were 48 million users; 44 percent of devices were smart, and there were 16 million mobile Internet users. On the other hand, Italy is among the last (in the Western world) to use electronic payments; there were "only" 25 million users of payment cards, and 90 percent of transactions were still in cash.

In 2011, 23 million users (76 percent of Italians between 18 and 54 years) made at least one payment via their mobile. The volume of business was worth a total of €700 million, of which €500 million related to the purchase of digital content (Mobile Content) such as news, games, music, phone cards, or donations. Mobile commerce involved over €80 million. This amount is steadily growing, often as an extension of e-commerce projects – while showing a very limited distribution and an implementation using proximity payment, despite the presence of some interesting initiatives.

The situation reflects the spending habits of the Italians:

- The Italians prefer cash, with 90 percent of the transactions settled thus (Source: Bank of Italy 2010) compared to about 80 percent in Europe (Source: ECB, 2010);

- There are "only" 25 million Italians with an active card, despite the large number of cards in circulation – 82 million in 2010 (Source: ABI, 2010);
- The Italians do not use e-money for everyday purchases, as confirmed by the lower number of transactions per inhabitant per year (25 in Italy against 63 on average in the Eurozone) and the high average value per transaction (€80, compared to €52 in the Eurozone) (Source: ECB, 2010); and
- The value of transactions using payment cards remained stable from 2006 to 2010, between €120 and €130 billion (Source: ECB, 2010).

Depending on the different aspects of mobile payments, there are different scenarios and possible developments.

The mobile commerce and Mobile Remote Payments (MRP) display a mature technology, which is more and more available, although in constant evolution. Examples of success of the second type (MRP) are (all data refer to 2010):

- In the USA, Fandango (movie ticket sales), downloaded by more than 20 million users;
- Mobile Starbucks (ordering while in the queue), with over 30 million transactions a year; and
- In France, SNCF launched with great success (3 million downloads) the application of Mobile SNCF, with over 3 percent of rail tickets purchased.

1.4.2.4   *Latest developments*

In the last few years, the emphasis has shifted once again. Some of the most important developments are:

- Social Networking and Community (SN & C). This is the use within companies of collaboration tools across the network. It includes all the initiatives that are aimed at promoting interaction and collaboration within and outside the financial institutions;
- Unified Communication and Collaboration (UC & C). This is the use of ever more integrated communication tools. They allow, for example, the integration of traditional telephony in an Internet Protocol (IP) network and the handling of different media. It refers to those initiatives supporting the management of each type of communication – internal and external – to the financial institution in a unified way, independent of the media used for conveying content; and
- Enterprise Content Management (ECM) or similarly the Big Data initiatives. This is the use of information systems and telecommunications for the management, processing, and storing of data and unstructured information, such as documents, email, voice, images, and video, internal and external, to the financial institution.

A research by ABI Lab in Italy showed that investment in these sectors has increased in recent years even when the Information and Communication Technology budgets, especially as regards investments, were either stable or declining[28].

Among the three sectors, Enterprise Content Management is the one in which financial institutions have invested in and will invest in even more in the future. Depending on the size of the institution, there have been investments ranging from the hundreds of thousands to several million Euros. The motivation is the efficient management of a large amount of heterogeneous information and documents, such as drawings, financial and management control reports, business information, contracts, customer files, form and press releases, paperwork, and quality indicators.

CIOs interviewed by ABI Lab attached a somewhat less important role to Unified Communication and Collaboration than to ECM, but UC & C is nevertheless definitely growing rapidly. Specifically, eight out of ten CIOs expect that this area will in the future play an important role in supporting the processes of their financial institutions[29].

An analysis of the level of maturity of the initiatives in the three fields shows that:

- SN & C applications are in their infancy;
- The scope of UC & C is going through a period of strong growth, and it is past the experimental phase. Some financial institutions have defined long-term development plans. They often also include a rationalization of the telecommunications infrastructure with a migration to Voice over IP (VoIP); and
- The ECM is located at a level of maturity higher than the other two areas. It is also in a phase of more structured planning.

In the current economic environment, the Intranet and the new paradigms of Banking 2.0 can be an impulse to the financial institutions to encourage interaction and collaboration by using SN & C. It will allow the rapid exchange of information and at the same time a looser structure between all levels of the organization. This can lead to greater efficiency and support the creation of new identities[30]. The use of these applications is initially internal. The plan is to extend them to the customers and other partners in a new paradigm of open financial institution. They correspond to the expectations of customers and employees that use these web tools in their private lives.

If one accepts these trends, it is worthwhile considering which infrastructure could best support them. This will be the subject of the following chapters.

Insurers finally get acquainted with cloud computing[31]

For New York Life Insurance Co., the option was to go to a cloud provider for agents' document management requirements. The corporation had a big giant system. Individual small agents could not have that, and it could not be rolled out to the field.

Through the cloud solution, New York Life is able to maintain the complete client files that agents have (the applications, fact finders and policy receipts, and illustrations). The corporation uses these contents also for reviews with the agents connecting with them in the cloud rather than in person.

1.4.2.5   Process improvement

Lean and Digitize improves capacity to manage information and processes in an integrated manner. Tools like Straight Through Process (STP) can enable customers to receive responses within a very short time, even for complex tasks such as the approval of loans. The choice of integration of new channels with the "old" ones is rather common in many financial institutions. Existing instruments are not replaced, but instead a complete re-assessment becomes necessary. It is important to re-engineer the distribution processes in the financial institutions.

Some financial institutions have built robust, scalable, and high-performing integration layers across the organization. Multiple service bus implementations help in re-engineering processes, leveraging the maturity of technologies such as those available in middleware, like Websphere, Tibco, WebMethods, etc.

Financial institutions have also invested and implemented new technological solutions such as:

- Service-based integrated solutions, for both internal and external purposes;
- Context-based functional services connecting financial institutions' applications with external service providers. They can help for functions related to Know Your Customer (KYC), card processing, originations, market data validations, securities processing, and so on;
- Process triggers and event-based functions have become common in some financial institutions; and
- Semantics applications to better interpret data and information. To use these technologies, data representations, use standards like FpML, MISMO, and so on.

In a Lean and Digitize approach, the introduction of new technologies must go hand in hand with the redesign of processes. The integration process involves changes in both aspects of internal management and external activities, with a significant standardization process in both areas. Current solutions are quite mature, and most of the further developments regard the provision of additional functions. Integration scenarios have reached such a level of maturity that the distribution of solutions can use standard models.

What distinguishes the various solutions is the degree of integration. Many operators have developed an online banking offer parallel to the physical financial services network, offering special benefits to customers who access them via the Internet. The implementation of a model of multichannel integrated banking requires a design and construction effort that is not comparable to the construction of a mere virtual trading service or a virtual bank; integration must be built into the technological, organizational, and commercial processes side. A Lean and Digitize approach is mandatory.

- From a technological standpoint, information systems of traditional financial institutions (legacy systems, client-server architectures of branch offices, and so on) must be integrated with virtual channels. Applications must be consistent. Customer information must be sharable; interaction between the channels must be granted by platforms integration;
- From an organizational standpoint, structures and processes must be adapted to the offer delivered through new channels; and
- From a commercial perspective, customers and branch operators must be able to manage the virtual offer, understand its benefits, and be able to exploit them. Virtual channels in this model represent the extension of the physical channels, and the financial institution offering incorporates multichannel access as an additional element of value.

The advantage of this approach is that it builds on the existing organizational and technological assets, aiming to expand internal collaboration without replacing it, and avoiding a loss of investments.

It is becoming increasingly and widely believed that to implement innovative solutions and new online services, it is necessary to create a technical and organizational setting capable of integrating the new solutions into the pre-existing financial institutions information system. It is not appropriate to develop autonomous solutions detached from the other information systems; the more integration there is across the processes, the better it is. In this way, one possibly could expect greater benefits.

Most financial services are now "virtualized services" in the sense that they have been de-materialized. It is possible for financial institutions to offer them remotely. For better results, financial institutions should base their multichannel strategy on technologies accessible in a simple way by the customers anytime, anywhere and with any device. Anticipating the diffusion of these technologies can result in some cases in a major competitive advantage in gaining market shares. This approach requires careful planning; it is necessary to avoid a scenario in which technology does not meet with great success and quickly becomes obsolete without having built a substantial market share. This would prove to be a loss of energy and economic resources.

1.4.2.6   Operational risks

The implementation of these new processes and new technology must also take into account the possible risks associated with them. Among the many risks faced by financial institutions, those derived from operational costs are important, especially in the light of the regulations connected with Basel II[32] and Solvency II[33]. The production of financial services implies the use of real resources and of support systems for back office. An operational risk is, as the name suggests, a risk arising from the execution of a business function. It is a very broad concept. It focuses on the risks arising from the people, systems, and processes through which a financial institution operates. It also includes other categories such as fraud, legal, reputational, physical, or environmental risks.

A widely used definition of operational risk is that contained in the Basel II regulations. This definition states that operational risk is the risk of loss resulting from inadequate or failed internal processes, people and systems, or from external events. As we have described, financial institutions have recently found in technology one of the best tools to address the growing competition. It is still not clear, however, what the correct combination between labor and technology for the delivery of services should be. For financial institutions, the issues of operational risks remain relevant, and financial institutions should evaluate them in connection with any Lean and Digitize initiative.

1.5   Conclusions

Customer proximity has become one of the major aspects in the new strategies of the financial institutions, and ICT can help with this to a marked degree. The following chapters will examine a certain, very powerful, technology that can support this transformation not only from a technical point of view but even more so from a business point of view: it is known as cloud computing.

2
Cloud Computing

2.1 Introduction

This chapter defines the concept and scope of cloud computing. It starts with a discussion on the origins of the model as well as the main evolutionary elements supporting its launch, such as virtualization and the spread of the Internet.

In order to provide a comprehensive definition of cloud computing, this chapter introduces the main distinctive features of this model. It shows how cloud computing is an advanced computing environment with three specific dimensions:

- Five essential characteristics;
- Three service models or service layers; and
- Four deployment models.

This chapter briefly describes:

- The main classifications of cloud computing;
- The benefits of such a model to both client and vendor, which justify the adoption of cloud services. Special focus will be given to the business-related benefits; and
- The potential risks and drawbacks, and the corresponding remediation, resulting from the adoption of cloud computing

2.2 Cloud computing in growth

Cloud computing in general terms refers to the provision of computational resources on demand via a computer network, possibly the Internet.

The term "cloud" derives from the symbol used in the past to represent the Internet. The cloud denotes a collection of servers and computers accessible through a network. A cloud vendor normally owns and operates these resources in multiple data center locations. These machines can run any number of operating systems (OP).

Cloud computing includes both the applications delivered as services over the Internet and the means via which those services are provisioned, such as the hardware components, servers, storage, and systems software in the data centers.

Cloud computing is a further advancement in the commoditization of investments in Information and Communication Technology[1]. It is the outcome of an evolution toward a utility business model[2]. In this model, computing capabilities are provided as a service[3], as the core element of the era of Web 2.0 in which Internet is used as a software platform[4], or simply as an application of the generativist power of the Internet[5].

The cloud is the result of the evolution, in terms of diffusion, speed, and availability, of the Internet. Today, consumers can access online a huge number of web-based applications as if they were applications residing in their own computer. Cloud computing introduces an innovative model, network-based, for the delivery and the consumption of ICT services. It is another example of ICT consumerization[6]. Cloud computing makes available to organizations content and services that have been available to millions of consumers for some time.

In his book *The Big Switch*, Nick Carr discusses his vision of an information revolution; it is very similar to the massive changes that occurred during the industrial revolution[7]. Carr draws a parallel between the genesis of cloud computing in the information age and the genesis of electrification during the industrial age. Before that, organizations had to provide their own power (water wheels, windmills, and so on), but with electrification, organizations no longer had to worry about how to procure power – they merely needed to plug into the electrical grid.

The cloud computing distribution rationale of new services would be similar to the supply of utilities such as electricity, water, gas, or the provision of telephone or postal services. Today, most organizations use their own computing resources. But they could simply plug into the cloud to procure the resources they need. Carr's underlying concept and vision of cloud computing can be traced back many years. In 1960, John McCarthy predicted: "computation may someday be organized as a public utility"[8]. It was not until the 1990s, however, that vendors started to offer cloud services as a networking infrastructure resource. As McCarthy and Carr point out, eventually the savings offered by the utility model will become too attractive to even the largest organizations to switch away from.

What cloud services might have in common with public utilities is that all of these services are delivered to the clients in a simple way. The client does not need to:

- Know about the technology behind it;
- Be experienced in how the complex underlying system works; and
- Understand how ICT plans, organizes, and delivers the services.

Cloud services encompass everything from computation to application, data access, and storage services, none of which require the end-user to have any knowledge of the physical location and configuration of the systems that deliver the services. Cloud computing is an advanced computing environment whose clients can outsource their computing needs to a third party. When the client needs to use the computing power, applications, and resources such as storage, processing, or servers they can access the resources via the Internet. This would be possible through a set of channels, just as if they were using software installed in their data centers. The client can access the applications whenever they wish via a network (possibly the Internet) and pay-per-use.

This is the origin and widespread use of the logic of cloud computing. It is a new model of distribution and utilization of ICT resources. It is an alternative solution to the problems of flexibility and complexity, and it attains interesting objectives in terms of the four Es: effectiveness, efficiency, economics, and the respect of compliance (ethics).

The key technological enablers for cloud computing are:

- Virtualization technologies, which phase out the one-to-one relationship between applications and hardware;
- Increase in Internet connection speed, which enables large amounts of content to be accessible and retrievable from remote locations at low cost; and
- Grid computing, which enables large numbers of computing devices to work together.

This virtualized set of physical resources can easily and automatically provide services. The high utilization rate of these resources contains the costs as a result of the economy of scale typical of ICT; it makes the model financially viable. Innovative metering and charging mechanisms give vendors significant cost savings, and this normally reduces cloud computing costs. For many organizations, cloud services have become viable and attractive options[9].

2.2.1 Definition and classification

There is still a large debate on what cloud computing really means. Since the term is an appealing one, vendors often extend its meaning for marketing purposes.

There are many definitions related to cloud computing for the:

- Concept;
- Scope;
- Content;

- Characteristics;
- Expectations;
- Strategies;
- Technologies; and
- Architectures.

Gartner, the world's leading information technology research and advisory organization, defines cloud computing as[10]:

> a style of computing where massively scalable IT-related capabilities are provided "as a service" using Internet technologies.

The National Institute of Standards and Technology (NIST), the American Standards Body, defines it thus[11]:

> Cloud computing is a model for enabling convenient, on-demand network access to a shared pool of configurable computing resources (for example, networks, servers, storage, applications, and services) that can be rapidly provisioned and released with minimal management effort or service vendor interaction.

Wikipedia's definition is[12]:

> Cloud computing is the use of computing resources (hardware and software) that are delivered as a service over a network (typically the Internet).

Vaquero provides a further definition of cloud computing[13]:

> The "cloud" is a large reserve of easily usable and accessible virtualized resources (for instance hardware, development platforms, and/or services). These can be dynamically reconfigured to adjust to a variable load (scale), allowing further optimization of the physical resources. Typically, resources are exploited under a pay-for-use model in which the infrastructure vendors offer guarantees through customized Service Level Agreements (SLA).

These definitions appear a little bit too simple. They do not explain what cloud computing actually means to the ordinary business or manager. They define what cloud computing "is," but not really what it "does" or "means" or especially "could do" to the people who work in the organizations. The result is that 42 percent of CIOs said their executive boards did not fully grasp the potential of the cloud[14].

Deutsche bank cloud strategy garners industry praise[15]

With the construction of its innovative new Infrastructure-as-a-Service platform, Deutsche Bank has gained the approval of its industrial colleagues with an award from the Open Data Center Alliance's "Conquering the Cloud Challenge." Its winning initiative was "Identity Management in the New Hybrid Cloud World."

The prestigious contest aims to identify the best practices in cloud computing implementation as judged by a diverse panel of experts.

According to Computerworld, the new platform will provide developers with the ability to rapidly create and deploy virtualized applications, running up to 2000 virtual machines at once. The versatile environment will embrace developers using Window, UNIX, Linux, and Solaris programming.

Additional innovation includes what organization officials have labeled "aggressive standardization" and automation. This would ultimately reduce client expenses and storage costs.

A useful definition for cloud computing could be:

> Cloud computing is not only a technology. It is a completely different way to see computing. It will lead in time to a complete revision of the products/services and processes of the organizations. The cloud computing model provides access to a delocalized, easily accessed, on-demand set of shared computing resources (network, servers, storage, applications, and services) which can be quickly acquired and released. The organization can use a variable workload while maintaining a minimal impact on operations. Clients can typically access this set of resources using a pay-per-use model. In it, the service vendor commits to provide certain protections through a Service Level Agreement (SLA).

Cloud computing is an evolving paradigm. Its definition is still evolving. It will change over time.

As shown in Figure 2.1, the NIST definition of cloud computing describes five essential characteristics, three service models and four deployment models[16].

The NIST definition includes five essential elements that define the cloud[17]:

- Self-service on demand: For the provision, monitoring, and management of computing resources, there is no client interaction with human administrators. The client can unilaterally provision computing resources, such as server processing time, storage, and so on, automatically and as needed, without requiring human interaction with the service vendor;
- Broad network access: Vendors deliver cloud computing resources over standard networks and heterogeneous devices, possibly the Internet.

ICT capabilities are available over the network and are accessed through standard mechanisms, including a large number of devices such as thin or thick client platforms (for example mobile phones, laptops, and smartphones);

• Wide elasticity: ICT resources can be provisioned to scale up quickly or be released rapidly to scale down fast. To the client, the capabilities available for provisioning might appear to be infinite, as they can potentially be purchased in any quantity and at any time;

• Resource pooling: The ICT resource vendors serve all clients using a multi-tenant model. Different physical and virtual resources are dynamically assigned and re-assigned according to the client demand. Examples of resources include storage, processing, memory, network bandwidth, and virtual machines (VM); and

• Measured service: ICT resource utilization is measured for each application and for each tenant for public cloud billing or private cloud charge-back. Cloud systems automatically control and optimize resource usage by leveraging a metering capability. This should be appropriate to the type of service (for example storage, processing, bandwidth, and active client accounts). Resource consumption can be monitored and reported, providing visibility for both the vendor and the client of the services used.

The possible deployment models of cloud services are (see also Figure 2.1):

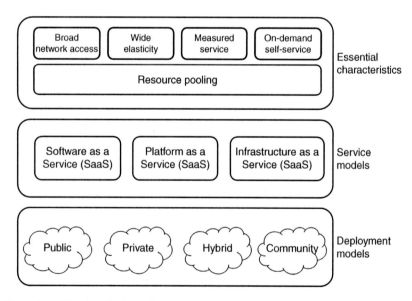

Figure 2.1 The cloud's three dimensions

- Software as a Service (SaaS): Vendors deliver applications through the cloud as a service (CaaS) to end-clients. There are hundreds of SaaS service offerings available today, ranging from horizontal organization applications to specialized applications for specific industries, as well as client applications such as web-based email;
- Platform as a Service (PaaS): The platforms are for the development and deployment of applications. Vendors deliver them as a service to build, deploy, and manage applications in the cloud. The platform typically includes databases, middleware and development tools. The network is the media through which to deliver the hosted applications. In the context of cloud computing, PaaS represents an intermediate step between IaaS and SaaS; and
- Infrastructure as a Service (IaaS): the infrastructure layer focuses on enabling technologies through the provision of storage capabilities, network services, and computing power. This makes sense, since more and more ICT infrastructures are becoming a commodity. The infrastructure hardware is often virtualized. Virtualization, management, and operating system software are also part of IaaS.

Over time, these service models have been enlarged to include other possible modes, indicated in general as XaaS, where X stands for a specific service.

BPaaS is particularly relevant in this regard. It is the provision of business processes as a service. It is a generalization of SaaS where the vendor not only provides the ICT systems but also uses the application to operate a full process on behalf of the client.

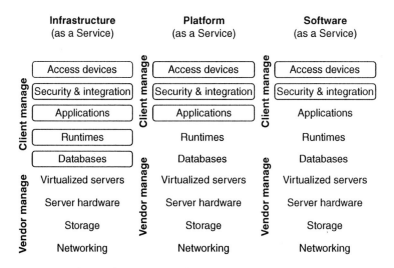

Figure 2.2   Breakdown of IaaS, SaaS, and PaaS

Table 2.1 Modes of use of cloud computing (2009)

Answer options	Response percent (%)
Individual software packages (SaaS)	34.2
Complete operating system and software package available via cloud services (PaaS)	28.8
Just infrastructure services such as storage, network capacity and so on (Iaas)	24.7
Security services in the cloud	9.6
Others	2.7

A survey conducted by Enisa (see Table 2.1) provides data on the current use of these diverse modes[18]. Data from this type of survey would change quickly over time.

When talking about cloud services, we generally refer to the "Public Cloud" type of delivery model. Actually, it is only one of the possible solutions available; there are at least four deployment models:

- Private Clouds: A single organization uses a dedicated cloud infrastructure. The organization itself can manage the private cloud. The hosting and operation of private clouds may also be outsourced to (or managed by) a third-party service vendor. There are some substantial differences on respect to the traditional data centers. Some of these features are:
  - Server consolidation and virtualization;
  - Shared pool of computing, storage, and network resources;
  - A way to quickly and easily decommission resources;
  - Centralized control and visibility;
  - Role-based access control and approvals;
  - Self-service portal for clients;
  - Catalog of standardized service options;
  - Integrated development platforms;
  - Automated provisioning and orchestration;
  - Policy-based controls and governance;
  - Metering and billing of services based on usage; and
  - Possible interfaces to public cloud resources.
- Public Clouds: The cloud is for use by multiple organizations (tenants) on a shared basis, and is hosted and managed by a third-party service vendor. The cloud infrastructure is available to the clients. It is owned by an organization that sells cloud services;
- Community Clouds: This is a cloud computing environment access to which is shared by a group of related organizations. The community shares some views such as the industrial sector, the mission, security requirements, policies, and approaches to compliance. It can be managed directly by one or more of the organizations or by an outsourcer; and

- Hybrid Clouds: This is when a single organization adopts both private and public clouds in order to take advantage of the benefits of both solutions. Two or more different delivery models make up the cloud infrastructure. They, albeit remaining separate entities, are connected together by technology, proprietary or standard, allowing for the interchange of data and applications. For example, an organization might run the stable workload of an application on a private cloud. When a peak in the workload takes place, such as at the end of the financial quarter or during the holiday season, they can use computing capacity from a public cloud. They return those resources to the public pool when they are no longer needed. Another option is that some applications are on a private cloud while others (for instance the Customer Relationship Management module) are on a public cloud. The organization can access the latter much more easily from many locations and devices.

Each of these models has plus/deltas and benefits in moving from one another (see Figure 2.3 moves from the Different Types of Cloud Computing).

There are also additional variations to the previous classifications. For instance, somebody talks about "Virtual Private Clouds (VPC)." In this case, a client uses an external vendor with a bespoke ICT system, fully managed by the vendor in a separate partition.

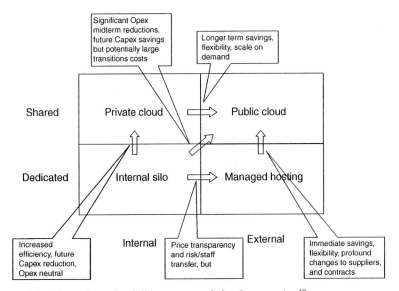

Figure 2.3   Moves from the different types of cloud computing[19]

ING Bank builds a hybrid cloud[20]

ING, a global banking and financial services organization with assets in excess of $1.7 trillion, is investing in cloud computing.

In 2008, ING had many data centers (16 in the Netherlands alone) which were obsolete, saturated and inefficient, with a fragmented architecture and slow processes. The costs were 24 percent above the market average. A first phase of a project to consider cloud computing brought the elimination of 13 data centers, virtualizing over 6000 servers and 350 applications. It has cut by 35 percent the number of managers and created new teams for the direct support to internal customers and delivery processes. In early 2011, new business pressures triggered another round of interventions; ING created a private cloud going down to six data centers. It has implemented a virtualization of the servers, desktops, and applications. Now the bank is considering becoming a broker of internal and external services on the cloud. ING's investment involves the construction of a large hybrid cloud. It combines the features of public clouds and private data centers. ING hopes that other banking and financial service organizations will use this investment.

The hybrid or shared ICT infrastructure helps to bring forth variable costs, scalability, flexibility, and on-demand availability. These benefits should help overcome the concerns of banks and financial services organizations. Those concerns are related to security, compliance, and performance procedures that financial services organizations follow in their internal data centers.

With a hybrid approach, ING will start with total control over the physical environment in which servers, storage, and applications reside. As public cloud service level agreements are better understood and as regulations develop, more solutions can shift to cheaper and easily scalable cloud venues.

Figure 2.4 shows another way to represent the cloud architecture offered by the NIST. As in the previous representation, a "Cloud Cube" has three key dimensions, relative to: three service models, five essential characteristics, and four deployment models[21].

2.2.2   The B2B cloud

An interesting variation of the deployment models is the so-called Business to Business (B2B) cloud. This solution helps in tackling the very important aspect of inter-organization collaboration and integration[22].

Cloud computing makes available opportunities as:

- Systems connected are live;
- Boundaries of classic systems disappear; and
- Capabilities are shared and transparent.

Organizations can use these opportunities to implement better B2B connections. This solution is of interest when[23]:

- There is a frequent need to exchange information between different organizations;

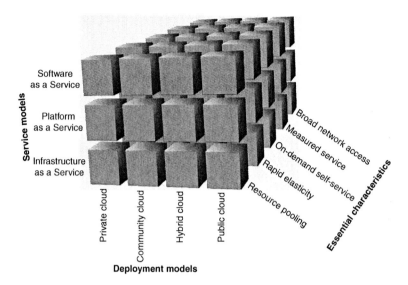

Figure 2.4   The cloud cube

- Each organization's system is locked up in their internal premises; and
- Standard data formats are available to connect disparate solutions.

In this situation, it is possible to implement an outsourced B2B partnering and trading community management[24].

ICT is used to handle processes and application mapping. Some of these tasks can be done in the B2B cloud. In this way, the ICT organization can focus on value-added activities such as R&D and innovation. Even more important, the organizations can improve their connections with their partners, be they customers, resellers, suppliers, research centers, or universities. To ease internal ICT requirements, look for a B2B solution vendor that has a large existing community of trading partners that the organization can plug into. The best solution might be, at least initially, a hybrid B2B solution. It would allow the organization to connect directly with the most important and demanding partners. At the same time, the organization can use a B2B cloud to connect with the remaining partners. By using the cloud, it also becomes easier to build a social network to improve the collaboration among partners.

2.2.3   Some of the vendors acting in cloud computing

Cloud computing has attracted several big technology players (see example in Table 2.2). They are spending large sums on the development of technologies that fit this model; this will ensure fast evolutionary development as well as reducing costs in the long run.

At present, there are several global and local vendors of cloud computing, and their number is increasing over time. Leading global service vendors such as Microsoft, Amazon, Google, Oracle, IBM, Salesforce.com, and others are expanding computing infrastructures and platforms for providing services for computation, storage, database and applications. The possible grouping of services offered is:

- Basic:
  - Infrastructure;
  - Storage; and
  - Database;
- Applications:
  - Business Process Management (BPM);
  - Marketplace;
  - Client Relationship Management;
  - Procurement;
  - Billing;
  - Finance; and
  - Accounting;
- Office:
  - Email; and
  - Office applications;
- Content (data, documents, and so on):
  - Content storing;
  - Content sharing;
  - Content processing;
  - Content certification (for legal and/or fiscal reasons); and
  - Web services for accessing the content.

Every day, vendors are introducing new types of utilization for cloud computing.

Many of the vendors mentioned have already built huge data centers. They have hundreds of thousands of servers available for current and future client needs. They have introduced cloud computing in several market sectors. Nevertheless, few players today are offering services that are really cloud computing according the NIST definition.

Amazon has been the pioneer in this field. They provide access to their platform Amazon Web Services (AWS), initially developed for internal purposes, to more than half a million application developers. Through their cloud computing service, Amazon provides small firms with the tools needed to start a cloud-based e-business. There is the possibility to scale out or, depending on demand, add extra virtual machines, or release them. For this reason, the name of the utility is Elastic Compute Cloud (EC2).

Google is also investing deeply in data centers. Google already provides online office applications such as word processing and spreadsheets.

Table 2.2 Comparison of some cloud computing platforms[25]

System property	Amazon Elastic Compute Cloud (EC2)	Google App engine	Microsoft Live mesh	Sun Network.com (Sun Grid)	GRIDS lab Aneka
Focus	Infrastructure	Platform	Infrastructure	Infrastructure	Software Platform for enterprise Clouds
Service type	Compute, storage (Amazon S3)	Web application	Storage	Compute	Compute
Virtualization	OS Level running on a Xen hypervisor	Application container	OS level	Job management system (Sun Grid Engine)	Resource Manager and Scheduler
Dynamic negotiation of QoS Parameters	None	None	None	None	SLA based resource reservation on Aneka side.
Client access interface	Amazon EC2 command-line Tools	Web-based administration console	Web-based Live Desktop and any devices with live mesh installed	Job submission scripts, Sun Grid Web Portal	Workbench, web-based portal
Web APIs	Yes	Yes	Unknown	Yes	Yes
Value-added service vendors	Yes	No	No	Yes	No
Programming framework	Customizable Linux-based Amazon Machine Image (AMI)	Python	Not applicable	Solaris OS, Java, C, C++, and FORTRAN	APIs supporting different programming models in C# and other. Net supported languages

Software and data are stored on the cloud; the Google App engine allows software developers to write applications that can run on Google's servers

Microsoft entered the market later; it is directing very large investments into the creation of new data centers. In 2008, Microsoft introduced a cloud platform called Windows Azure, which is able to provide a number of new technologies: a Windows-based cloud environment for data storage and applications deployment in Microsoft data centers. It launched another solution in the cloud, labeled Office 365; and in 2012, it reached an agreement with Sage to make available an Enterprise Resource Planning (ERP) solution in the cloud.

Other software and hardware companies have been actively investing in cloud computing; 3Tera and Saleforce.com are particularly active. Oracle has introduced a cloud-based version of its database and applications.

Social networks have moved in the same direction, turning into social platforms for client-based applications. At the time of writing, Facebook is in pole position, and Yahoo! is developing server farms as well.

2.2.4   Standardization and cloud computing

As the number of organizations turning to the cloud increases, there is a concomitantly increasing need for a clear and widely accepted set of industry standards.

There is a lively debate between those people in favor of the implementation of cloud standards and those who argue against them. At the center of the debate is a clear need to balance the benefits of a standard against those of a sustained pace of innovation.

The arguments against the adoption of cloud computing standards are that standards are simply unnecessary; according to this perspective, industry-wide uniformity and standardization are seen as something that would suffocate innovation; they would divert attention from more important problems. In short, they would introduce bureaucracy. According to this stream of thought, different vendors need to be free to develop solutions that best fit their distinctive domain and their client needs, without any restriction on them.

The opposition sees the lack of standards in the cloud industry as a serious concern. The arguments are that:

- If the industry is not acting in accordance with any commonly accepted standards, there will be no control over service vendors. As a result, potential and existing clients will have little objective information on which to base their buying decisions. With the markets ever more congested and in absence of clear standards, it will become complicated for clients to distinguish between a well-architected delivery infrastructure and a poor one. These circumstances will make it increasingly difficult for clients to navigate their way through the plethora of cloud services on offer;

- The main benefits of cloud computing come from using similar components, such as standard applications. More customizations will mean fewer benefits from cloud services;
- A deficiency of inter-cloud standards would limit the options available to people who want to migrate on another cloud or vendor (lock in), or use multiple clouds. The lack of fluency and interoperability among vendors could create a communication barrier. This would be very difficult, if not impossible, to overcome. It should be possible for organizations to move their data to any cloud vendor without being tied up for the foreseeable future; and
- There is considerable confusion around the term "cloud." Among vendors, there is a visible trend towards "cloud washing"; some organizations re-label their products as cloud computing for marketing purposes and not for their real characteristics, creating an overestimated perception of the benefits and concealing existing underlying deficiencies, both technical and non-technical.

The issue of standards is no longer being sidelined. There are debates and working groups in a large number of organizations, with contributions from some of the industry's top decision-makers and influencers. Among these, the most influential bodies are:

- The European Telecommunications Standards Institute (ETSI);
- The National Institute for Standards and Technology (NIST);
- The Open Grid Forum (OGF);
- The Open Cloud Consortium (OCC);
- The Organization for the Advancement of Structured Information Standards (OASIS);
- The International Standard Organization (ISO);
- The Banking Industry Architecture Network (BIAN); and
- The Interactive Financial eXchange Forum (IFX).

Organizations need to consider them as a reference. They should actively support these bodies by accepting their standards, conventions, guidelines, and protocols.

Moreover, the creators of any new cloud-based technology obviously do not want to see their project fail. Organizations dealing with vendors that do not apply strict standards to their business should be very cautious; good vendors should welcome standards, because they have nothing to fear from best practice rules.

The "Data Lifecycle" is one of the more important standards. In previous years, when a client bought software they installed it directly on their computers; if the vendor disappeared, the client could keep running the software until they found an alternative or the software functionality was no longer acceptable. But with a cloud, how can a client ensure they can continue to have access to their data if the vendor goes out of business or a competitor buys it? The increasing number of organizations moving to the cloud means that there is a need for data lifecycle standards, especially as the onus is currently on the client to check the financial health of their vendors.

For most people, it is simply a question of when, not if, cloud standards are established. But while the debate continues, organizations need to ensure that they are aware of the perils and pitfalls associated with adopting a cloud service. They should take on the burden of carrying out their own research, and they should continue to monitor the environment to ensure that their chosen technology is robust, properly architected, and secure.

2.3   Benefits and expectations associated with cloud computing

Currently, the market supply of ICT services is devoting a lot of effort and resources to advertise to potential clients the many benefits arising from the use of a cloud service. The benefits are essentially:

- Flexibility of provision and use. This would be particularly important when there are load variations over time, as happens for instance with software development projects;
- Economies of volume;
- Financial aspects, mainly connected with moving from investments to variable costs;
- The overcoming of the inertia and many of the consequent delays that accompany the release of new services;
- An easier access through the Internet. This would be particularly valuable when the workforce is distributed and is web enabled (as happens with a flexible or remote workforce);
- A great support for collaboration, inside or outside any one organization. Cloud computing is not only "computing"; it is also a powerful tool for communication. It can easily make available new facilities such as Unified Collaborative and Communication (UCC)[26]; and
- A general higher efficiency in service management and security (for instance a full compliance with ISO 27001).

There are two perspectives for cloud computing:

- The client perspective: Standardization, automation, and self-service access to a catalog of defined services; and
- The vendor perspective: Virtualization and resource optimization.

2.3.1   Benefits to the client

Cloud services entail the adoption of significant economic and financial benefits, such as the ability and potential to:

- Reduce the start-up costs of a system;
- Reduce capital investments (Capex) against higher running costs (Opex);
- Size systems and applications according to the normal workload. It is possible to manage peak loads through the ability to scale, typical of the cloud infrastructure; and
- Optimize costs in terms of computational resources and financial resources, and in terms of human resources, capabilities, and management.

2.3.1.1   Increased pace of innovation

Cloud services encourage organization innovation, as they enable organizations to explore the new ICT organization functions more quickly and economically, with very good scalability.

Cloud services allow financial institutions to accelerate innovation. The low cost of entry to new markets and products allows start-up organizations to succeed by giving greater chances to deploy new products quickly and at low cost. This allows small and medium size organizations to compete more effectively with traditional and established organizations whose deployment process in-house data centers can take more time. The market rule is that increased competition helps to increase the pace of innovation, so the entire industry will benefit from the impulse introduced by cloud computing.

2.3.1.2   Focus on organization strategy and organization agility

Cloud services offer an unparalleled opportunity for organizations to focus on core competencies. This brings a real competitive advantage[27]. Two key factors contribute to this opportunity[28]:

- The dynamic nature of resource allocation in cloud computing, which allows for a closer alignment between ICT and business strategy; and
- A reduction or removal of the distractions associated with internal ICT management. In this way, the ICT organization can re-focus its resources and management efforts to the core business[29].

Organization agility is the ability of an organization to adapt rapidly and cost-efficiently in response to changes in the business environment. According to McKinsey and Company, the benefits of agility include[30]:

- Faster revenue growth;
- Greater and more lasting cost reductions; and
- More effective management of risks and reputational threats.

It is often difficult to tell whether organizations are agile because of the agility inherent within ICT, or whether an agile culture in the organization influences ICT. Regardless of the reasons, the management in agile organizations understand the importance of tightly coupling organization and ICT agilities.

Forward thinking CIOs are deploying cloud services as a strategic tool. The benefits are not only for ICT. Cloud services enable a full organization transformation. It can eventually change how the organization operates.

For organizations with agile ICT functions, business and ICT managers agree that infrastructure and technology are the primary drivers of that agility. Agile organizations that have already adopted organization wide cloud deployments are paving the way for their ICT organizations to become more responsive and flexible to the demands of the organization. An open technology and business environment, enabled by cloud computing and new outsourcing models, creates a radically new approach to the delivery of business services and processes. The result is a new and more flexible operating platform.

As Jimmy Harris and Stephen Nunn explain in a chapter on cloud computing[31]:

> Today, an open and agile technology environment, and the relentless expansion of outsourcing into most ICT functions and business processes, is changing the nature and the economics of service delivery. The ultimate benefit and competitive advantage delivered through this new platform and design is greater organizational agility.

An agile operating platform enabled by outsourcing models and by an ICT infrastructure that expands or contracts to meet demand can help organizations be more responsive to the marketplace. It would create a more open environment for innovation.

2.3.1.3 Mobility

Ubiquitous access implies access anytime, anywhere, and from any device. For the organization wanting to offer 24/7, or global, access to their customers or partners, cloud computing offers a variety of opportunities to meet these demands. For staff who are dispersed and/or required to travel, this can mean working out of normal business hours, or in a range of time zones. Cloud computing creates an even faster, more responsive and connected environment.

2.3.1.4 Elasticity: a flexible and scalable technology model

A major business advantage of cloud computing is the bringing of elasticity to the organization[32]. It makes trade-off decisions more fluid. The elasticity offered by clouds serves to transfer risk to the cloud vendor. They can accept it thanks to the variety of their clients.

NIST's definition of elasticity in the context of cloud computing is as follows:

> Capabilities can be rapidly and elastically provisioned, in some cases automatically, to quickly scale out and rapidly released to quickly scale in. To the client, the capabilities available for provisioning often appear to be unlimited and can be purchased in any quantity at any time[33].

In other words, cloud computing provides the ability to add or remove ICT resources in a fine-grained way and with a short lead time rather than weeks or more. It matches resources to a variable workload much more closely.

Normally, advanced ICT infrastructure and application services would be accessible only to large organizations with huge budgets available to develop and sustain the ongoing use of these resources. But with cloud computing, small and medium organizations can access these as well. Moreover, these resources can be added to, changed, or removed in a very short time. This fact potentially allows for exponential improvements in operational efficiency. Organizations are also moving to the cloud because it offers them the flexibility they need to adapt to the ever-changing business climate. The cloud makes possible for them to access technology quickly and to offer in a short time solutions that they do not have themselves.

Cloud services can speed up transformation and close performance gaps that require support from ICT services. Thus, cloud services may allow for rapid business reconfiguration at times when organizations need to be able to adapt their organizations and delivery models globally to meet market evolutions and change accordingly.

2.3.1.5   *Adoption of best-of-breed security solutions*

From the security point of view, cloud services can bring several benefits to the client, including the ability to enjoy:

- Superior security solutions compared to their own internal standards;
- Security around the organization which is difficult to achieve in their own internal reality;
- Services and open standards that exceed the typical proprietary approaches; and
- Professionalism that is otherwise difficult to acquire and maintain over time.

Cloud service vendors can benefit from economies of scale for the creation of much more advanced and high-performance security solutions compared to those that are implementable with the same investment by entities making multiple smaller investments. The commendable features that cloud solutions can provide are, for example:

- Redundant and geographically distributed architectures;
- Monitoring of services with high granularity and automation;
- A very short reaction time to accidents and emergency;
- Ability to scale resources to respond to any distributed denial of service attacks;
- Better outputs in terms of physical and organizational security; and
- Consistency and coherence of the various security solutions.

As regards openness of solutions, cloud service vendors, in their relationships with multiple and diverse subjects, must target their services to the standard and open modes of delivery. This implies, in terms of security perspective, the availability of a greater ability of direct and indirect control over the infrastructure. This has clear positive effects on the capability of execution.

Many cloud vendors use and follow security standards, some of which are connected with certification schemes. The unique features of the cloud contribute to limiting the side effects of the shared nature of such an environment. Standards and certification help to increase security levels, and they provide guarantees to the cloud computing clients on how the vendors manage security.

2.3.2   Benefits to the vendor

Cloud vendors provide their services from large data centers. They can enjoy significant economies of scale in three areas:

- Supply-side savings: Large scale data centers reduce costs relating to both hardware and software;
- Demand-side aggregation: Aggregating demands for computing smooths overall variability, increasing computer utilization rates; and
- Multitenancy efficiency: A multitenant application model with an increasing number of tenants reduces the application management and ICT cost per tenant.

2.3.2.1   Supply-side economies of scale

The management of ICT systems require high upfront costs for infrastructure investments and skilled personnel. Only large organizations have enough resources and the aggregate demand that justify the huge investment needed to achieve significant economies of scale, continuous innovation, and capabilities.

The cloud vendor can transfer to cloud clients (particularly small/medium organizations) true economies of scale and efficiency, exceeding those of a dedicated ICT infrastructure.

Such economies of scale are the result of achievements by the cloud vendor in the following areas:

- Greater purchasing power, which enables economies of scale. Cloud vendors purchasing hardware can get discounts of up to 30 percent compared to smaller buyers;
- Lower infrastructure management costs: A cloud data center administrator can operate thousands of servers, whereas a traditional organization ICT administrator, for the same cost, can service up to approximately 140 servers. Not only does the cloud ensure a greater return on the costs of ICT equipment, but also it promotes more efficiency and more effectiveness in the technical staff; ICT personnel costs alone can account for up to 70 percent of an organization's budget[34];
- High autonomy: Cloud computing eliminates most of the time usually needed to sort and deliver ICT resources. Moreover, cloud computing can considerably reduce labor costs through the automation of repetitive management tasks;
- Lower electricity costs: Cloud vendors are able to achieve cost savings by building data centers in locations with an inexpensive electricity supply and by using bulk purchase agreements. In contrast, the operators of small data centers pay a higher rate on average for electricity than large vendors, who pay less than a quarter of the national average rate. Moreover, further research has shown that operators of multiple data centers are able to take advantage of the geographical variability of electricity rates, which can reduce energy costs further:
- Greater security and reliability: Large cloud vendors are often better able to bring deep expertise into this area than can a typical corporate ICT department. Cloud systems tend to be more secure and reliable. Security is often raised as an issue when discussing the adoption of cloud computing; however, a cloud vendor's very survival depends on its adoption of good security; any inadequacy or deficiency in the service provision would be detrimental to its brand and to its own existence. As a result, cloud vendor security access and data protection measures are far superior to those that many other organizations are capable of putting in place. However, presenting the cloud as a secure environment may be a questionable, if not even hazardous, move. The consequences of a security failure in the cloud could create serious problems, and the result would be far more damaging than the breakdown of an in-house ICT infrastructure;
- Multitenancy economies of scale: Instead of rendering a specific application to each client in a multitenant application, multiple clients use a single instance of the application simultaneously. This brings important economic benefits. The impact of fixed costs is considerably reduced since labor costs and overheads are shared across a large set of clients;

- Ongoing Research and Development: The large aggregate scale of these larger data centers can justify considerable and ongoing R&D to continue running them more efficiently; and
- Overall Impact: In cloud computing, the combination of supply-side economies of scale in hardware capacity (amortizing costs across more hardware), demand-side aggregation of workloads (reducing variability), and the multitenant application model (amortizing costs across multiple clients) leads to large economies of scale.

2.3.3   Benefits to society: pollution reduction

The sustainability agenda of many organizations is more and more a core strategic priority. Now, executives will often examine the entire organization to detect ways in which they can operate more sustainably.

Cloud services allow financial institutions to use their hardware more efficiently, improving their efficiency per kWh. The result is a reduction in the usage of non-renewable energy and the generation of greenhouse gases. Two factors allow cloud computing to improve system efficiencies[35]:

- The packing of many sessions from different clients into the same machine (multitenancy); and
- The computing capacity of multiple machines into a smaller number of machines (virtualization), which increases the average loads on the physical machines.

In addition to these savings, cloud computing support to telecommuters may contribute to a significant reduction in staff travel.

The precise balance of all these factors is different in every situation. Some surveys help in an initial evaluation. The independent analyst firm Verdantix conducted research in this field, sponsored by AT&T[36], then the Carbon Disclosure Project (CDP) presented this research as an addendum to the study they launched in June 2012 "Cloud Computing: The ICT Solution for the 21st Century."

ICT is a key area of focus for achieving sustainability goals. Computing requirements have accelerated rapidly over the last ten years. Back in 2006, the USA Environmental Protection Agency (EPA) estimated that data centers consumed 1.5 percent of total US electricity, and suggested that this was double their 2000 consumption. The growth of data centers continues; the USA Department of Energy believes that in 2012 data centers may be consuming up to 3 percent of total US electricity.

It is estimated that by 2020, large USA organizations that use cloud computing should be able to achieve annual energy savings of $12.3 billion, and annual carbon reductions equivalent to 200 million barrels of oil – enough to power 5.7 million cars for one year. By 2020, large UK organizations that use cloud computing could achieve annual energy savings of £1.2 billion, and annual carbon reductions equivalent to the annual emissions of over 4 million passenger vehicles. With the forecast move to cloud computing, large UK organizations can reduce CO_2 emissions associated with their ICT capacity by 50 percent compared to predicted levels without the adoption of this technology.

The above-mentioned report also looked at the French market. It showed a disparity between the annual CO_2 savings that can be achieved by 2020 in France (1.2 million metric tons) and the UK (9.2 million metric tons). The most likely reason for that difference is the currently higher proportion of electricity in France generated from nuclear and renewable sources.

The report finds that an organization that adopts cloud services can:

• Reduce its energy consumption;
• Lower its carbon emissions; and
• Decrease its Capital Expenditure (Capex) on ICT resources while improving operational efficiency.

The report came out of in-depth interviews with multinational firms in diverse sectors. All study participants had adopted cloud services for at least two years. Many of the firms interviewed reported cost savings as a primary motivator, with anticipated cost reductions as high as 40–50 percent.

2.4   Risks and mitigations of cloud computing

There are several risks and challenges, both real and perceived, on the journey to the cloud. These are largely associated with:

• Not fully understanding the concept;
• Architecting the right solution;
• Ensuring that security is appropriate, and governance is in place; and
• Managing procurement carefully.

The correct experience and knowledge of the technologies involved is subject to change, as are the organizational needs, as well as education, and stakeholder engagement could mitigate these pitfalls. These are all critical elements to enable a convincing and effective cloud services solution.

There is a need for specialist skills and experience for assembling and customizing multiple cloud services from different vendors in a flexible, changeable way, while maintaining security, backup, and governance mechanisms. To this end, applications offered in a cloud computing environment will need to become more loosely coupled. They should be programmed to act with an integration layer and a server bus, not with the underlying hard-coupled piece of hardware.

Some key issues and risks to consider include:

- Vendor lock in;
- Loss of governance;
- Contracts not always adequate;
- The impossibility of negotiating contractual terms or inadequacy to do so;
- Applicable law and competent courts;
- Difficult or poor network connections;
- Standardization, which might hurt competitive advantages; and
- Risks of the unavailability, or interruption, of the services provided by the cloud.

The following sections will examine each of these aspects.

2.4.1   Vendor lock in

Vendor lock in means the difficulty for the client to change cloud vendor once it has been with its original vendor for a certain period. A client should have a guarantee to be able, and should be put in the right situation, to:

- Change its cloud vendor;
- Insource any service operated by an external cloud vendor; and
- Entrust to an external cloud vendor a service handled internally in its own private cloud.

All this processes should take place without any particular problem. Clear contractual terms should take these aspects into account. They should specify in a clear and comprehensive way all the terms and operating procedures for exiting from the service and transiting to a different environment (the so-called transfer back), with particular reference to:

- The modes through which the data are given back to the client;
- The delivery methods followed by the cloud vendor to support the migration; and
- The time, effort, passage conditions and any transitory steps envisaged.

It would also be useful to define best practices and internationally accepted standards that make the migration of data and applications across several clouds truly viable and efficient.

As pointed out by the Vice President of the European Commission, Neelie Kroes[37], interoperability is crucial in the field so that this new market becomes fair, open, and competitive, and therefore be able to express its full potential.

2.4.2 Loss of governance and third-party data control

In the context of the services supplied by the cloud vendors, loss of governance is an ever-present risk to the client. The factors influencing this aspect are mainly related to the "way to use" proposed by the vendor, possibly formalized in special clauses, Service Level Agreements, and contractual terms.

Another important aspect refers to the specific security practices considered normal in outsourcing relationships, such as assessments (technical and procedural) and audits; these must be included in cloud computing service contracts. Furthermore, the use of subcontractors by cloud vendors may make it increasingly difficult to assess the impact of this type of risk.

It is necessary to take into account the requirements of compliance with:

- Relevant legislation;
- Regulations;
- Standards; and
- Best practice.

These guidelines may contain requirements related to control and governance whose compatibility with the cloud is difficult if not impossible to satisfy.

The loss of governance on data and applications could also result in potential risk of infringement of the legislation regarding data privacy.

2.4.3 Contractual aspects

The cloud services market is new. Vendors that offer public cloud services have not yet thoroughly developed a diverse offer based on the types of market and client; in most cases, cloud service vendors offer standard contracts applicable to all their clients.

Often cloud vendors, in order to simplify their contract agreements, do not meet the different client requirements. This translates into clauses that do not always protect clients with higher security requirements, so cloud vendor and client should address these aspects from the initial stages of preparation of the agreement.

Another difficulty is negotiation of the contractual terms. The real driving force of economics in the cloud is economy of scale, so cloud vendors are keen to establish a standard contract applicable to all their clients. They insist on no negotiation or, at the very least, a highly restricted possibility.

Chapter 4 examines these aspects in more details.

2.4.4 Applicable law and competent courts

In many countries, organizations must meet data sovereignty requirements that strictly limit the locations where it is possible to host data. The CIOs must consider what type of cloud may be compatible with such systems, or rather what is necessary to bring them into compliance.

Separate mention is required for the law applicable to the handling of personal data, identified by special legislation, which the parties cannot rescind or inhibit. Similarly, in the framework of a business-to-client contract, it is the jurisdiction in force in the country where the client resides that should, with very limited exceptions, apply.

Within the framework of the services provided by public clouds, data and applications can be physically located in a multiplicity of data centers distributed around various countries worldwide. International vendors choose countries to build their data centers based on:

- Economic criteria (for example in countries with low staff costs, financial or tax incentives, or low cost of energy and land);
- Geographical criteria (such as in colder regions, where it costs less to keep data centers cool); and
- Technical criteria (for example in countries with large availability of skilled labor).

These criteria may lead to choices that are inappropriate for some types of clients who prefer or need only those options that ensure a large degree of security.

The immaturity of the cloud market also depends on the current lack of defined and widely recognized standards by the market. In the field of security management particularly, there is a lack of certain guidelines for the support of cloud service clients in the assessment of the approaches proposed by the vendor.

Another crucial point for the possible acceptance of cloud computing in organizations is the security of critical data, in terms of both transfer and storage. Large organizations will not be willing to support the cloud concept while there is no visibility about where the data is stored and how it is protected[38]. Reasons for such concerns include respect for foreign laws (which could possibly allow foreign governments to access the data), and domestic insurance contracts (which might demand that data and/or applications be stored only in certain regions). Providing this required visibility would contradict in some ways the whole rationale of cloud computing. It is unclear how the large cloud vendors will tackle this concern, at least in terms of information of where the data resides at any given moment, and the provision of updates on when and where the data is moved.

The respect of the laws on data transfer would apply also to multinational organizations for the data of the organizations in the group, even if they were adopting a private cloud.

Some vendors have introduced a new breed: public sovereign clouds. With them, the vendors undertake the obligation to keep the data within a specific region[39].

2.4.5 Security

It is a fact that for all industries showing interest in approaching cloud solutions, the issue of security appears to be the major impediment to rapid adoption of cloud technologies. It is on this subject that supporters of this technology mostly conflict with its critics, the latter wanting to emphasize the many sensitive and potentially damaging aspects that could arise from its adoption.

For an organization, the retention of its information, applications, and hardware in its own premises provides a level of confidence that for many people would be lost in a cloud. This does not mean that cloud services are necessarily insecure. It means that new relevant considerations come into play. There is the need to identify and use more modern security models. Organizations are now highly concerned with end-to-end security; firewalls are no longer considered as the only solution for their internal procedures such as password control and maintenance.

With the growing demand for cloud services, security incidents could emerge with increasing frequency. However, many of the incidents that could occur in a cloud environment, and so be regarded as a concern relating to cloud security, would in fact merely reflect most of the traditional networked application and data-hosting problems; the underlying issues continue to be the well-established challenges such as phishing, downtime, data loss, password weaknesses, and compromised hosts running botnets.

On the positive side, cloud clients can potentially take advantage of a concentration of security expertise at major cloud computing vendors. These vendors can adopt a wide range of security measures, ensuring that their entire ecosystem employs security best practices. On the other hand, in a cloud computing environment a single subverter could disrupt many clients; for example, spammers subverted EC2 and caused Spamhaus to blacklist a large fraction of EC2's IP addresses, causing major service disruptions.

Security, data privacy, and compliance are also important elements. In this field, the international regulators will play an important role; they will dedicate more attention to the standardization of procedures and "forensic" instruments for control over the cloud world. In this way, police forces may have the ability to efficiently gain secure and reliable evidence on whatever might happen.

It is nevertheless desirable that homogeneous and harmonic regulations be enacted by the various States. They should not limit the possibility of intervention inherent within the international distribution of the data centers in the cloud. These regulations are a necessary precondition for being able to effectively counteract the phenomenon of cybercrime, particularly in the world of cloud computing.

Security needs standards. This is one of the major sources of concern for clients wanting to transfer data to the cloud, and it needs to be urgently addressed. Some vendors take this topic into account; they are deeply concerned about security and any potential security breaches. As a result, most vendors go to extreme lengths to protect their clients' data. Security breaches would inevitably hinder the reputation of a vendor. Just one problem could cause a vendor to fall into disrepute. In the worst cases, it could mark the end of their business altogether.

Deutsche bank completes cloud computing overhaul[40]

Deutsche Bank has performed a major cloud computing overhaul aimed at improving the development of internal applications.

The German bank has set up an Infrastructure as a Service (IaaS) development platform. The aim of the new platform is to enable developers to rapidly create and deploy virtual environments, running up to 2000 VMs at any one time. A variety of collaboration and knowledge management systems support these environments.

The VMs are available for development in Microsoft Windows, UNIX, Solaris, and Linux environments.

Using the new system, costs for end users are lower than their running a dedicated PC for development, partly through "aggressive standardization" and partly through automation. Additionally, storage costs were cut by not providing automated backup. There are instead "flexible" data repositories to protect and manage applications.

Deutsche Bank has also developed new modular data center designs and elastic computing platforms. It has implemented access to the IaaS platform underpinned by its core identity management platforms.

Any authorized permanent employee requesting a new virtual machine can visit a particular website. S/he then selects an operating system and clicks three buttons. The new "machine" will be available "within an hour."

A system records the user's cost center and details in a configuration management and billing database.

2.4.6   Difficult or poor network connections

Poor network connections currently constitutes one of the biggest difficulties in the generalized use of cloud services for all organizations. Unfortunately, broadband is not available everywhere. There is the option to resort to satellite communications, but they are expensive and of low quality.

In time, this obstacle will disappear. However, it remains a problem for now, especially for organizations with dispersed facilities or with remote workers or mobile workers. The way to overcome this difficulty is to get the help of a telecommunications company; they will respond if there is enough business.

In a survey, 56 percent of respondents said they expected cloud computing to have a big impact on their business. There were significant concerns over security (voiced by 61 percent of respondents) and uptime (37 percent). This is undermining the perceived benefits that the cloud can bring[41].

2.4.7   Standardization which might hurt competitive advantages

Some organizations gain their competitive advantages from specific and proprietary applications. These are not suited to SaaS implementations on public clouds, since the organization would run the risk of losing their advantage. This would not, however, prevent their use of IaaS or PaaS. For greater protection, an organization could resort to virtual private clouds – bespoke applications hosted in a public cloud, but with strict restrictions in terms of access by other tenants.

The best way to overcome this limitation is by making a thorough analysis of which application really provides a competitive advantage.

To be fair, in some cases it is precisely the opposite; to remain with a bespoke system brings higher maintenance costs in its wake, and in some cases the use of an obsolete application with outmoded functionality can damage a business. In such a case, not using a public cloud would bring a competitive disadvantage – and this is the case more often than most people believe.

2.4.8 Cloud vendor default or interruption of service

Clients should consider very carefully the risks related to the cloud vendor failure or interruption in the provision of the service. This is important especially if the cloud service is selected for critical data and applications. Vendors adopt advanced technologies as a guarantee of service continuity, and they should give protection through appropriate contractual SLA. The cloud clients should not, however, believe that all possible problems have been tackled.

An extreme circumstance associated with this kind of risk is the possibility of bankruptcy or termination of the cloud vendor or of its services. The cloud market is still in its early stages. Therefore, it is likely that over time natural selection of the various competitors will lead to bankruptcies, cessations, mergers, and reorganization to a greater degree than in other, more established, sectors.

Moreover, given the lock in risks previously analyzed, it may prove to be very difficult and costly for a client to find alternative solutions should their cloud vendor decide to interrupt the delivery of its services or be forced to do so.

The reasons why public clouds are most at risk are that cloud vendors:

- Are often international players with logics of business and management systems that may be incompatible with those of the cloud services clients;
- May use a cloud infrastructure located outside the European Union;
- May offer a lower degree of visibility with respect to security measures and resilience than the more conventional outsourcing models, or with respect to internal ICT solutions; and
- May not have an interest in declaring a possible loss of data or fraud. In addition, a legislative obligation to disclose security incidents may not exist. All this could be incompatible with the client's aims and objectives. In this respect, in May 2011 the Obama Administration proposed new legislation imposing an obligation to report incidents involving the loss or theft of personal data. The proposal, called "Data Breach Notification,"

stems from the idea that the use of encryption on stolen data nullifies the risk and hence concludes with the non-applicability of guarantee norms including the obligation to notify the event[42].

A specific aspect to protect in contractual terms is the "ownership" of the data in case of default of the vendor and also the possibility to reclaim it from a legal point of view.

2.4.9 Higher costs

In certain specific cases, if an organization decides to operate its activities in the cloud, some of the stated cost benefits of cloud computing may not apply. In fact, it could be that in some contexts it could be cheaper for the organization to have its own data center. Take the case of fiscal laws. In some countries, these laws prevent financial services from reclaim the VAT between revenues and costs, and so moving from an internal data center to an external vendor could create the additional cost of the VAT.

Nevertheless, in many cases a fully scalable architecture such as that allowed by cloud computing could still be justified. This could be the case when, for instance, the organization decides to launch a pilot on a new product or service. With the cloud, the service can be:

- Launched quickly;
- Market tested in a low-risk way, before hardware and software is acquired; and
- Be insourced later as a longer-term solution with a more proven investment case.

Migration from a traditional architecture to a cloud based one requires a new set of skills and processes, so the organization may need help in the short term. Organizations should explore the opportunities and test cloud services as early as possible. In this way, they can build experience and gain confidence with lower risk. Examples could be in areas such as backup, peak application demand, and disaster recovery solutions.

Backup and business continuity at Narragansett Bay Insurance[43]

Narragansett Bay Insurance specializes in homeowner policies. The company is based in Rhode Island, RI, USA which is in the path of many hurricanes, and they need to ensure that they are available to their policyholders during hurricanes. They want to be supportive in the event of a hurricane, and at those times their biggest issue is claims; during a hurricane, they are not selling policies but are servicing claims. For that reason, the company operates two remote, cloud-based data centers, providing resiliency. All of Narragansett Bay's operations – including its phone systems – are in the cloud.

2.4.8.1   Cost savings

Cloud services may lead to significant cost savings[44]:

- The cloud client may achieve savings by avoiding the cost of capital purchase or leasehold of hardware and software. Economies of scale available to the cloud vendor make it feasible for the client to offer their services cheaply, through load balancing and improved efficiency of resource use[45];
- As pointed out by Grossman[46], cloud computing allows the use of the exact capacity required, paying only for the computing power required. In other words, there are also savings in terms of opportunity cost for the capital that would otherwise be invested, without the option of the cloud, for the acquisition of greater computing capacity to meet the potential growing demand. Avoiding such capital-intensive expenditures may be even more important during the early stages of the life of a business, when contingency may be speculative and cash may be limited[47];
- The efforts and costs associated with energy, space, security, plants, and equipment required to house, transform and adapt the workplace to ICT equipment requirements may be reduced or eliminated altogether;
- ICT support costs, including maintenance, backup, helpdesk services, and similar, may be reduced or be provided more cheaply by the cloud services vendor;
- Much ICT equipment is prone to obsolescence over a short timeline. Cloud computing offers a model to reduce these costs[48]; and
- Normally using cloud services brings an increase in network costs. Organizations' corporate networks are seemingly being overlooked and not incorporated into a cloud strategy. While 43 percent respondents in a survey stated that their organization networks would need to upgrade to make the most of cloud, just 20 percent said that this was actually a key part of their strategy[49]. In some cases, cloud computing can bring savings in the telecommunication costs. Take the example of a central office that sends regularly heavy files to their branches or remote offices. With cloud computing, the originator would send these files just once, to the cloud. The cloud vendor would distribute them via the Internet. Yamamay, a global apparel producer, experienced this situation[50]. They used to send heavy files with the latest collections to their stores around the world. Now they periodically send just one file to Google, which distributes them to all the remote locations.

Clearly the precise balance of these components and hence the potential savings will differ from one situation to another.

2.4.8.2   Cost efficiency and cost control: capex v. opex

Cloud services clients can avoid or drastically reduce many expenses related to personnel, software, hardware, real estate, ICT infrastructure cooling, power, software licenses, and maintenance costs. With cloud computing, organizations may no longer need to maintain the large, specialized ICT staff and resources responsible for the maintenance of expensive computing and storage systems. Apart from the direct costs, the issue is that internal personnel need to update frequently, since ICT technology is still very much in development. These updates bring additional costs and, in some cases, redundancy costs.

In addition, the vendor rather than internal personnel would apply most patches, fixes, browser application updates, and other expensive and time-consuming trouble-shooting procedures. The potential for reduced hardware and software costs means that the cloud services client can free up capital for use elsewhere, for strategic corporate goals.

Cloud computing is often described as converting capital expenses (Capex) to operating expenses (Opex). Cloud computing enables the sharing of ICT resources. It makes the total cost of a service variable with use (pay-per-use), enabling ICT costs to be accounted as an expense rather than as an investment. The pay-per-use model reduces investment and the associated Capex and Opex. In addition, it reduces the risk of over- or under-investing. For example, most traditional data centers are built to handle peak demand, whereas the cloud allows purchase on demand of the peak processing, for just the time or capacity needed at any specific moment.

Most ICT organizations are accustomed to Capital Expenditure (Capex) models; organizations invest significantly upfront. The cloud model, in contrast, is based on an Operating Expenditure (Opex) model with faster times to benefits and more accurate evaluations. This change in the business model will affect all parties. Special demands will be made on the software publishers, hardware vendors, and systems integrators, who will need to adapt rapidly. By radically changing an organization's infrastructure, cloud computing can help organizations bring new products and new markets to clients faster, by reducing the time to market.

An additional benefit arising from the cloud is the opportunity to minimize infrastructure risk[51]. ICT-driven organizations can use the cloud to reduce the risk inherent in purchasing hardware, because when migrating an application out to the cloud, the risk of purchasing too much or too little infrastructure becomes the cloud vendor's responsibility. Typically, a cloud vendor has volumes that would allow it to absorb the growth and workload spikes of individual clients to balance loads, and in this way, the vendors can reduce their financial risks.

Highly optimized and virtualized ICT infrastructure facilitates cost efficiency and control by enabling organizations to leverage the correct and diverse hardware components. They can thus manage their computing needs as a function of real time usage, rather than having to design and run them with maximum capacity, redundancy, and resiliency upfront.

2.4.8.3   *Speed-to-market and lower cost of entry*

There are several facets of cloud computing that help new players reduce the costs of entering new markets and launch new products or services:

- The infrastructure is rented, not purchased. Hence the costs can be monitored while the capital investment can be limited;
- The pay-per-use formula; and
- The cloud vendor will offer huge capacity on request.

Many cloud services are standard applications, and can be customized via parameters rather than changes in the code. This reduces preparation times, and also helps reduce the time needed to reach the market. It potentially gives to the organizations using the cloud services the opportunity to take the lead over their competitors. At its core, cloud services offer standardization, flexibility, and business model innovation. Their use can:

- Change the competitive landscape within an industry; and
- Lower barriers to new entrants on a global scale.

For example, setting up the infrastructure necessary to launch a new business is simpler and cheaper with cloud services; a fast, stable Internet connection is all that is needed, as through the Internet the client (and its customers, resellers and partners) can access a full suite of business services almost instantly.

2.5   Migration paths

The evaluation of whether or not an organization should go to cloud computing is not an easy task – albeit worthwhile – to perform[52]. It must start with a clear understanding of the problems or opportunity to address, whether at the strategic, organizational, or operational levels. Only once this has been achieved in full can it become feasible to negotiate and contract for cloud services.

The use of cloud computing requires complex management in order to balance risks and benefits. The usefulness of hybrid approaches, together with the issue of vendor dependence, suggests that a modular approach may reduce risk. This would imply:

- Staging the implementation;
- Retaining some capacity in house; and/or
- Contracting with multiple vendors to provide different elements of the services (in particular, backup services should be provided separately).

The organization may be able to divest itself of some or all of its ICT operations. There will be a critical dependency on the new relationships with cloud vendors. Managing these relationships adequately will require the client to have (or to acquire through consultancy) the following competencies:

- Strong contract negotiation skills and experience;
- Sophisticated understanding of cloud computing concepts and practices;
- Sound understanding of the complex security considerations; and
- Strong governance method and capabilities (as analyzed in Chapter 4).

The cost savings will be unique to every situation. Each organization needs to do a proper Cost Benefit Analysis. In addition, the costs charged by cloud vendors may change significantly in the future, as the industry matures. The client should take into account the risk of increased charges at the first contractual renewal when evaluating the financial aspects of cloud services.

The cost savings could be real. But reaping the benefits of cloud services will almost certainly require changes to be made in the organization's existing technologies, leaving it with little or no possibility of making alternative arrangements in the event that the cloud vendor fails to deliver the service or fails altogether. Clients should consider this as a risk when designing an implementation, selecting a vendor, and negotiating the contract.

Nevertheless, cloud computing offers a means to:

- Start with minimal infrastructure costs;
- Expand incrementally in response to demand if required; and
- Avoid the costs of obsolescence.

Cost reduction is important, and cloud computing brings many more benefits, as discussed in this chapter. Hence, in order to detail requirements and analyze benefits adequately, and to evaluate the challenges of the migration, organizations should consider a Proof of Concept (POC) or pilot. This option has often been considered too difficult or too expensive to take; however, cloud computing now offers a means to temporarily deploy appropriate infrastructure rapidly and to scale up as required, to meet the needs of analysis as well as operations. It is necessary to provide the opportunity to tighten the benefits analysis, planning beyond what has previously been available, and put in place the appropriate remediation.

Suitable use cases for a cloud computing POC may include[53]:

- Lighthouse application. This should be relative to an application for which POC results will be meaningful to the organization. Business-critical applications, however, may not be the best choice – whereas success with a high-visibility application will promote broader adoption and acceptance of cloud solutions as the organization moves forward with the rollout;

- Lifecycle phase. This should be a standard development or test environment in the cloud. Giving developers fast access to non-production environments meets a specific need and helps build confidence before the organization moves to production solutions;
- Variable usage. The choice should be with a workload with scalability requirements that highlight the unique capabilities of a cloud. The POC should be set up in a non-production test bed to allow for experimentation that yields as much learning as possible about how the workload and cloud technology operate; and
- Resource intensive. This is the case with workloads that consume scarce human resources. They may be workloads with a high business priority. Or alternatively, they might be workloads that steal scarce resources from priority projects.

The case of a medium-size financial institution[54]

A medium financial institution in Italy, Istituto per il Credito Sportivo, decided at the end of 2009 to create a fundamental transformation in its ICT environment. Its roadmap can be seen as an interesting example of moving towards cloud computing. After a couple of years, it had successfully implemented several steps in this direction:

- At the lower level it had moved all its servers and desktops to a virtualized environment;
- It had outsourced its core banking applications to an external vendor;
- It had moved the disaster recovery center for its internal servers to a cloud vendor; and
- Finally, it had moved its email system and web site to the cloud using a true cloud computing operator.

The benefits in terms of costs have been substantial. Apart from that, the Istituto per il Credito Sportivo has been able to prepare for the launch of new financial products in a short time. Finally, from a security point of view it has now a much more secure environment than it could have afforded by going it alone, due to its limited ICT staff.

A side effect, important for the social balance of the institution, has been an improvement in its environmental impact in terms of CO_2 emission (albeit limited, taking into account the limited size of the Institute).

2.6 Conclusions

There are several ways of looking at cloud computing:

- An incremental improvement to what ICT is achieving today;
- A disruptive innovation that can change the way ICT is managed and, much more important; and
- An introduction of new business models into an organization.

The last approach requires a concerted effort by the part of the entire executive team of the organization. The COO, CFO, CMO, and indeed the CEO should all be involved.

A possible sequence to follow in the implementation of a cloud computing strategy should consist of the following steps:

- Increase the organization skills/capabilities in Business Process Re-Engineering (BPR);
- Define what the organization should be in the next five years;
- Establish the true cost of ICT as a baseline;
- Consider a greenfield ICT landscape to support the "new" organization;
- Research/tender for potential transition and future operations;
- Re-assess what could actually be achieved through a six-month to a two-year plan;
- Redesign processes and procedures;
- Renegotiate existing applications and infrastructure contracts;
- Select and pursue an appropriate transition strategy; and
- Incorporate benchmarking and flexibility in the new contracts.

The VMware Global Cloud Adoption Study questioned over 1000 ICT decision-makers at organization companies[55]. At the top of the results was the fact that respondents indicated that they plan to spend almost one third of their 2012 ICT budget on cloud computing. In percentage terms, this represents 31 percent, up from 26 percent in 2011. It underlines that organizations are looking to become more agile, connected, and productive.

3
Cloud Computing in Financial Institutions

3.1 Introduction

This chapter focuses on the potential impact that cloud computing can have on the financial services industry by examining the current context and looking at various considerations connected with the adoption of cloud services.

Financial services institutions are at the forefront in terms of the adoption of new technology and also of cloud computing. They can benefit significantly from the capabilities of cloud computing as a result of its characteristics:

- Processing of large amounts of information, from various sources;
- A high degree of business process automation;
- A mature, functional portfolio;
- Straight Through Processing (STP); and
- Proven benefits from technological outsourcing.

This situation arises for:

- The nature of the business and its dependency on technology;
- The amount of ICT investment; and
- Their exposure to changing market and economic conditions.

3.2 Financial institution outsourcing trends

The use of Information and Communication Technologies (ICT) infrastructures by financial institutions varies with the size of the organization. Financial institutions can be divided into three groups based on size: large, medium/large, and small/medium.

- Financial institutions with a large number of branches fall within the large group. This is the case with Citibank, HSBC, Barclays, BNP, Deutsche

Bank, Santander, BBVA, Intesa Sanpaolo, Unicredit Group, and so on. ICT management is predominantly carried out in house;
- Medium/large financial institutions – those with more than 500 branches – follow a predominantly in-house type of ICT management. However, facility management solutions and several applications (such as card processing) are often outsourced;
- Small/medium financial institutions – those with 500 branches or fewer – predominantly follow a full outsourcing model for the management of ICT applications and infrastructure. They have a certain propensity toward Business Process Outsourcing (BPO) for some of their other activities as well, such as payroll or collection. This approach is spreading to the other two groups of financial institutions.

In general, in many countries a proportion of financial services operators already entrust their information systems to an outsourcer. The financial services industry is therefore one of the most advanced examples of information systems outsourcing. The diffusion of the full outsourcing model depends on its significant cost efficiency, as it gives its users considerable savings and full compliance with strict and changing regulations.

According to an analysis based on the financial services financial reports Fiscal Year (FY) 2009[1], the financial services industry is one of the sectors that has the highest impact of ICT costs on its revenues. In this sector, as much as 5.01 percent of revenue goes into covering the costs of ICT, as against much lower percentages in other sectors: around 2 percent in telecommunications, 1.7 percent in insurance, 0.57 percent in transportation, and 0.42 percent in industry, down to the service sector where only 0.18 percent of the revenue is used to cover ICT costs[2].

Based on the same survey, the incidence of ICT expenditures on financial services costs is significantly higher in large and medium/large financial institutions than those of smaller operators. ICT expenditures for large and medium/large size operators affect, respectively, 0.184 percent and 0.141 percent of the intermediated funds, whereas in small financial institutions the amount is set at around 0.103 percent; this corresponds to a cost saving of around 27 percent. Large financial institutions therefore spend approximately 30 percent more on ICT, with peaks of inefficiency that sometimes result in even higher spending, compared to financial institutions such as the small ones which follow a full outsourcing model.

The data shows that the financial services industry is:

- The industry sector that spends the most in percentage terms on investment in ICT. This explains its interest in experimenting in new solutions such as cloud computing, which allows a move from investments to costs; and

- Characterized by the presence of many small/medium entities. Compared to the big players, these are turning largely to outsourcers to support ICT in their business. The fact that in these financial institutions the level of use of outsourcing solutions is already high and widespread makes them potentially prepared to move to cloud solutions;

Small- and medium-size financial institutions are turning to financial services outsourcers to become more efficient and compliant. Large financial institutions spend more both in percentage and in absolute terms[3]. They are also attracted by cloud services as a useful means of achieving reduction in ICT investments and costs.

3.3 Cloud computing scenario for financial institutions

The financial services industry is taking its first steps towards the adoption of cloud computing, leveraging years of experience on topics such as virtualization, automation, outsourcing, and security.

A survey shows that in 2011 financial services were the second sector using cloud technology, following the computer, electronics, and telecom equipment industries (see Figure 3.1).

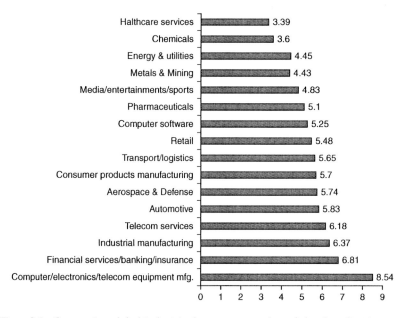

Figure 3.1 Comparing global industries by average number of cloud applications per company/industry (2011)[4]

The unique characteristics of the financial services ICT portfolio are closely dependent on:

- The range of products and services offered;
- The customer target; and
- The widespread geographical presence.

The following specific factors must be considered:

- Business processes automaton and digitization, which are a feature common to all functions of financial institutions. Almost every business functionality, change or improvement, is the result of a significant technological contribution;
- The set of ICT technologies is complex. There are several platforms, infrastructure, development languages, applications, and tools. In a large institution, it is not unusual for ICT to use almost all that is offered by technology;
- The ICT portfolio is not merely complex; it has reached maturity in different competence areas, such as organizational structure skills and competencies, the System Development Life Cycle (SDLC) model, integration among business processes, development languages, investment, governance, and technology partnerships;
- Change management processes, which are well defined and established. These are influenced by several factors such as mergers and acquisitions, constant adaptation to changing market and compliance demands, and most important, the adoption of continuously evolving technologies;
- Financial services outsourcing, which is widespread. Financial services institutions value outsourcing as the main way in which to achieve rapid efficiency and agility across the organization. In terms of a function providing technology and service, ICT is also considered the way to benefit from unique capabilities by exploiting the competencies and expertise of partners;
- Products, Pricing, and Business models, which can use ICT in a highly innovative manner – as a means for growth, differentiation, and innovation; and
- The financial services business sector's pressures push for the design of ICT-driven processes in order to achieve greater effectiveness, efficiency, economics, and optimization in the conduct of operations. Hence, ICT is one of the fundamental ways to deal with economic variations, economic fluctuations, changing customer behavior, and challenging regulations.

Financial institutions consider each technological innovation with great interest, and in many cases adopt them. Cloud computing could also have a great impact due to the complex laws and regulatory policies combined with an expansion of the products and their geographical coverage.

On the one hand, the benefits are exponential, but on the other, there are significant challenges in adopting cloud services. The challenges are:

- Legal concerns;
- Issues around security and performance;
- Reliability;
- Complexity of processing;
- Operational control;
- Governance; and most importantly; and
- Evidence of the economic benefits promised.

Despite these obstacles, many financial services are considering the adoption of cloud services. Research conducted by Temenos in 2011 supports this view, with only 29 percent of bankers confirming they would completely rule out running applications in the cloud, compared to 41 percent in 2009. In the long term, we will see larger banks requiring standardized technology components in the cloud[5].

Another 2009 survey shows that in the insurance sector this percentage was slightly higher, at 51 percent[6].

The primary reason for considering cloud services is that the most advanced financial services have innovative and flexible business models. Cloud computing is potentially a disruptive innovation, and financial institutions are interested in examining this change. The expectation is that, in the near future, more and more financial institutions will take advantage of cloud computing. Their internal business and technology operations will move into a comprehensive range of on-demand, flexible, and scalable platforms covering three key dimensions of technology development:

- Core Business Services and Products;
- Customer-oriented functions for multichannel and integration services; and
- Business-enabling processes and corporate services, such as Finance, Human Resources, Legal, and Marketing.

Financial institutions see cloud computing as an evolution of (and in some cases a revolution with respect to) the traditional service models. They are evaluating what types of computational loads to migrate, and focusing on ensuring that business applications are in compliance with internal and externally mandated security policies. The attention of the financial services is turning particularly towards areas where such an approach seems at present to be capable of bringing the greatest benefits most quickly. This can be achieved with widely distributed technological facilities and the ability to disengage from the usual logic of the acquisition of software, in order to move on to a model of ICT as a service.

Large financial institutions are showing increasing interest in developing an approach to private cloud computing within their own ICT organizations, aiming to optimize the use of the internal resources already available to them. In financial institutions, there are high transactional loads, so, it is necessary for them to evaluate the adoption of technologies and ICT architectures, specialized according to the relevant workload to be managed. The next step is the evolution of systems towards hybrid Cloud Architectures (Cloud Arcs), even if this will create a challenge in terms of integration of operational processes. Service-Oriented Architecture (SOA) will play an increasingly important role as the primary mechanism of interaction with the cloud services. The interface between the two clouds (private and public) will require a service bus and secure Internet Protocol Security (IPsec) networking.

3.4   Expectations of cloud-based solutions

Financial institutions follow an increasingly dynamic and flexible technological pattern. The aim is to meet the diverse and changing needs of the business. The objectives are to:

- Take advantage of the technological resources and functionality provided as services and on demand. In this way, they can have what they need when they need it, rather than having to plan upfront for solutions, capacity, and availability;
- Achieve cost efficiency and scalable services from the utilization of optimized and virtualized infrastructure. With cloud services, financial institutions can leverage the right hardware components, and manage computing requirements as a function of real usage, rather than design and run with maximum capacity, redundancy, and resiliency upfront; and
- Finally, yet importantly, reduce the operational risks (as requested by the Basel II regulation). Cloud computing involves a radical restructuring, avoiding many of the execution risks connected with internal ICT departments. These were due, for example, to the limited number of skilled resources available internally.

Financial institutions demonstrate significant maturity in terms of business architecture, process deployment, and standard operating procedures to drive operations, technology adoption, and service delivery. They are also one of the biggest spenders on innovation with significant business potential.

The following considerations would accelerate the adoption of cloud-based solutions within financial services:

- Promise of business agility, with the ability to scale and respond to business variations as needed rather than building redundant capacity;
- Initial success of virtualization and on-demand solutions in the infrastructure space. Most financial institutions today are focusing on consolidating their servers and data centers. They are implementing organization grade virtualization solutions, with excellent Return on Investment (ROI) benefits;
- Success of outsourcing at all levels pushes to entrusting significant parts of the business and technology operations to multiple service vendors; and
- Standardization and service-based model of the business functions, products, and services.

Cloud-based solutions can offer the next stage in the evolution of the outsourcing paradigm for these institutions. As the financial institutions consider next-generation technology solutions, they are looking at a deeper alignment of business functions, operations, and technology; they are moving from technology systems to business processes optimization and management.

The analysis of the financial organizations and their business operations shows that there is no single cloud solution model that can meet all requirements. Rather, financial institutions will create and manage a federated ecosystem of cloud-based services along with non cloud-based solutions. In some functionality, they should leverage the abstraction control provided by public, private, and community cloud deployments. A federated ecosystem can:

- Leverage multiple types of implementations;
- Deliver flexible capacity to match business requirements; and
- Provide an incremental adoption path, building on the success of each previous step.

This will also enable external business service vendors, who would themselves start offering their product solutions on the cloud, to seamlessly integrate with this ecosystem.

As institutions evolve into the cloud-based model, internal business operations would be organized around five specific categories[7]:

1. Service Development, which encompasses functional, technical, and operational development. This includes all aspects of ICT services

development within a financial organization, and would cover application and infrastructure development, deployment and maintenance services. While there is a significant diversity in the technologies and tools used within the organization, there has been steady movement towards the use of commercial software packages rather than developing software in house. The internal task will be to define the architecture, manage the integrations, and innovation projects and customize/parameterize services to the internal requirements;

2. Customer Services, which refers to all aspects of customer engagement, sales, servicing, and interactions[8]. It also includes the internal employee functions that are enabled to perform customer-focused activities. Most financial institutions are developing and offering mobile-based services, and cloud-based solutions are a big enabler in this direction. Examples of near-future developments in this direction are Unified Communication and Collaboration systems[9];

3. Core Business Services, which includes core business processes covering retail financial services, commercial financial services, payments, treasury, investment financial services, asset and wealth management, fund management aspects, and other functions such as cards and payment services, governance, risk management, and compliance services. Product vendors which provide Commercial Off-The-Shelf solutions (COTS) today will gradually move towards a cloud-based model, as the concept becomes widely adopted by their customers. The cloud will cover several aspects of the processes. While these are parts of the core functionality today, they will evolve in the future, to become business processes enabling new and old services;

4. Business-Enabling Services include a set of business functions that are essential to complete the business processing[10]. Initially, these functions were intricately embedded within the core functions; over time, however, most institutions have extracted and delivered them as shared services across different business lines. The set of enabling services will increase as financial institutions reconsider aspects of differentiation. These services provide real, rich, and practical opportunities for leveraging the benefits of cloud-based solutions. This will further force financial institutions to replace their internal service platforms with external services; and

5. Corporate Services functions, which include functions that enable the business existence and legal operations, including finance, HR, procurement, legal, asset management, marketing, and performance management activities. Most of these functions, embedded processes, and technology platforms have been standardized and abstracted into well defined service lines. Most financial institutions have already outsourced portions of these platforms. Technology vendors have consolidated into a small number of large players. These vendors are aggressively looking to deliver these services on the cloud. Some of these vendors already have

SaaS versions of their platforms. They are currently catering to small and medium size financial institutions, and in time, they will scale up to support larger institutions. An example of this trend is marketing, currently extensively disrupted by the influence and impact of Web 2.0 and social media; this is expected to increase significantly. Financial institutions will move towards digital marketing models, leveraging social media, and enabling marketing services to be delivered from the cloud.

Benefits with a public cloud[11]

LPL Financial is the United States' largest independent broker/dealer. It has US$3.1 billion in annual revenue, and delivers proprietary technology, brokerage, and investment advisory services to more than 12,500 financial advisors around the USA. It also provides comprehensive clearing and compliance services for advisors. It supports these services with independent research, practice management programs and training, and technology.

For the past ten years, the organization has experienced huge success. In advance of the Initial Public Offering (IPO) in November 2010, the management made a large investment in the internal systems, including general ledger, human resources, and procurement systems. The finance organization wanted to have the systems ready within six months (in order to coincide with the IPO) and to use a team with the necessary depth of expertise.

Historically, back office applications were supported internally. The capacity of the support team was limited, and LPL management, with the IPO on the horizon, had to take a long, hard look at how best to develop and maintain these systems.

External vendors gave LPL strong support for their security services, technical expertise, and the ability to have their systems managed effectively through the cloud.

The management calculates that moving their finance applications to the cloud gave LPL Financial's finance organization stronger ownership of the system implementation and use. They are now maximizing the usage of these systems.

3.5 Aspects accelerating the adoption of cloud-based solutions

Financial institutions should demonstrate significant maturity in terms of business architecture, process deployment, and standard operating procedures in order to drive operations, technology adoption, and service delivery. They are also among the biggest spenders on innovations that bring significant business potential.

The following sections summarize which aspects of the adoption of cloud services would benefit financial institutions more:

- New Delivery Channels;
- Multiproduct Integration;
- Customer Sales and Services;

- Customer Relationship Management;
- Social Networking and Community;
- External Interfaces (B2B);
- Transaction Processing (TP) Systems;
- Corporate Functions and Common Supporting Services; and
- Application Infrastructure and Application Development.

3.5.1   New delivery channels

Delivery channels refer to all the different channels through which financial institutions provide access to their services, such as:

- Front-office applications;
- ATMs;
- Online financial services;
- Telefinancial services and touch screen financial services terminals;
- Exchange services;
- Trade services; and
- Mobile financial services.

The following scenarios are of particularly interest in their break from traditional approaches:

- Thanks to technology integration, the majority of functional capabilities, such as user interfaces and process flows, can be standardized across all channels. All means of interaction, both back-end and front-end, have evolved through the years. Most financial institutions have implemented multichannel integration capabilities to provide enhanced customer experience. Financial services integrated functions can be established across channels regardless of the point in the lifecycle stage;
- Technology tools at the level of channel platforms have attained a high degree of standardization. This is achieved through a series of functional products used for business process management, customer relationship management, decision management, and core financial services platforms, thanks to tools such as Java and .NET technologies. Rich Client platforms are currently deployed using technologies such as Adobe Flex and Microsoft Silverlight;
- Self-service solutions for digitization and workflow optimization have enabled automation of almost all services connected with retail financial services, commercial, and capital markets. "Do-it-yourself" capabilities are increasing rapidly, with the aim of enabling customers to virtually perform almost any operation they need; and
- Several functional activities are currently outsourced to partners as business services, and this trend is increasing. These solutions align well with a proposed move to a cloud-based delivery model.

3.5.2 Multiproduct integration

The capacity to manage information and processes in an integrated manner covers all aspects of financial services. Straight Through Process-based solutions (STP) are now widespread in all aspects of the financial services systems; they enable very rapid response times, even for complex tasks such as the origination of loans or mortgages.

By using common and reliable transport mechanisms for transferring service information, a financial institution can exchange data on loans, mortgages, term deposits, investments, and retail transactions between two or more systems. This approach helps alleviate the "silo" problem that financial services have faced for years as a result of the incompatible systems from multiple vendors used in different parts of the organization. Both middleware and enterprise platform solutions are widely used in the financial services systems.

Financial institutions have built robust, scalable, and high performance integration layers across their organization[12]. The integration process involves changes in both aspects of internal management and external activities with a significant standardization process in both areas. Current solutions are quite mature, and most of the further developments regard the provision of additional functional capabilities. Integration scenarios have reached such a level of maturity that the distribution of solutions follows standard models.

3.5.3 Customer sales and services

Cloud services can support better customer sales and services:

- Customer service integration can provide an integrated service for the delivery of customer solutions. These solutions cut across multiple divisional products such as deposits, loans, cards, wealth management, securities management, and so on. This integration also supports Common Services such as Charges, Statements, Collateral Management, Card Issuance, and others. These services used to be embedded within specific functions, but over time, financial institutions have extracted, consolidated, and re-integrated information and tasks, and as a result they now operate these as a set of common services covering all product lines. A good example in this direction is the so-called Payment Hub, which allows processing and consolidation of different forms of payment processing; and
- Outsourcing of conventional customer services is becoming more and more common. In recent years there has been a sweeping change in the way that financial institutions operate. Growing competition in the financial services sector has forced financial institutions to outsource some of their activities to maintain their competitive edge. Financial institutions tend to outsource a number of services, since functional aspects have evolved to such a level of

maturity that no noticeable differentiation in the type of service is present any longer. Such services become common to many financial institutions, and the expectation is that more and more of these services will move into the outsourcing domain. Such outsourced services are often grouped together according to the functions they perform; for instance, a financial institution may decide to outsource the ICT infrastructure, application development and maintenance, administrative processes, and business processes.

3.5.4 Customer relationship management

Over the last few years, financial institutions are moving from a product-oriented environment to a customercentric model. Most financing institutions are starting to use Customer Relationship Management (CRM) systems, which allow the financial services to gain an integrated view of the customer, product profile, associated risk, and value ratings from an organization perspective.

CRM systems are at present implemented for the support and management of the entire customer relationship. They range from service interactions across channels up to the customization of service delivery. Organizations make many efforts to improve and boost the level of integration of communication channels and data sharing among the different parties within the service chain, and there is a combination of commercial and custom-built solutions. In many cases, Customer Account Data Engines (CADE) of several institutions hold duplicate customer and relationship information, so financial institutions are starting to use data synchronization mechanisms, data dedupe tools, and master data management.

Some retail financial institutions see parts of the CRM functions as commodity elements that can be delivered as a service by external vendors, and are increasingly moving towards this model. Financial services now consider customer information and relationship management as standard for customer service. Meanwhile, financial institutions are evolving towards relationship-based products and pricing models which enable differentiation and personalized engagement.

The availability of these tools from other industry sectors (such as retail) and their distributed nature favors their use in a cloud computing environment.

Bajaj auto finance adopts cloud-based CRM and increases productivity by 50 percent[13]

Bajaj Auto Finance is an Indian non-banking financial corporation financing automobile and industry machinery. It started to use a CRM in a cloud model. It was able to reduce the time for approving a loan from 19 to 15 minutes. Thanks to the cloud, Bajaj Auto Finance was able to manage an increase from 1600 to 8500 transactions a day.

3.5.5 Social network and community

Several related trends affect the operating environment of financial services. Financial institutions are more and more interested in interacting with their customers in a more direct and innovative way; this leads to an increase in the use of tools for social networking and communication in the financial services sector.

Social networking has become a trend in the field of collaboration and communication that has exploded in the workplace, even in the financial services world.

According to a survey conducted in Italy by Convenzione Interbancaria per i Problemi dell'Automazione (CIPA) and Associazione Bancaria Italiana (ABI) on the state of automation of the financial services system, approximately one third of the financial services groups have already launched social networking applications with the intent of improving communication and collaboration in the workplace. This trend is expected to double in the next two years[14]. According to this survey, financial institutions use Social Network and Community for multiple purposes (see also Table 3.1):

- As a way to improve communication and collaboration in the workplace;
- As a communication strategy used for communicating both internally and outside the organization;
- As a channel dedicated solely to external customers for the expansion of the target, and to strengthen customer loyalty and brand; and
- Simple Syndication (RSS), wikis, social networks, social bookmarking, and social voting can be considered as financial services tools because once they have been introduced they are used by users multiple times daily.

The expectation is that the business market for social collaboration, content, and communication tools is booming[15]. Cloud versions of social media tools can help balance openness with acceptable risk. Today, each of the technology trends can be valuable individually. The combination of two or more of them, for instance social networks and cloud, can help accelerate progress towards a new set of business capabilities. It can enable a new set

Table 3.1 Important potential benefits of collaboration

Potential benefits of collaboration	Percent (%)
Increased productivity	87
Better informed decision making	83
Alignment between employees, teams and management	82
Increased end-user satisfaction	80
Reduced costs (including travel expenses)	75

of business rules for organizations in marketing, operations, performance, and competition.

BBVA banks on the Google cloud[16]

BBVA, one of the largest financial institutions in the world, announced that it is adopting Google's cloud-based collaboration and communication suite to increase productivity and drive innovation.

Over 35,000 BBVA workers in Spain will start to use the productivity tools integrated into the Google Apps suite. By the end of 2012, BBVA expects to migrate 110,000 employees in over 26 countries to Google Apps.

BBVA chose a cloud solution to increase efficiency and to help its workers collaborate more easily regardless of their location. BBVA's new global intranet is the main technology project undergoing a big transformation thanks to these collaboration tools. It will enable the Intranet to be changed from a corporate communications and process management site to a place where all employees will be able to share, contribute, and manage knowledge globally. In addition, BBVA will create a social network to improve communication and explore new ways of working.

BBVA was looking for a technology that would transform their business operations – not just increase efficiency. The employees will be able to access the information they need at any time from any internet-connected device, anywhere in the world, and any time. In this way, they will be able to be more flexible and mobile. The collaboration tools will allow them to communicate and share ideas more easily – working in an innovative way. On the cloud, for example, many people can simultaneously work on a single document – increasing productivity by removing the need to update constantly different versions of a document.

3.5.6   External interfaces

External interfaces typically supply data necessary to the financial services organizations, such as market data, credit bureau ratings, regulatory information, price, rates, and other relevant information. This has evolved and matured into a near-real-time-based model with Service-Oriented Architectures (SOA). Financial institutions have built bi-directional pattern-driven solutions for external interfaces. Most of the data service vendors have standardized the languages and integration architectures. In this way, in several cases, formats are common across different financial institutions.

Commonwealth bank Australia CIO talks cloud computing[17]

The Commonwealth Bank of Australia (CBA) is serious about cloud computing; it wants to buy software and infrastructure as a service over a network. The Bank has set up an Enterprise Cloud Leadership Council. The key elements of the bank cloud computing strategy are the need to buy software and infrastructure as a service over a network. The bank wants to pay for what it uses on demand. The ultimate objective is to supply their customers with the services they want and to do that with good value.

To reach this target, the bank has taken some important steps. The first was to define standards; the virtual private cloud or a public cloud was created by using existing technology and exporting some of those activities outside the corporation. Once the bank had developed and tested those capabilities and they were operating in full production, the bank could determine whether they should stay outside in the public cloud or be brought back in house.

The bank has in the past introduced a stream of innovative technology-based services to its retail and other customers; it must find ways to economize on ICT. Four years ago, the bank launched a core banking modernization program for its huge number of information systems. It also identified applications that should go into public clouds, a private cloud, or a hybrid of the two.

By shifting dozens of on-premises applications to the cloud, the bank has reduced its operational costs. This has freed up money that the bank has reallocated into delivering new services. To reduce costs, CBA has created "As a Service"/ cloud offerings in sales, customer service, Human Resources, operations, and ICT applications and environments. Some of these are:

- Core organization systems, for instance salary and talent management;
- Pilots and proof of concepts such as "Big Data"; and
- Support environments such as development and testing.

It has developed a single payment solution to be used across the bank, from front office to back office, with standard interfaces. In this way, CBA has achieved significant savings in system integration, development costs, and time to production. Components of the solution's modular architecture, such as SWIFT (for international money transfers), have also been extended to CBA group entities across Australia and Asia.

The bank has also become a vendor of cloud services to its customers. For example:

- It has collaborated with pharmaceutical, manufacturing, and distribution companies, and even other banks, in the creation and provision of cloud-based databases "as a service"; and
- It provides cloud infrastructure services running on CBA servers or a cloud vendor's servers. With these services, CBA develops and tests new computing applications used internally and externally.

The bank categorizes the benefits in three ways:

- Cost reduction. For example, "as a service" storage has cut CBA's cost of computing storage by around 40 Percent. Even more impressively, the "as a service" overdraft offering has reduced the processing time for standard overdrafts by 90 percent. In this way, CBA declares that it is saving tens of millions of dollars and [potentially] hundreds of millions [over the next three or four years] from buying services on demand, paying a unit price for them and having flexibility;
- Faster development of computer applications. The bank refers to this benefit as one of "agility." The bank's payment system – which combines a stack of technologies required to offer payment services (the application, its underlying

middleware, operating system and other infrastructure, and the server and storage hardware) – is a case in point. No longer does the bank need to build a new payment system every time a business unit or department asks for one; and

• Culture shifts from getting business units to share ICT applications. CBA's HR function has adopted a talent management application to better understand trends in turnover, recruitment, hiring patterns and future hiring needs, absenteeism, and other areas. CBA has created a cloud-based talent management application that any of its banking units – for instance, Bankwest (a 2008 acquisition) and ASB (its New Zealand bank) – could adopt. This has drastically reduced costs.

ICT infrastructure cost savings from cloud computing is freeing up time and money for innovation. The bank is launching new banking services, many of them online. These services let customers do things such as getting offers on financial products in real time. This is because more bank staff can now focus on evaluating customers' individual needs and pricing products and services based on their risk profile and loyalty.

Shifting technology spending from the back office to the front-office applications is necessary because in explosively expanding areas such as mobile payment, banks are no longer competing against just other banks.

3.5.7   Transaction processing systems

Transaction processing systems represent the core processing portfolio of systems for financial institutions; they cover the functionality for deposits, cards, mortgages, lending, wealth management, and securities processing. Functional aspects, including regulatory requirements, are abstracted and implemented as functional products. Most of the large financial services institutions have implemented products from leading vendors, and integrated them within their ecosystem, hence, multiple products and versions co-exist. Financial services have implemented channel solutions to provide a front-office user interface and thus enable better products, faster delivery cycles, and customercentric capabilities. Some of the product vendors are moving towards a service-based model, but the inherent complexities of the business, products, services, and the core nature of the business make this evolution very slow. Financial institutions are increasingly outsourcing business processing services, including niche areas like underwriting and collections.

IBM teams up with Nawanagar cooperative bank to implement core banking solutions on the cloud[18]

The Nawanagar Cooperative Bank has selected IBM to deploy core banking solutions on a hosted cloud services model. As part of the agreement, IBM will be remotely hosting and managing the ICT and networking infrastructures of the

bank. IBM is offering Smart Cloud Resilience Service for a core banking solution to the bank in partnership with InfraSoft Technologies.
The Bank has the objectives of scaling up their ICT. The objective is to improve operational efficiency for delivering consistent, uninterrupted services in a cost-effective, secure, and compliant manner.
The core banking solution scales up the bank's business and centralizes the management of its mission-critical operations, including front office, middle office, and back office processes. It includes the implementation of real time transaction processing. This will help the bank to better cater to the customer requirements. It will also help reduce the burden of upfront capital expenditure by allowing the bank to spend on a flexible operational expenditure or pay-as-you-go model.
The innovation is important to support in the highly competitive segment of cooperative banking in India. It makes a big leap from legacy branch banking to online/anywhere banking.

3.5.8 Corporate functions and common supporting services

Common supporting services include those functions that enable business existence and support operations, including finance, HR, procurement, legal, asset management, marketing, and the associated performance management activities. They also cover technology services such as content management, digitization, and workflow. Most of these functions, embedded processes, and technology platforms are standard and abstracted into well defined service lines. Most financial institutions have outsourced significant portions of these platforms.

Corporate functions have become fully commoditized, and most financial institutions adopt either SAP, Oracle, or other ERP platforms. Often, lower-level functions like payments are outsourced as a platform service[19]. Technology vendors have been consolidated into a small number of large players who are aggressively seeking to deliver these services on the cloud. Some of these vendors (such as SAP, Oracle, and Sage) already have SaaS versions that are currently catering to small and medium organizations. They have scaled them up to support larger institutions.

Financial institution wide governance, risk, and compliance propositions are being enacted in order to ensure full coverage, standardized platforms, and homogeneous procedures. Growing external compliance requirements is influencing this trend.

The Spanish bank Bankinter uses a cloud service as an integral part of their credit risk simulation application[20]

Bankinter develops and run complex algorithms to simulate diverse scenarios for evaluating the financial health of its clients. This requires heavy computational power to process at least 400,000 simulations in order to get realistic results. By using the cloud, the bank was able to carry out a simulation reducing the time on the average necessary from 23 hours to 20 minutes.

Technology functions like workflow, document and content management, digitization, and integration are now mature functionalities. Product vendors have consolidated, and most implementations are routine and standardized across institutions and geographies. Business processing services are increasingly moving to the cloud. These include niche areas like research and analytics (the so-called KPO, Knowledge Process Outsourcing).

AmBank places sourcing function in the cloud[21]

Malaysia-based AmBank Group moved its sourcing function into the cloud after signing a deal with a third party service vendor. The financial services institution wanted to optimize procurement and spend management, and to drive savings and efficiencies across its operations. AmBank decided to use a cloud services vendor in order to use best practice processes to improve the effectiveness of its operations.

The solutions enable AmBank to identify opportunities for significant savings opportunities across a number of spend categories and to incorporate visibility and rigor into its internal processes,

---

3.5.9   Application infrastructure and application development

Financial institutions have built all-encompassing infrastructure in order to deliver a full range of technology services to support their departments. The infrastructure runs on large data centers; many financial institutions have moved to a consolidated model in the last few years. Procurement costs for infrastructure and software typically absorb over one third of the total ICT budget[22]. Due to the evolution in technology, most large financial institutions possess all types of hardware, software, and devices that they introduced several decades ago, so the most relevant part of ICT expenditures (70 percent and more of the total budget) is spent on running these systems and ensuring that they continue to be functional, as the cost of technology refresh is high and intrusive. For this reason, many services have been extensively outsourced. Outsourcing was frequent in financial institutions in earlier times, with entire data centers run or managed by service vendors.

Application development services have undergone significant change in the last decade. Financial institutions today, even when they are very large, retain a smaller portion of technology development. Some institutions are now moving into the cloud for their development infrastructure; ICT service vendors that specialized in building test and production environments offer these in a flexible and cost-effective way.

North American bank experience[23]

Many banks see cloud computing as a way of bringing new capabilities to the market quickly, with a variable cost structure. Banks are looking at the infrastructure they use for development and testing. They are looking to access and leverage lower-cost environments they can tap into via cloud. One North American bank mandated that all application development and testing be done through its virtual environment, so it can provision infrastructure in hours rather than weeks.

3.6 Dilemma of financial services institutions: private v. public cloud

The relation between the cloud and the financial services sector is still very delicate because of the specific issues outlined above. Some financial institutions are still hesitant to adopt cloud environments for their core business services. On the other hand, there are public cloud environments that deliver services to a large number of users. Functionalities are offered in an open and shared manner. In this situation, financial institutions CIOs are seriously concerned that putting sensitive information in a virtual public place could lead to problems in terms of security and regulatory compliance. Characterized by high critical business data and by the complexity of infrastructure, the level of adoption of the public cloud could therefore remain low in the financial services sector over the short and medium term. However, if the private cloud is considered as an internal information-sharing environment, with no need to migrate the data, and above all with the security to maintain the information within its own structure, the picture changes radically.

Information and Communication Technology in the financial services sector must always ensure high levels of security, partly, as mentioned above, because of the normative landscape that has established strict rules in many countries. This is perhaps the most crucial aspect to be addressed, not only to achieve implementation of cloud solutions, but also for the development of cloud services tailored to financial institutions. In the case of this sector, the services currently provided by different vendors need to be improved in terms of data security and compliance. An example of this situation is the difficulty of moving certain data outside regional borders.

However, these security problems can be solved:

- From a technological standpoint, with the introduction of advanced security and secure access systems; and
- From the legislative point of view, with modifications that will meet this changing way of doing business.

At this time, then, public cloud computing has limited application in the financial services sector. It can, however, be implemented in, for example, the organization's or community's data centers. The important is to overcome the "silos" architecture that is still widely diffused both at the level of applications and in management terms. In the short term, financial services might mainly go onto private clouds for their core applications.

In its applications in the financial services sector, private clouds must anyway meet specific industry regulations and requirements related to security and reliability.

In the short term, the approach to private clouds for core applications offers benefits when compared to the public cloud, not only with regard to

Table 3.2 Private cloud in some financial institutions[24]

Financial services institution	Private cloud benefits
Lloyd's	Lloyd's, the world's only specialist insurance market, virtualizes environment to cut operating costs, increase resource utilization, and take advantage of its new data centers.
DnB NOR	Norway's largest financial services group, new platform for credit evaluation process.
Auva	Auva is Austria's largest social security and emergency hospital insurance provider. It maximized service availability through virtualization.
Urban Lending Solutions	Financial Services provider uses Hyper-V for speed with $1 million savings.
Banco Central do Brasil	Virtualization solution helped Brazil's Central Bank to cut power costs by 20%, boost productivity by 20%, and increase processing speed by 50%.
Banque de Luxembourg	Private bank virtualized data centers for ICT, business and environmental benefits.
Bank of Hawaii	The bank updated the aging environment in its mission-critical Operations Group, while reducing the risk of business disruption.

security issues but also with respect to the expectations of speed required by the financial world.

Several financial institution groups have already organized themselves to manage their technology assets through internal clouds, which are often adopted for all different departments or controlled companies (see Table 3.2).

For example, the public cloud can help financial institutions build closer relationships with their customers, and also help with further development of closed financial services systems. In the meantime, the number of vendors of solutions in the public cloud for financial institutions is growing (see Table 3.3 which names a few of them). This will help the financial services move to the cloud with a hybrid cloud approach, adopting an incremental approach. The sequencing in the case of applications could be done taking into account[25]:

- Possible showstoppers;
- The potential of each application; and
- The characteristics of the application, which would make it prime for consideration.

Table 3.3 Financial services scenarios with public cloud[26]

Scenarios with cloud	Financial services examples
Organization productivity and collaboration	Aviva and Aon
Sales and service	Axa, Century Payments, Accenture, Rdt and Figlo
Core processes and efficiency	NVoicePay, Mysis and Temenos
Risk analytics and reporting	RiskMetrics Group, Open Text and Kynetix
Data insights and monetization	Alteryx and Xignite

For example, a financial institution could leave its customer data in house, and cloud computing power could be used for analytics and high performance computing. Chapter 5 will examine successful migration strategies to the cloud.

Cloud computing appears to be an approach that is also valid for organizations in the financial services world, which, having created virtual environments, can then make resources available to their users, and enable on-demand access for them. This would respond to a common interest of business and ICT, to reap the benefits through the paradigm of cloud computing.

A financial institution should not expect to purchase cloud services off-the-shelf. It is important that when making a contract with the vendor an organization should take into account many factors, including compliance and regulations. In order to be successful with cloud services, the cloud environment should have at least the same quality of service and protection of resources that had been adopted in the traditional environment.

Bank of America use of the cloud[27]

Nearly 50,000 of Bank of America's 300,000 employees use Salesforce.com's CRM application. The bank has also tested Chatter, a free collaboration service that Salesforce.com is adding to its sales and service applications and cloud platform. The service embeds social networking style collaboration alongside existing Salesforce.com functionality. It integrates with popular public networks including Facebook and Twitter.

Bank of America values its customers, and it is eager to allow them to communicate with the bank using whatever channels they desire. The objective is to collaborate in real time with them.

One of the biggest challenges the bank faces is deciding among internal cloud solutions, external private cloud, and external public cloud. The question is how much data the bank feels comfortable moving. This depends on the prices, service level agreement and data security guarantees it can obtain from internal, external private, and external public cloud offerings.

3.7   Conclusions

The move by financial institutions to the cloud is an important trend, not only from a technological point of view, but is becoming more and more important from a business point of view.

This move must be governed, and the control of cloud computing is a strategic aspect of this transformation. This will be the subject of next chapter.

4
Governance of Cloud Computing

4.1 Introduction

With cloud computing, organizations delegate direct control of all or part of their ICT organization to an external party. The responsibility of governing the third party and its actions remains with the delegating organization. This aspect is particularly relevant in the case of financial institutions; the regulatory bodies (normally the central banks) still lay the responsibility for any wrongdoing on the financial institutions. Cloud services bring benefits; nevertheless, before using them, an organization should go through a conscious and active evaluation and, if necessary, remediation of any possible risk connected with this choice. Cloud computing does not mean purely and simply a transfer of assets to support a business; cloud computing is also a partnership relationship, in that the two parties intend to achieve common benefits, and the risks and opportunities are shared between them. As with any outsourcing relationship, cloud computing brings with it the serious issue of the procuring entity's loss of knowledge of the activity outsourced. Such a partnership is always subject to the threats of the relationship not being an equal one; one of the parties is in a dominant position, due to the skills with which it handles certain processes. This is especially true in the case of cloud computing, since should problems arise it would be very difficult to insource the services moved to the cloud. Financial institutions should take particular care with the governance of the relationship of cloud computing.

To reiterate and thus emphasize, cloud computing is much more than a technology. It is a completely different way of running a business. In order to move to cloud services, it is essential for the client organization to redesign their processes; this is the only way to reap all the benefits of cloud services. In other words, migrating to cloud computing requires a method that we call "Lean and Digitize"[1]. To use the technology that constitutes the foundation of cloud computing, it is necessary to "lean" the processes that are to be partially or entirely supported in the cloud. Once this has been achieved, it would become very difficult to go back to the previous setup, and the only real alternative would be to move to another cloud services vendor. Such a migration would bring its own problems in its wake, since another vendor would normally require other types of process in order for it to provide its cloud services.

This being the situation, before taking the decision to move to cloud services it is essential to take all possible risks into account, design an effective governance process, and implement it.

This chapter intends to analyze how to design governance in a cloud computing relationship. Cloud computing governance consists of a set of rules, procedures, and organizational structures aimed at ensuring compliance with the organization's strategy and the achievement of the following targets:

- Effectiveness, efficiency and economics of the business processes (planning, administration, operations, delivery, and so on);
- Safeguard of assets and protection against losses;
- Reliability and integrity of accounting and management; and
- Compliance of operations with laws, regulations and supervisory policies, plans, norms, and internal procedures.

4.2   Planning and controlling cloud computing

The responsibility for the quality of the service/product provided (such as the ability to meet the requirements of the client and of the regulatory bodies) rests on the delegating organization. The organization must ensure that processes in the cloud are subject to the same degree of governance as that which applies to their own internal processes; this is the only way to ensure compliance with internal requirements or certification, as for instance in the case of the ISO 9001[2]. The governance process must include the following activities, in accordance with Deming's Plan-Do-Check-Act (PDCA) model (see Figure 4.1)[3]:

- Planning;
- Monitoring;
- Examination of the results obtained;
- Taking any subsequent actions to put the activity on the right course; and
- Improve continuously.

This definition of governance leads us to the way in which a financial institution should manage a relationship with a cloud services vendor. This approach brings with it the need to reconsider governance as a whole; it is not an independent process, but a tool for defining and implementing

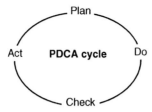

Figure 4.1 The PDCA cycle

the strategy of moving to cloud computing. ISO 9001–2008 notes, with stronger emphasis than in previous releases, the importance of controlling and monitoring the outsourced activities that affect:

• The final characteristics of the product/service provided; and
• The quality perceived by the customer.

Appropriate governance requires the following steps (see also Figure 4.2):

• Definition of the control system of a cloud service vendor. This activity is pervasive; it affects all the processes of the organization – the different phases of definition, design, development, operating, and monitoring of the ICT processes. It also includes a thorough analysis of risk areas in the processes. There should be a consistent identification of appropriate points of control, and the definition of Key Risk Indicators (KRI). This would be a first-level control. The cloud service vendor should follow this procedure in all its activities. The client must verify its effectiveness and receive a periodic report;
• Verification of the adequacy of control systems of the vendor of cloud services. This activity aims at assessing the effectiveness of the overall system of internal controls. It goes through an analysis of the organization's processes and their changes over time. It is necessary to verify the completeness of the mapping of risk areas and the related definition of adequate steps to remediate and monitor them. This phase should feature a process of synthesis carried out on a parallel set of internal audit activities relating to the different areas of the vendor and client organizations. This process, depending on the faults/issues discovered and their levels, allows the financial institution to make an adequate assessment of the effectiveness of the controls. It is a second-level control. It is the responsibility of a vendor manager in the client organization;
• Verification of the regularity of operations. This is composed of activity audits aimed at identifying anomalous trends, and violations of internal and external procedures. The internal audit department of the client

organization should conduct such audits periodically or on special occasions. The internal audit is carried out in connection with the personnel of the client information systems department and of the internal audit of the vendor. It involves a complex system of checks – including remote or on-site visits – on the planning, and confirmation of the elimination of anomalies previously reported;

- Reporting on controls on the vendor of cloud services to the client executives. This activity consists of periodic reports submitted to the executives and board of directors of the financial institution. These must contain information about the activities planned for the year, including priorities, methods, goals, and so on. There should be reports of the progress achieved during the year (quarterly, semi-annual, annual, and so on). They should include specific cases of relevant anomalies discovered and the actions taken to remediate them. The reports must show indications of possible specific actions, organizational or technological changes, and so on. They should also include an overall analysis of the control system of the vendor of cloud services and of the client organization. The source of this analysis should be the results of an audit carried out previously. The analysis should include an evaluation of the Key Performance Indicators (KPI) and of the Key Risk Indicators (KRI) and their variations in time. In the optimum situation the analysis should be carried out by a third-party consultancy organization and paid for by the vendor;
- Follow-up on findings and anomalies. This is the verification of the regular execution of the actions and remediation identified and agreed between client and vendor for overcoming deficiencies and areas of weakness identified. The client and the cloud services vendor should cooperate to achieve this.

4.3   Data processing regulatory obligations

With cloud computing platforms, financial institutions may be able not only to outsource their technology operations and resources to the cloud, but also enhance their ability to improve their processes and please their customers by offering financial products and services anywhere, anytime, with a significantly pared down physical infrastructure. Web-based and mobile financial services are already rapidly increasing in both availability and customer adoption; rapid technological developments and globalization have made profound changes worldwide. At the same time, these services have generated new challenges relating to the protection and privacy of personal data.

Complexity has grown due to the globalization and technological developments. Cloud vendors are increasingly operating in several countries, providing round-the-clock services and assistance[4]. The Internet enables vendors established outside the European Union to provide services

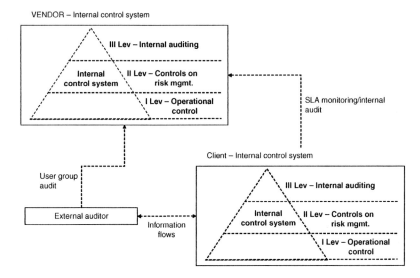

Figure 4.2   Relationships between client and vendor control systems

remotely, and they can also process in real time. When using these vendors, it is not easy to ascertain at any given time the location of personal data and the equipment used.

Cloud services enable users to share and store data or applications on hardware operated by third parties, which can be accessed through the Internet. This brings advantages in terms of cost containment and efficiency gains. However, from a legal point of view, a source of concern is the flow of data that travels to the cloud and resides within it.

Currently any organization that decides to use cloud services has to deal with the many different, and often conflicting, regulations in the countries involved. This is especially true of the EU, which reputedly has the world's most stringent data protection laws.

One of the five essential characteristics of cloud computing in the NIST definition is "Resource pooling"[5]. This relates to the situation in which the vendor's computing resources are pooled to serve multiple consumers. There is, thus, a sense of independence of location, in that the client generally has no control over – or, indeed, knowledge of – the exact location of their resources; the client may, nevertheless, be able to specify a location at a higher level of abstraction (for example, a country or region of the world) for resources such as storage, processing, memory, network bandwidth, and physical machines.

This basic aspect of cloud computing, whereby data can reside in, and at intervals be moved between, locations unknown to the client might in some cases clash with the requirements of the EU Commission stipulating that organizations should know where the data in their possession is located, and that in any case they should be subject to EU regulations.

The success of cloud computing will depend largely on how the regulatory bodies, both national and international, pass laws to regulate this matter.

4.1.1   Cloud computing and compliance

The issue of compliance and the related risks are of great concern when a financial institution moves part of its operations and functions to a third party.

Financial institutions make considerable investments either to be in compliance for competitive advantages or to meet industry standards or regulatory requirements. These investments may be at risk with a migration to the cloud if the vendor:

- Cannot provide evidence of its own compliance to the relevant requirements; and/or
- Does not permit audits by the client.

A bad compliance risk management may result in[6]:

- Audit or certification not being available to clients;
- Storage and transmission of data in multiple jurisdictions and lack of visibility about them;
- Lack of standard technologies and solutions;
- Certification schemes not adapted to cloud services; and/or
- Lack of completeness and visibility in terms of use of computing resources.

A financial institution in the EU can decide to outsource its technology and operations to a cloud services vendor located outside Europe. When considering such a transaction, the financial institution has to evaluate:

- The capabilities of the cloud services vendor to ensure integrity, security, transmission capability and reliability;
- Its ability to ensure compliance with the regulations applicable to financial services; and
- Above all the respect of the laws and regulations of the EU institutions, especially with reference to Data Privacy.

At the international level, the most relevant regulations are currently:

- Markets in Financial Instruments Directive (MiFID);
- USA Sarbanes Oxley Act;
- Basel (various numbers) International Agreements;

- International Accounting Standards and International Financial Reporting Standards (respectively IAS and IFRS);
- Payment Services Directive (PSD);
- SEPA (Standard European Payments Area agreement) to go into full effect on February 1, 2014;
- The International Safe Harbor Privacy Principles; and
- The EU Data Protection Directive[7] and the Convention for the Protection of Individuals with regard to Automatic Processing of Personal Data (ETS Convention No.108);

The following paragraphs will attempt to clarify the mandates of some of these regulations; we recommend getting more precise information from legal advisers.

The implementation of MiFID[8] for financial intermediaries is very complex and requires a major effort from both organizational and technological standpoints. This is especially true when a financial institution decides to adopt cloud services. From an organizational point of view, financial institutions must perform:

- A critical revision of their front end processes, support, and governance functions; and
- The quantification and implementation of investments for the governance functions (compliance, risk management, and internal audit).

From the technological point of view, the impacts are even greater:

- Review of the SLA with the vendor;
- Possible implementation of new systems for data management; and
- Review and preparation of a new disclosure to be released to the customers if required[9].

The US Sarbanes Oxley Act (SOX)[10], when applicable, affects not only the financial side of the corporation but also the ICT departments storing corporate electronic records. The SOX states that all business records, including electronic records and messages, must be saved for "not less than five years." The consequences of non-compliance are fines, imprisonment, or both. ICT departments are increasingly faced with the challenge of creating and maintaining this corporate records archive in a cost-effective fashion. With such a premise, the implementation of a cloud-based solution becomes difficult, since the premise for it is an "on demand" and fast service usage.

The purpose of the Basel agreements is to ensure stability of the financial services system and to change the relationships between financial institutions and their customers. Basel II is the international agreement that dictates capital requirements for financial institutions. On this basis, financial institutions of the adhering countries should maintain equity in proportion to the risks deriving from various credit relations, as assessed using the rating tool. The Basel II agreement defines the financial institutions' capital requirements in relation to the (market, credit, and operational) risks undertaken. Regulations that are even more stringent are connected with Basel III.

The Single Euro Payment Area (SEPA) projects an area in which customers, companies and other economic operators, independent of their location, will be able to make and receive payments in euros within a single country or outside national borders. In both cases, there should be the same base conditions and equal rights and duties[11]. SEPA will contribute to enhancing European integration and market efficiency, and this might be a further accelerator to the adoption of cloud services by financial institutions. The SEPA assumption is that all euro retail payments are "domestic," negating any distinction between national and cross-border payments within the Eurozone. SEPA consists of:

• Harmonized payment instruments (credit transfers, direct debits, and payment cards);
• European infrastructure for the processing of payments in euros;
• Technical standards and common business practices;
• Harmonized legal basis; and
• New, evolving customercentric services.

The International Safe Harbor Privacy Principles consists in a scheme negotiated between the US Department of Commerce and the EU Commission. The Commission recognizes that US entities which publicly sign up to the scheme will offer appropriate protection to personal data. As a result, US-EU Safe Harbor is a streamlined process for US organizations to comply with the EU Directive 95/46/EC on the protection of personal data. Organizations that adopt the Safe Harbor scheme must, among other things, send notices to subjects whose data are collected relating to the purposes of their processing and potential intended transfers. They must also provide individuals with the opportunity to opt out of disclosure of their personal data to third parties. In addition to this, organizations relying on this scheme must ensure that individuals have access on a reasonable basis to all information that might be held about them. Such a protocol establishes specific limits to the processing of data. The validity of such a protocol does not apply automatically in case of data processed through cloud computing since:

• Each EU Member State might not have transposed the protocol within their own system of rules;
• The EU Member State may, after having transposed the protocol, voluntarily perform any necessary checks on the lawfulness and fairness of the

transfers and processing of operations prior to the transfers themselves. The Member State could inspect the enforcement of these standards, as well as adopt any measures to block or ban transfer. It is not clear if in this case such protocol applies to cloud computing service provision[12];
- The Safe Harbor Protocol, with its principles regulating transfer of data to the USA, cannot be extended to other countries outside the EU.

A further important impetus was given by the European Treaty Series (ETS) Convention No.108[13]. Article 1 expresses its main objective:

> To secure ... every individual, whatever his nationality or residence, the respect for his rights and fundamental freedoms and in particular his right to the privacy, with regard to automatic processing of personal data relating to him ("data protection").

The Agreement is effective for all EU Member States that signed it. It regulates important issues such as:

- Quality of data undergoing automatic processing;
- Data security;
- Cross-border data flows; and
- Mutual Assistance Principle and Cooperation between EU Member States[14].

Still there is an urgent need for the government and international agencies to be proactive in dealing with the unique challenges presented by the cloud computing environment.

Each of the mentioned regulations and regulatory bodies, as well as several other applicable regulations, reveal that a financial institution must conduct extensive due diligence in selecting its cloud services vendors. At least, it should use reasonable efforts to manage and monitor the compliance with applicable guidelines and regulations of its third party vendors.

The European Commission, in a recent communication to the Parliament[15], identified cloud computing, along with social networks, among the emerging phenomena. There is an urgent need to revise the EU regulatory framework concerning data protection in ICT systems. There is the need of adapting the existing legal regulations to the methods for sharing and managing the personal information whose development has *de facto* undermined the system seal ability of existing regulations.

A study confirmed that there seems to be a convergence of views among Data Protection Authorities, business associations and client organizations. Risks to privacy and the protection of personal data associated with online activity are increasing[16].

It is necessary to wait for interventions that fit the existing legislation concerning the protection of data against the challenges generated by the market in the field of cloud computing. In the meantime, there are factors relevant to competitiveness for cloud services vendors, including:

- Visibility, both at the time of establishment of the contractual relationship (with respect to the data center locations and the privacy policy), and during the relationship (through the prompt notification of any unauthorized access);
- The provision of adequate guarantees in terms of security measures (that is, through accredited certification bodies); and
- The provision of adequate guarantees and penalties in the event of unauthorized access to, theft of, or loss of data.

4.1.2   Private data localization and transfer

As far as the regulators are concerned, it will ultimately be the responsibility of the financial institution to handle the private information of its customers, employees, and suppliers in accordance with the applicable guidelines and regulations. To this effect, it is not important if such information resides in an in-house system or a third-party vendor system.

Cloud computing is associated with a range of serious and complex privacy issues.

To provide a useful discussion of the specific privacy issues that arise from cloud computing, it is necessary to distinguish two types of cloud structure:

- Domestic clouds (also sometimes referred as Sovereign Clouds); and
- Cross-border clouds.

A domestic cloud has the entire cloud physically located within the same country. Domestic clouds will not give rise to any cross-border issues. However, such clouds can still give rise to privacy issues such as:

- Whether the collection of data is performed in an appropriate manner;
- Whether the data is used appropriately;
- Whether the data is disclosed only where disclosure is appropriate;
- Whether the data is stored and transmitted safely;
- How long the data will be retained for;
- The circumstances under which the data users can access and modify the data; and
- Whether the data owner is informed sufficiently and appropriately about these matters.

The organizations should consider these matters in all cloud services, whether or not the cloud is domestic. When clouds act cross-border, there are additional privacy issues. In approaching these issues, it is useful to draw a distinction between those associated with:

- Cross-border cloud services vendors and
- Cross-border cloud services clients (such as, for example a financial institution using a cross-border cloud service affecting client information).

Western countries and those in the European Union have developed regulatory systems for the protection of personal data rarely found in other countries. In this situation, it can be very complex for a cloud services vendor to reconcile the demands of compliance relative to the protection of personal data with a geographically optimized distribution of data and applications. This applies in particular to European countries where such rules are more stringent, based on the "principle of territoriality."

An example of such regulations is probably the "EU Directive 95/46 on the protection of individuals with regard to the processing of personal data and on the free movement of such data"[17]. This Directive regulates specifically the manner in which information can be collected, recorded, used, and disseminated. It imposes requirements on the physical transfer of data to countries outside the EU.

Article 2(a) of the EU Data Protection Directive defines 'personal data' as:

> Any information relating to an identified or identifiable natural person ('data subject'). An identified person is one who can be identified, directly or indirectly, in particular by reference to an identification number or to one or more factor specific to its physical, psychological, mental, economic, cultural, or social identity.

The same Directive in Article 2(b) defines "processing of personal data":

> processing of personal data shall mean any operation or set of operations which is performed upon personal data, whether or not by automatic means, such as collection, recording, organization, storage, adaptation or alteration, retrieval, consultation, use, disclosure by transmission, dissemination or otherwise making available, alignment or combination, blocking, erasure, or destruction.

With regard to the free movement of such data, Article 25 of the same Directive states that:

> The EU Member States shall provide that the transfer to a third country of personal data which are undergoing processing or are intended for processing after transfer may take place only if, without prejudice to compliance with the national provisions adopted pursuant to the other

provisions of this Directive, the third country in question ensures an adequate level of protection.

Article 25 plays a crucial role in privacy protection. In fact, the legislation of many EU countries prohibits the transfer of personal data to countries outside the EU that do not provide an adequate level of protection. This applies unless the organizations have prior to the transfer made adequate safeguards, including those of contractual nature, for the protection of data privacy. This type of provision seriously limits both the degree and modes in which cross-border cloud services can be used, demanding that the clients of cloud services should know the geographical locations in a specific cloud. This law creates a fundamental tension between the law's focus on geographical locations and the ubiquitous nature of cloud computing, and this tension may represent the largest obstacle to widespread adoption of cloud computing. Cloud services vendors should make it possible for European financial institutions to have their data stored on servers within the European Union only. Consequently, the way forward seems to be for cloud services vendors to develop services that are geographically limited (the so-called sovereign public clouds). Moreover, within Europe itself, in spite of the presence of a central nucleus of shared principles, detailed regulations vary from country to country; this is the result of the greater or lesser rigor adopted by each EU Member State when transposing the EU directive to its local legislation. The related obligations that mandate to the holder to ensure full compliance in terms of the treatment of personal data laws also vary from one EU Member State to another.

This matter should be addressed from an international perspective. The market is crowded with cloud services vendors, and networks of data centers in various countries both within and outside the EU can form a cloud. Hence, the first problem is to understand which:

- Law(s) will regulate relations with the vendor, in terms of data protection; and
- Court shall have jurisdiction over any vendor infringing the law.

For this reason, cloud computing is an interesting environment in which to observe the interaction between the law and technological developments. On the one hand, regulations such as the ones described, aim at sound goals, but on the other, they will inevitably restrict the dissemination of solutions such as cloud computing. Such situations highlight the need for modernization of this type of regulation.

4.2   Governance

In using cloud infrastructures, the financial institution necessarily cedes to the cloud vendor the control of aspects that may affect security. For example,

Terms of Use may prohibit checks on the quality of the security measures being made through port scans, vulnerability assessment, and penetration testing. Or there may be conflicts between the client's security procedures and those of the cloud environment. On the other hand, SLAs may not offer a commitment to provide such services by the vendor, leaving a gap in security defences.

In the case of cloud computing, data transfer from local computers to remote systems owned by third parties, present, along with potential benefits, the following aspects that need attention:

- The financial institution, by entrusting its data to the systems of a remote vendor, loses direct and exclusive control;
- The selected services could be the result of a chain of transformation of services provided by other vendors, who could be different from the vendor with whom the financial institution has contracted its cloud services. Thus the financial institution, in the face of complex chains of responsibility, may not always be able to know which of the various operators of intermediate services can access certain data; and
- The service, in the absence of appropriate guarantees about the quality of network connectivity, may occasionally be downgraded in the presence of extreme peaks in traffic. It might even become unavailable when anomalous events occur, such as network breakdowns. Such cases would temporarily prevent access to some or all the data.

It is important to be aware of when the cloud services vendor in turn outsources or sub-contracts services to one or more third parties. These unknown vendors may not assume the same obligations, in terms of the service provided, to be in compliance with the law. Another case may be that the control of the cloud services vendor changes, so the terms and conditions of their services may also change.

The loss of governance could lead to:

- The impossibility of complying with the security requirements;
- A lack of confidentiality;
- Problems with the integrity and availability of data;
- A deterioration of performance and quality of service; and
- The introduction of compliance challenges.

4.2.1 Vendor manager

The Vendor Manager's job is an essential one within the structure of the client organization in a cloud computing scenario. S/he should carry out the following tasks: Part 0 – Basic Tasks

- Manage the contract and any problem that might arise in the performance of the services;

- Manage from a technical, functional standpoint the administrative and technical relations between the parties;
- Verify the respect of the scope and characteristics of the agreed services and authorize payment of the vendor's invoices;
- Control the level of services provided by the vendor. In particular, verify compliance with the contractual Service Level Agreement (SLA);
- Verify the vendor's monthly reports on their activities;
- Verify daily that the batch procedures have been processed regularly;
- Report faults and anomalies to the functions and control structures, and to the executive board, if necessary;
- Liaise with the vendor regarding upgrades to and periodical runs of the Disaster Recovery and Business Continuity tests, and agree the relevant procedures with the vendor;
- Manage and agree the improvement of services and functionality required by the organization;
- Work with the vendor for the continuous improvement of the services provided; and
- Follow the meetings organized by the vendors to report and improve their services.

Part 1 Checks on direct applications. These are the controls in connection with the financial institution structure:

- Manage and control network access and user profiles;
- Perform operational controls on the system administrators by using tracking software;
- Carry out periodic reviews on a sample basis to verify respect for the data privacy of customers, employees and suppliers;
- Set up the database of the loss data collection, and monitor the operational losses in conjunction with Internal Audit;
- Support the financial institution Risk Manager and Committee in the execution of the regulatory processes and processing of the reports;
- Support the executives for the drafting of public disclosure (Basel II – Pillar 3); and
- Be the point of contact for certification actions (for example SSAE 302) of the vendor of cloud services.

4.3   Cloud computing controls

4.3.1   Risk management

Financial services possess critical and/or confidential business information. It is therefore essential to consider the potential loss of control, at least in part, over data, and all associated risks.

Financial institutions today must be more attentive to the optimization of organizational processes and to the introduction of specific solutions at the base of the effectiveness, efficiency and economics of the financial institutions.

Schiaffonati, Capgemini's Vice-president for Financial Services, highlighted that[18]:

> Risk management is acquiring an increasingly central role in the management processes. A Risk Manager is no longer a simple controller of the levels of risk or a producer of information for the benefit of top management and the Board, but rather is becoming an authoritative partner actively involved in the processes of strategic decision making.

Before signing a contract with a vendor of cloud services, and periodically, it is important to perform a risk management assessment. The objectives are to:

- Identify as far as possible all potential risks;
- Guarantee that potential problems be addressed as soon as possible;
- Specify actions to reduce the probability that risks will materialize, or eliminate the causes and therefore the possibility that they will become problems during the implementation and use of cloud services;
- Develop plans of actions, both preventive and contingent, to reduce the impact of the realization of a risk; and
- Improve capabilities to sound an alert relating to the possible realization of a risk.

The basic steps of risk management are summarized in Table 4.1.

Table 4.1 Steps in risk management

Step	Description
Step 1	Identification of risks: To identify and describe all possible types of events that could occur during the implementation and use of cloud services.
Step 2	Risk quantification: To assess the probability of occurrence, the potential impacts, and the possibility of advance alerts of each event identified in Step 1.
Step 3	Identification and implementation of countermeasures: To define the actions useful to mitigate the risks and their consequences.
Step 4	Monitoring: Along all the use of cloud services, to implement preventive measures, to assess their returns and possibly update the original plan.

The first three phases are used to produce reports to be included in a Quality Plan for the provision of cloud services. The organizations should conduct the stages of Identification, quantification, and design countermeasures at the initial planning stage of the project. These steps are replicated along the life cycle of cloud service provisioning. This ensures permanent control over the state of every risk. It helps to improve the ability to take preventive action promptly in order to reduce the probability and the potential effects of the risk in question.

4.3.2   Certifications

During the evaluation of a cloud services vendor, it is important to identify its certifications, thus abbreviating the phase during which the controls and audits are contracted. Below there is a list of some relevant certifications. The characteristics of the services offered by the vendors of cloud services, the type of markets they address, and the size reached by the organizations show the usefulness of certifications that would ensure:

- The certainty of the correctness of the processes used by the vendor regardless of the knowledge/experience of staff; and
- Controls that these methods are not only correct, but also always carefully implemented.

Some useful certifications are:

1. European standards series EN ISO 9001/2008, issued by accredited bodies under the rules of the European standard EN 45000 EA33 "information technology";
2. ISO/IEC 27001:2005, important from the point of view of security;
3. ISO/IEC 42010, relating to systems and software engineering – Architecture description;
4. ISO 27001 Lead Auditor, for staff resources;
5. Personnel certified by suppliers of hardware and software;
6. Staff resources certified in the area of ICT Governance;
7. SOC II focused on the general controls of information systems ("General Computer Controls"), detected through the use of the COBIT framework (Control Objectives for Information and related Technology). COBIT is a framework published by ISACA (Information Systems Audit and Control Association). It identifies four domains, 34 ICT processes and 214 control objectives on the specific area of information systems general controls.

The American Institute of Certified Public Accountants (AICPA) has defined three new report types[19]:

- The SOC-1 or SSAE 16, which replaces the SAS 70. It concerns only the accounting systems;

- The SOC-2, which is a more technical report, dedicated to one or more elements (security, availability, integrity, confidentiality, and privacy). Its associated controls are described in a document labelled "Trust Services Principles and Criteria"; and
- The SOC-3 is a kind of summary of SOC-2. It is intended for publication. It can be compared to the ISO/IEC 27001 with a logo that can be published on the vendor's website.

More and more accurate details can be found on the web.

8. Cloud services must include the provision of different types of digital certificates:

- To sign documents;
- For trading online;
- For encryption;
- For managing certified emails and digital signatures; and
- The certification of the servers.

9. There are some emerging cloud security standards (for instance Cloud Security Alliance (CSA), Shared Assessments Program, and Federal Risk and Authorization Management Program (FedRAMP)). They may lead in time to certification programs.

4.3.3 Contract

A fundamental tool for the governance of a cloud vendor is the contract. To ensure that a cloud services contract is clear and capable of achieving the objectives that led to the choice of outsourced activities and processes, all aspects should be treated both comprehensively and independently. In this way, it is possible to avoid unclear or even contradictory situations. The most important thing in defining a contract with a cloud services vendor is to have clear business goals for the cloud initiative. It is necessary to take into account some basic considerations[20]:

The management of the security requires a plan and a control system;

- To mitigate key vendor vulnerability, identify, and select alternative locations and/or vendors to re-deploy to in the event of service interruptions; and
- To mitigate dependence on a single vendor, a separate vendor may be selected for Disaster Recovery services;

The monitoring and management of the SLA:

- It might be considered worthwhile for either the vendor or the client to use software that can automatically monitor SLA. This would be a fast, effective way of obtaining measurement of the desired services dynamically and cheaply; and

- The client organization might want to use an external consultant to monitor services.

4.3.3.1   Importance of cloud services contracts

The negotiation of the contract with the vendor is an important element for the control of cloud services[21]. At one of the cloud computing world summits, 30% of the participants reported negative results from cloud computing projects; they had not reached their goals. The main reason for these failures is the incorrect setting up and management of the relationships between client and vendor. One of the fundamental causes of such negative experiences is the fact that the increased use of cloud services has not seen a similar increase in the capability of the organizations to manage these contracts and their complexity. So it is important that for each vendor selected, an organization should:

- Check their track record, financial status, and stability;
- Obtain a written quotation for the services under consideration;
- Understand the jurisdiction under which the contract will be enforced;
- Negotiate ownership of data, the right to retain it when the relationship terminates, and agree the format in which it will be returned; and
- For key applications, obtain the rights to the source code (in order to run the system) and to reclaim all the data (including historical) in the event of vendor failure.

The amount of negotiation and contracting is often underestimated. Some organizations let the vendor write the contract, but this might lead to complex supply agreements being managed through simplified and inadequate clauses, often favouring the vendor. The processes of negotiation and contracting of services and activities are rather high value-added processes. They are keys to a successful relationship with the vendor, smoothing the management of the contract and avoiding strained relationships. The contractual arrangements with the vendor must focus on the scope and the perimeter of the service. But rarely do they clearly define roles and responsibilities, and sometimes they do not cover, either fully or partially, topics such as the SLA (Service Level Agreement). Even worse, they do not contain pricing models or description of the change management (for example how and when to transition, termination, and so on). With respect to the management issues in the contract documents, the approach that guarantees the best results and optimization efforts is pyramidal. The cornerstone is a Master Service Agreement (MSA), which represents the legal architecture to which the parties will refer in the course of the life cycle of the relationship. The MSA should include clauses such as:

- The objectives;
- The duration;

- The reasons for termination of contracts and the consequences for the client; and
- The governance:
  - System of governance;
  - An auditing mechanism to monitor the service, especially with respect to data privacy;
  - The responsibilities of the vendor and the client[22];
  - Clarification of relationships, rights, and responsibilities between the vendor and any brokers or resellers that may be involved; and
  - The organization in terms of account (on the side of the vendor) and vendor management (on the side of the client);
- Confidentiality;
- The liabilities, especially those relating to data loss. The contract should spell out clearly and unambiguously which losses are covered, and whether the vendor will increase the cover it offers if the customer agrees to pay more or agrees to a different service package;
- The insurance which the vendor should have;
- Ownership of the systems used and their respect of recognized industry standards;
- Limitations on unilateral changes in the contract;
- No automatic renewal; and
- The legal clauses, with special attention to the choice of the governing law and location.

The MSA should not deal with procedural and operational aspects; these should be defined in the annexes. The MSA should, however, include a detailed description of all the elements and phases of the life cycle of the cloud services from a procedural and functional point of view, including all phases from the handover of the activities to the vendor of cloud services (the project plan and transition) to the definition of all activities and responsibilities at the termination of the contract. In order to have a comprehensive contractual framework, the key annexes to the MSA are[23]:

Scope of services:

- Identification, in a clear but not rigid way, of the domains and the business processes within which the vendor of the cloud services must operate; and
- A complete and specific description of services: identification and description of functionality, technologies, services to be supplied.

Service level agreements:

- Definition of the SLA associated with each service. They should be based on concepts that are clearly measurable and relevant. There should be in a specific and quantifiable way a set of parameters to measure the level of service provided. The failure to meet an SLA incurs a penalty. It should be a share of the fee equal to the weight percentage of that failure with respect to the SLA itself;

- The remedies and penalties available to client and vendor if the terms of the SLA are not met;
- How the SLA will change over time;
- Method and targets for continuous improvement and innovation.

Pricing model:

- Basic fees;
- Level of service provided, and costs for moving (either way) to a different level of service;
- Charges for change requests;
- Inflation or productivity reduction over time;
- Benchmarking with best of breed in the market;
- Costs for continuation of the contract at its natural termination; and
- And so on.

Data management

- Legal ownership of data and rights of access. Data should always be accessible and reserved;
- Rights of the customers, suppliers, and employees of the financial institution;
- Geographic location of data and data transfer;
- Isolation of personal data from other data in case of law enforcement actions; and
- Data retention, storage, and deletion protocols.

Security and compliance

- Disaster recovery and business continuity arrangements, including frequency and storage location of backups;
- Security protocols, data classification systems, data encryption standards and application (in transit and/or in storage), reporting of security incidents and support during such incidents offered by the vendor;
- Specification of regulatory requirements to respect, and protocols for demonstration of compliance with regulations and certification;
- Protocol for reporting service level breaches by the vendor to the client;
- Project migration; and
- Maintenance standards, procedures and timeframes.

Termination of the contract:

• Assistance processes available from the vendor in case of termination of the contract; the so-called lock in must be avoided. This expression refers to the client's dependence on the vendor, and it must not be too strict. In other words, it should not prevent a change of vendor and therefore compel the acceptance of unfair terms at contract renewal or termination. The contract should clarify the obligations of each party, pricing, and maximum duration of such an event; and
• Commitment to erase all client data, documentation and programs at termination.

4.3.3.2 Legal concerns

In cloud computing, financial institutions transfer data, programs, and business processes in the cloud. They should ensure that the contract is solid and fully respectful of applicable laws and regulations. It is also necessary to assure that the legal and law enforcement systems and the apparatus from the jurisdiction in which the cloud services are provided are sound, reliable, and trustworthy.

If considering, for instance, an EU organization receiving cloud services from a vendor outside the EU territory, the transparency of the vendor is very important. The presence of physical servers in another country may allow the judicial authorities of that country to mandate the production of evidence, plus access to data or detention of it, where there are serious legal grounds under the laws of that country. In contrast, referring to those same databases, the organization's national judicial authority could attain the same results only by means of complex international requests.

The situation becomes even more complex in the extreme but possible scenario in which the financial institution itself operates in multiple countries. The requirements and reporting would be complex and multi-jurisdictional. Difficult and overwhelming regulatory requirements would reduce the perceived benefits of cloud services. In such confusing circumstances, it would be difficult, if not impossible, to determine or regulate features, functions, services, applications, databases, and the like, in a cloud computing environment.

The consequence is that an organization operating in multiple countries is exposed to extraterritorial claims of jurisdiction and extraterritorial applications of privacy laws.

Similarly, vendors of cloud services expose themselves to the laws of all the countries in which their services are provided and used. In such unclear situations, decisions by the European Union Regulators would be needed to clarify the position, with appropriate interventions.

4.3.4   Control over the governance and the definition of operational plans

Within the supply of cloud services, there might be specific projects that include the initial migration plan, the transition plan at termination, and so on, and in these cases the relevant controls must be put in place. They are relative to the governance and the definition of the operational plans and to the processes for the overall management of the ICT projects. They should include accurate knowledge of the performance and the cost of each activity in the plans. All these elements should be included within the larger organization's strategic plan. The provision of changes or modification in the systems should be a consistent and coordinated set of the activities required to ensure that the client organization objectives are met. They would normally be part of a statement of work, as agreed between the client and the vendor. It is essential, in this context, to:

- Define roles and responsibilities at different levels;
- Follow an appropriate project management plan, with reference to the contract or to specific requests; and
- Assure a proper exchange of information.

The goal is to be ready to solve any problem that may arise during the implementation of the project. The client organization must put in place a series of actions to meet the requirements of the control system fully. The general criterion adopted should be based mainly on the principles of reliability, professionalism, and timeliness:

- Reliability: The work statements should define the referrals to individual areas and unique services, the relevant staff having specific roles and responsibilities, competence and appropriate experience, a positive attitude towards cooperation and a pro-active attitude. This aspect provides an element of assurance for the financial services organization of the availability of reliable partners to whom they can make requests, and to find solutions and answers to the problems arising in the provision of cloud services;
- Professionalism: The needs of cloud services providers include a variety of technologies and activities. This requires professional resources with multiple skills and experiences; and
- Timeliness: The ability to provide the professional resources in the shortest possible time is a specific commitment that the vendor needs to undertake. In this way, it is possible to:
  - Overcome the limitations of running the outsourced system or process inside the organization, and gain maximum flexibility in management;
  - Manage the priorities for change as much as possible independently of the resources of the vendor.

The organizational model must be able to ensure the success of the project as a whole. It would be ideal if it:

- Complied fully with all the specifications on how to conduct the planned activities;
- Offered a direct interface between the executives of both organizations. This would assure maximum ease and simplicity in decision making involving the two parties;
- Ensured enough flexibility in the management of resources to:
  - Solve any unexpected needs of the financial institution which cannot be postponed; and
  - Manage mission-critical situations which may arise during the course of the supply;
- Added further significant value through the sharing of specific skills, assuring the optimal approach to the achievement of:
  - Functional integration in such a way that the results are in line with the functional design of the overall system; and
  - Fairness of products/services provided.

Between the client and the vendor of cloud services there must be a layer of a governance structure; this should be able to guarantee 100% continuously the quality of the services provided. It is essential to control, plan, and monitor the services with a proactive approach and ability to coordinate. The goal is to represent the needs of the client better. The tasks of this structure will be to:

- Set the objectives and the quality of services to be provided, as an agreement between client and vendor;
- Define the modes of organization and execution of each process;
- Develop and/or consolidate the organizational structure of the service;
- Plan the implementation and delivery of products and services;
- Estimate the resources and time required to achieve the objectives agreed;
- Implement work plans which dynamically allocate human resources, logistics, and instrumental activities; and
- Monitor and measure results.

It is important that a Project Management Office (PMO) should govern the project according to the contract. At the time of initial migration and improvement projects, this unit must:

- Provide support to the project team;
- Define and respect effective and efficient standards;
- Document the project phases;

- Monitor the situation;
- Identify and assess potential risks, and the problems that might occur; and
- Suggest possible corrective actions and solutions.

4.3.4.1 *Control systems of the project*

The effectiveness of any project (such as migration) is controlled and monitored continuously using the following tools, which the vendors of cloud services should make available to their clients:

- Periodic monitoring of the progress of activities (with payments on reaching milestones) as defined in the project plan;
- Close control of the data mapping and migration between the two environments. The vendor of cloud services should provide all the necessary tools to the client. In this way, the financial institution can verify and certify the correctness of the migrated data in the new system. The standard method of acceptance is dependent on the number of recycles for migrating the data and on completing the functional tests on the migrated systems;
- Certification of the migration of individual data streams including justification for the differences. The vendor of cloud services should provide all the tools required for the client to verify and certify the correctness of data in each single "migrated" stream;
- Involvement of the working groups defined by the project plan as being responsible for the correct migration of data. An immediate escalation to the Steering Committee should be possible if issues arise relating to the attainment of the proposed organizational coordination necessary for the success of the migration; and
- Definition, in cooperation with the client, of the checklist of activities and checks to be carried out during the migration, generated from templates previously used by the vendor.

4.3.5 Control of the operational management

The term "ICT Operations Management" refers to the management of the ICT services in terms of delivery, and monitoring of the same. This includes the verification of the proper provision of services by the cloud vendors. The following paragraphs describe the methods of control and verification of the effectiveness of performance of the quality of service and the associated procedures. As part of the service, there are systems and methods to measure it. The following paragraphs provide a brief description of the tools used.

4.3.5.1 *Reporting system*

The general reporting of the service should be based on the system activity data generated from the processing of the records and logs produced by the systems. The metrics should be collected daily, then consolidated by being loaded into a single database that is regularly checked and queried. Statistical applications software is a tool that can help in these tasks. The statistical system used by the vendor of cloud services must have elements enabling the user to monitor, probe, verify, and investigate data and events related to the managed information systems. It is a set of broad spectrum statistical objects ranging from high profile statistics for client management, such as:

- Balanced Score Card (BSC) with drill-down information at the level of procedures, functions, and departments;
- Statistics for the extensive analysis of possible indicators of waste;
- Computer performance (for example MIPS, Microprocessor without Interlocked Pipeline Stages) and number of transactions both monthly and daily with the possibility of drilling at the level of procedure/user;
- The operational statistics (produced shortly after the event);
- Large and abended transactions, with the option of displaying the input of the completed transaction; and
- Operations management, with statistics on the operational control of the servers and the helpdesk activity.

The phases for the supervision of management activities related to the processing system are:

- Operational support of the console team, control infrastructure, storage management, system monitoring, and so on;
- Management procedures for opening and closing systems, consistent with the needs of the situation and according to information provided by the client;
- Verification of the correctness of the operational sequences;
- Implementation of processes;
- Systems logs;
- Activation and closing of the system resources;
- Responses to pending system requests;
- Operational activities on the systems (installation and removal of hardware, input processing robots, and so on);
- Management of the operating system and its configuration;
- Tracking of all activity made available to the client; and
- Information on the status of systems or services.

The control system must:

- Develop/update procedures for startup/shutdown of systems;
- Develop, test (demonstrably), and put into operation procedures for the control of systems, database, and the TP monitor management software;

- Develop and test (demonstrably) procedures and instruments for the control of infrastructure components, such as: hardware and software, use of main memory, file system, controller, physical/virtual tape library robotic units power, Wide Area Network (WAN) interfaces, operating system processes, and subsystems (for example, DB2). Information from the monitoring procedures will be essential in the complex process of problem determination and resolution in the presence of malfunctioning applications whose root causes are not easily detectable; and
- Report on time 24/7, signal errors, anomalies, and more generally issues related to the operation of:
  - Technical components (hardware, operating system, subsystems, WAN interface, and so on);
  - Backup and archiving processes; and
  - Procedures for hardware control.

Daily archives from all systems should be downloadable and loaded in a database. A report of hardware/software control should be produced on demand. The operation team of the service vendor must check the status of the systems. Should serious errors occur, they will call the maintenance teams of the suppliers of hardware, software, or network. At the same time, they should alert the client organization and their vendor manager.

4.3.5.2   *Tools to monitor, manage, and control*

The vendor of cloud services must have available a set of tools that allow investigation of the operation of applications. Starting from a careful analysis of the data arising from these tools, the vendor's engineers should be able to provide the maintenance areas with information for the optimization of performance and consumption of resources. The vendor should perform periodic checks on the performance on both the system components and the application component, and then store them. The vendor should send the results of this analysis periodically to the system designers and application areas. These areas should take action, when necessary, on the system processes and applications in order to optimize the resources used. The services provided for monitoring the systems in real time should perform these operations[24]:

- Actively monitor service delivery to the client, including response times and outages. There should be an appropriate frequency and coverage of this monitoring;
- Develop a plan for redeploying to alternative sites in the event that service delivery is compromised;
- Train the client team in the plan, and rehearse it;
- Monitor for collecting information on the resource usage in the systems;

- Monitor for collecting information about the transaction processing service. Produce reports related to the critical response time for groups of transactions, server usage per transaction or globally on the system; and
- Produce a failures journal.

Batch processes should be monitored and followed with the standard tools provided by the automatic scheduling systems. In the event that the client deems it necessary, the vendor should make available advanced solutions to monitor the nightly batch scheduling and provide estimates on the duration of the processing steps by identifying critical paths. This is particularly important for services with night or maintenance windows when systems would not be available to users.

4.3.6 Control of maintenance and support

Control of ICT maintenance and support refers to the process of planning, development, and monitoring of the technical support and management of hardware, software, network, and any other cloud services, to ensure customer satisfaction. It should include:

- Corrective maintenance for the elimination from the services provided of errors and/or failures (blocking or not), or the restoration of functions in the face of errors and/or inconsistencies. For some cases which are difficult to resolve, the vendor should be able to make some workarounds available;
- A maintenance statement for the provision of all variations and/or additions to the services under contract; according to the Service Level Agreement; and
- Control systems based on applicable standards.

4.5.6.1 *Control systems and performance verification*

The monitoring and verification of the performance and quality of the service is done with three instruments: SLA, surveys, and statistics of total/open tickets:

- It is necessary to verify compliance with contractual service levels (SLA). This represents the reference to the "ideal" situation, as formalized and agreed with the client;
- There should be an annual verification of the quality of the services provided. This could be done by an annual submission by all clients of a "Questionnaire on the degree of satisfaction of service." The best way to conduct this would be through an independent third party. The survey should touch on all aspects of the service provided by the vendors. This questionnaire can help in targeting improvements to people, processes and systems; and

- Periodically, there should be an examination of the statistics of the tickets reporting problems in the services provided. This procedure helps in targeting remedial actions with the highest effectiveness and precision possible. It is also useful for the correct dimensioning of the resources necessary for the provision of the services.

4.6   Security

The protection of data assets and information is a requirement of great importance at the operational level. This is true especially because the vendor of cloud services manages data which can be personal, sensitive, and/ or critical. The client must pay particular attention to the security measures used by the cloud services vendor; they are crucially important, and vendors will not always give enough attention to these aspects.

The vendor must have a Security Manual that includes the goals and principles that underpin the security rules, regulations, operating procedures, and organizational arrangements for providing the services.

Security concerns fall into two buckets: logical and physical.

- The physical security is intended to achieve confidentiality, integrity, and availability of corporate assets by adopting measures:
  - Active (systems able to detect and report an event, halt it, and turn on assistance to *ad hoc* personnel);
  - Passive (measures, usually of a physical nature, designed to resist passively to possible dangers, delaying their effects as much as possible); and
  - Organizational (a set of procedures for prevention and control applied by external staff guards, police, or employees to make better use of the defensive measures installed);
- The logical security is aimed at obtaining confidentiality, integrity, and availability of data and information through the use of measures:
  - Technical (for system access control, antivirus, firewall, intrusion detection systems, and so on);
  - Organizational (policy development, security, user profiling and related ratings, and so on); and
  - Procedural (processes to be followed for security purposes);

The control system should allow access to authorized users through an authentication server single sign-on. The client security staff should manage the definition of access profiles centrally.

Security must ensure the consistency of the measures to comply with laws and regulations. Accesses must be logged., and they should be inspectable by authorized personnel. The security office should be able to provide files that show the activities performed by the users and security violations brought about by any user, and in particular by the system administrators. The profiling also runs the distinction between single view and management changes. Through the possible profiles, the client can define any level of competency for its users. The physical security of premises or the vendor of cloud services is also important. The security of the vendor of cloud services should also:

• Prescribe regulations governing access to the buildings and to protected spaces; and
• Collaborate with the "Administrative Management" (administration, finance, procurement, infrastructure management, and secretariat) for the determination of structure and processes for making the intrusion detection systems and remote surveillance (Closed Circuit Television, CCTV) effective.

There are several regulations that need to be respected. An example deserving of attention is The Federal Information Security Management Act of 2002 ("The Federal Information Security Management Act (FISMA)," 44 U.S.C. §3541, et seq.); this is a USA federal law enacted in 2002 as Title III of the E-Government Act of 2002 (Pub.L. 107–347, 116 Stat. 2899). The act recognized the importance of information security to the economic and national security interests of the USA[25]. The act requires each federal agency to develop, document, and implement an agency-wide program to provide information security for the information and the information systems that support the operations and assets of the agency, including those provided or managed by another agency, contractor, or other source.

FISMA has brought attention within the federal government to cyber security. It explicitly emphasized a "risk-based policy for cost-effective security." FISMA requires agency program officials, CIOs, and inspectors general (IGs) to conduct annual reviews of the agency's information security program. In FY 2008, federal agencies spent $6.2 billion securing the government's total information technology investment of approximately $68 billion or about 9.2 per cent of the total ICT portfolio[26].

4.7 Technical tools

The vendors of cloud services in the management of their activities should follow the Information Technology Infrastructure Library (ITIL) guidelines, inspired by the best practices in ICT Service Management (ITSM)[27]. They provide guidance on the provision of quality ICT services and processes, and the resources needed to support them. The operational management control of cloud computing must be using the tools and standards provided by the client for the specific delivery of macro-classes:

- Change planning must be done through packages of planning and control of projects (such as MS Project, Primavera, Open Project, and so on);
- Analysis of the processes, requirements, and design can be carried out using tools in line with standards UML 2.3 and XMI 2.1 (for example Altova UModel 2011, Magic Draw);
- Configuration Management (CM) can be done using one of the several specific systems available; and
- Monitoring can use tools such as Knowledge Tree.

As for the audits (at the third level of governance, as described at the beginning of this chapter), the intrinsic characteristic of immaterial information to be collected requires the adoption of methodologies and tools developed specifically for this purpose. Computer-Assisted Audit Techniques (CAAT) include analysis and tests performed with generic software to help with reviewing (ACL, IDEA, software for database management server or mainframe, Access, and so on)[28]. Their use is recommended to facilitate audits carried out by the clients.

4.8   Communications management

A cloud services vendor's documentation is expected to provide support for operational management (plans, requirements documents, manuals, specifications, use cases, and so on). It must be managed through appropriate tools.

The management of communications and collaboration between client and cloud services vendor must be optimized, using the functionality provided by computer tools.

There should be a system that acts as the repository of all the information, and there should be proper safeguards to prevent unauthorized alteration of the documents in the repository.

The information (documents, minutes of meetings, decisions, plans, risks, activities, and so on) must be accessible directly within the repository. Interested persons must be notified automatically when information/documents are available and/or are updated. The types of objects in the repository must be defined in agreement with the client. The vendor should populate the environment for the duration of the contract and must provide:

- The verification and real-time control of all activities;
- The subsequent versions of the documentation;
- Service-level reports; and
- All other documents related to the provision of the service.

The information must be made available through a simple and intuitive interface. The client should have the ability to aggregate data and information. Access should be through distinct profiles according to the different types of user.

4.9   Conclusions

Cloud services can bring benefits but also create risks; in this situation, governance is essential, and it requires efforts to be made by both vendor and client to create a partnership. With increasing technical and organizational complexities and internal/external threats in the future, there will be more and more requirements for improved governance.

An Enterprise Cloud Leadership Council has recently been set up to focus on these concerns. Credit Suisse and the Commonwealth Bank of Australia are some of its members[29].

For the reader interested to know more about controls in cloud computing, the recommendation is to download the Cloud Control Matrix from CSA[30].

5
The Future of ICT in Financial Institutions

5.1 Introduction

Society has changed drastically in recent decades, especially in the economy and finance. Financial institutions have started to change in response, and the expectation is that this transformation will accelerate in the next few years. The question often perceived, then, is how can ICT support such a transformation?

We believe that the paradigm is different. The question should be: How can ICT shape the future of financial institutions? ICT must take a much more active role in the their transformation. As a paradox, ICT, and cloud computing in particular, is already the place where financial transactions are managed, and will become more and more so in the. The word "managed" is different from "processed"; in other words, ICT will become more and more part of the core business of the financial institutions. This is the subject of this chapter.

Organizations should consider cloud computing as much more than just a technology. It is a completely different way to do computing and especially to innovate in business. This is true in general but especially for service organizations, such as financial institutions; Gartner claims that cloud computing can drive a "creative destruction" for financial institutions[1].

Data from an Assinform[2] survey confirms that the majority of financial institutions are planning to take advantage of cloud computing. This model offers many opportunities[3]. The survey specifically points out that the use of cloud services by financial institutions will aim to optimize the resources available and extend the potentially achievable audience of users and applications.

5.2 New challenges for financial institutions

The last few years have been very challenging for financial institutions. The future will be no easier for them; they will face many challenges such as:

- Further consolidation of the markets;
- International competition;
- Entrance of new players (such as PayPal and Payment Institutions); and
- Decreased customer trust due to the credit crunch.

Following the upheaval that has redefined and simplified the sector, financial institutions now give priority to efficiency and the creation of innovative customercentric products and services. They must work continuously to be compliant with national and international regulations. Security is of paramount importance. The financial institutions are working to strengthen security systems.

Financial institutions face many challenges; the four principal challenges are the four Cs:

- Cosmopolitization;
- Customers;
- Compliance; and
- Cost.

This section will analyze each of these challenges and discuss how cloud services can help. The chapter will also examine how an additional C (Cloud) can help to create new opportunities.

5.2.1 Cosmopolitization

Until the mid-1990s, a sparse presence of foreign players and a high fragmentation of domestic operators characterized most national financial systems. The operations were mainly limited to the domestic market and, very often, to a limited territory (such as in the case of the Sparkasse in Germany, the Credit Unions in the UK, the Banques Populaires in France, or the BCC in Italy). Several factors have for a long time limited the definition and implementation of internationalization strategies (to which we refer with the word "cosmopolitization") by these domestic financial institutions, such as:

- The average modest/small size of financial institutions, and the very small number of banks and insurance companies operating as global players;
- A scarce international vocation also due to the huge resources, increased risks, and knowledge required to enter in other advanced financial systems;
- The existence, for many years, of stringent national regulatory and currency constraints on penetration in foreign markets;
- A low level of efficiency, with a limited range of products and services normally not characterized by marked innovation;
- Good profit margins in the domestic markets; and
- A very localized culture in many institutions.

This scenario was not optimal. It suited an industrial system characterized by small and medium-sized businesses with a demand, essentially, for local financial services. So there was no strong incentive for foreign investments. Businesses were not able to guarantee a level of profitability sufficient to make foreign investments viable to financial institutions, meaning there was no justification for a strong international presence. This trend has, however, changed over the past decades. Globalization has become more and more a reality, so the process of internationalization of the domestic financial systems has significantly intensified.

Local financial institutions have in recent years developed new initiatives aimed at expanding their foreign distribution network and setting up internationalization strategies. These strategies, especially when directed towards Central and Eastern Europe, are important. However, at the time of writing the international presence of financial institutions remains relatively limited; the internationalization process has mainly affected a few large banking and insurance groups. This situation will change in the next few years[4], as there are many factors pushing for internationalization – the financial services system is influenced by:

- A gradual market enlargement;
- The growth of emerging economies; and
- The need for volume growth, rationalization, and greater efficiency.

In the past, the expansion of financial institutions at the international level has been directed mainly towards emerging countries. There, despite relatively small investments, the financial institutions have captured significant market shares, especially as a result of the backwardness of the local financial systems. The sum of these events has led the largest financial institutions to identify the countries of the new Europe and those adjacent to them as the most attractive markets. Apart from the many theories on financial institution internationalization formulated by scholars[5], the choice of the major banking groups to target Central and Eastern Europe for their internationalization process was almost unavoidable. But the approach to the markets of Central and Eastern Europe, albeit imposed upon them, has turned out to be truly visionary, profitable, and in many ways, ideal in terms of its timing. Domestic financial institutions in this part of the world became part of the foreign players that were better positioned to accompany those countries on their path to growth, development, and democracy.

The financial institutions later began to be interested in new geographical areas such as the countries of the former Soviet Union and most recently countries in North Africa, Asia, and Latin America. But now we are experiencing the reverse: Chinese and Arab financial institutions are moving westwards, leading to further growth in the scale of foreign activities[6]. In the last few years, the concentration process of the financial systems has intensified because of competition; some medium-sized financial institutions are starting to be active, especially cross-border, alongside the major players.

At present, many national financial institutions are facing new and growing challenges; market competition has increased and economic growth is weak. Very probably, there will be a long period of continued slow growth. Until now, the financial sector has been resilient enough to cope with weak economic growth, but it will have to become able to withstand and react to the continuing unfavorable macroeconomic scenarios.

Furthermore, foreign players are entering into the domestic markets, and the consequences have been a shrinking of market shares due to strong competition. Citibank, Barclays Bank, BNP Paribas, HSBC, Deutsche Bank, Unicredit, Santander, and ING Direct are just a few of the well-known names investing in many foreign markets. All these operators have played a major role in accelerating the process of innovation in the mortgage, funding, and investment market. Santander, Barclays, and BNP Paribas, for example, are taking advantage of the financial crisis to increase their overseas presence[7].Competition has not yet been fully reflected in the pricing and quality of the core services offered.

Competition in the domestic financial sector will intensify in the near future. A more intense struggle for market superiority between foreign intermediaries would help strengthen efficiency and competition in the domestic markets. Revenue generation will remain a key priority, as debt losses are increasing and commission income is stagnating. The latter aspect is due to the strong competition generated by the growing activity of foreign financial institutions in the domestic markets. With the increasing penetration of foreign financial institutions in other countries, control over a slice of domestic market will be challenged more and more.

The financial system in Europe is undoubtedly backward. It lags behind US financial institutions and in some cases behind the financial institutions of certain emerging countries. This situation will most likely increase competition and boost innovation benefiting the end customers.

A growing number of financial institution customers, investors, and supervisory bodies, the latter involved in the protection of the interests and rights of customers, believe that in only some countries in Europe are financial institutions offering low costs and convenient banking services[8]. With the pressure caused by competition, the number and weight of foreign financial institution branches has increased. EU financial institutions and other important non-domestic subjects have been able to acquire control over foreign financial institutions of significant size, so the share of assets held in each country by foreign financial entities is in turn reaching a significant size.

Both the current legislation and supervisory bodies have taken a more open attitude over time, and they are now more open to the entrance of foreign operators. Some of them are pursuing the objective of making other countries their second domestic market[9].

Today the European economy operates more and more in an open and international context. Competition is encouraged and efficiency rewarded. The national banking and financial systems are now more and more part of the European market, alongside financial institutions of international stature.

From a systemic point of view, the expectations are that in the future:

- The market will no longer be controlled almost exclusively by domestic operators;
- Competition will gather momentum as management strives to meet the expectations of stakeholders. Acquisitions and cross-border mergers and acquisitions, a phenomenon of great relevance, will modify the morphology of the financial systems;
- Even in domestic financial systems, significant developments are still to be expected in the internationalization process; and
- European initiatives, like the SEPA (to go into full effect in February 2014), or international ones like Basel III or Solvency II, will further accelerate the internationalization process.

It is widely believed that financial institutions that maintain a foreign presence in a large number of other countries are more likely to experience an above average probability of distress, and research conducted in this field confirms this statement[10]. One reason is that maintaining a large international financial services network is costly. In the face of such challenges, cloud computing can offer a great opportunity to enhance revenues and reduce costs through ICT reorganization, consolidation, and innovation. For instance, such benefits may be achieved by migrating the domestic financial institutions' foreign branches into a single ICT system, as Santander Bank is doing. Besides the benefits in terms of savings, the adoption of cloud services in the financial industry represents a compelling business case that may prove how web-based ICT resources can improve the workflow management of not only branches but also different channels. Many financial institutions are exploring alternatives to the conventional data center concept, especially cloud computing. In Europe, a certain number of organizations are moving towards a pay-per-use cloud computing model, and many financial institutions are initiating pilot projects in this area[11]; although financial institutions might not be ready yet for the public version of cloud computing, the private cloud can be a strong enabler in order to move in the cloud computing direction. Hybrid and Community clouds will be the next step.

5.2.2 Customers

Customers are changing drastically. They are becoming much more informed, technology savvy, cost aware, mobile, and sophisticated. Cloud computing can help financial services to acquire new customers, serve them, retain them, and satisfy them in many ways. Above all, financial institutions can empower the customer with the support of cloud services.

5.2.2.1 Customercentric approach

The survival of all financial institutions depends on the improvement of the customer experience. The adoption of cloud computing can help quite a bit in this direction. It supports strategies for achieving the efficiencies linked to:

- Know Your Customer programs (KYC): Cloud computing helps financial institutions to anticipate the moment of contact with the customer and improve the relationship to their mutual benefit. KYC programs can help the organization to understand customer needs and characteristics. Today, the financial institutions wait until the customer contacts them for a loan by making a request at a branch. However, it is necessary to anticipate and be capable of perceiving the customer needs before s/he turns up to inquire about the service; the financial institution should forecast the moment (and contact the customer) when the customer might need credit. This might be the case when s/he searches through the Internet looking at other offers by the competition, or when starting to think of living in a larger house. On the other hand, KYC programs are also essential for compliance with anti money laundering regulations;
- Simplification can transform services from paper-based to customer-based. Simplicity is a competitive advantage, as illustrated by Steve Jobs' Apple products;
- Integration and change in management can help to eliminate silos and overcome the traditional counter concept; and
- Moving from communication to conversation: according to recent research conducted globally, most people trust the opinion of other customers more than traditional advertising[12]. New communication channels with customers, such as Twitter, Facebook, and LinkedIn, together with new business models, are important. More and more financial institutions are adopting social media[13].

Future financial institutions should take into account the evolution of the customer by putting technology into the heart of customer service and focusing on the latter, to make it a positive experience.

5.2.2.2   *Management of customer relationships*

There are different ways for financial institutions to review their business strategies by following a customercentric perspective. One of the most interesting ways is for them to place the Customer Relationship Management model at the heart of their strategic initiatives. In this context, ICT can offer a fair amount of support. In the past, financial institutions' CRM investments focused on tools and initiatives that mainly sought to reduce operational costs. These initiatives were very often technology driven and did not maximize the benefits on the business side. Moreover, the lack of coordination between the functions involved, combined with a lack of clear vision in the medium–long term and appropriate interventions in change management, resulted in a perception of failure in many cases. The use of basic indicators for the measurement of CRM activities and customer satisfaction, although important, is a symptom of the lack of integration of information; these indicators do not provide any direct link to the value generated for shareholders. In contrast to this, the adoption of integrated models and appropriate support systems allows for the use of indicators with a direct impact on value. Such benefits are measurable in terms of[14]:

- Return on investment for each initiative in the market;
- Customer lifetime value; and
- Internal efficiency.

Customer care is a fundamental and strategic resource when it comes to highly competitive market sectors such as that of the financial institutions, and even more so with the spread of remote banking or online insurance, be it via the web or mobile devices. The assessment of the quality of service and customer satisfaction may in fact be the basis for consolidating the relationship with customers and enhancing the identification of new needs, expectations, and desires.

An effective Customer Relationship Management places the customer as a key element in the making and communicating of strategic decisions and driving business processes. This tool allows the definition and adoption of the best way to identify, attract, serve, and develop customer loyalty. "Customer insight" does not refer solely to the customer's personal information; it is enriched with sociodemographic and behavioral information. In the future, it will represent the starting point for the facilitation of marketing, sales, and retention efforts by the financial institutions.

It is crucial that a financial institution's CRM model pervade the entire organization; it should not be limited to the front-office functions. ICT systems can support the required professional capacity in an integrated way, having now reached a reasonable level of maturity. However, the complexity of implementation is a major obstacle, given the intrinsic complexity of the inherited systems currently in use by many financial institutions. From this perspective, the adoption of Service-Oriented Architecture (SOA) allows interventions to be planned and implemented in a modular and incremental manner.

The adoption of CRM models based on cloud computing represents a unique opportunity for financial institutions to:

- Manage their customer contact channels in an integrated manner;
- Monitor customer experience constantly via the different channels to fit customer needs;
- Define, plan, execute, monitor, and measure the results of multichannel campaigns;
- Carry out analyzes of customer information, integrating information from the financial institution with external data sources. In this way, the financial institutions' customer knowledge can be enriched, driving target definition and related commercial and retention actions appropriately; and
- Support the operator's real-time decisions while interacting with the customer, both in-branch and remotely.

Financial institutions can use the cloud to design their customer behavior analyzes and analytics in order to achieve faster results and maximize the return on investment. Cloud CRM solutions will enable the financial institutions to analyze, understand, predict and influence customer behavior throughout the entire customer life cycle. CRM strategies will be a priority for financial institutions as long as they remain capable of improving the quality of their relationship with customers. This would mean:

- Capitalizing on the information resources collected; and
- Enhancing interactivity.

From this perspective, the enablement of innovative channels of communication, such as the Internet, social networks, or mobile phones, will be crucial for the success of ongoing and future projects.

5.2.2.3 *Multichannel*

With the convergence of new technologies such as mobile devices, tablets, cloud platforms and social media, financial institutions have a tremendous opportunity to improve existing customer relationships (loyalty, brand awareness, niche marketing, and so on). At the same time, these technologies can contribute to lower costs. To seize these opportunities, financial institution executives should consider how their customer strategy fits within the context of the challenges associated with:

- Leveraging new mobile devices, tablets, and cloud CRM platforms to help improve sales effectiveness, revenue, and customer loyalty;
- Working on social media, since these media are effective in reaching a certain number of customer segments at the right time with the right offer;
- Aligning customer tools and applications with a cloud computing strategy and platform to enhance delivery and overall customer experience;
- Using real-time cloud-based analytics to gain insight into a diverse and ever-changing customer base; and
- Leveraging technologies, platforms, and analytics to enhance customer acquisition and retention, while helping to reduce operational costs to drive profit and shareholder value.

The points of sale are now called "terminals." But their name should be "initials." They are not just an endpoint – they are also the place where a new communication process can start. The point of sale, be it physical or virtual, is a device that comes into direct contact with the customer. It is the point of exchange in the value chain. The financial institutions should use it for what the word means: a real point of sale. This should be true not only for retailers but for the financial institution itself.

The Credicoop Cernusco switch to Google apps[15]

The Credicoop Cernusco is a small/medium size bank based in Northern Italy. It has adopted Google Apps for business solutions based entirely on the web. Through an integrated email management, instant messaging, chat and audio/video tools for sharing and collaboration on documents and files, the bank wants to renew the way to communicate and collaborate.

The choice has fallen on a cloud solution for three primary reasons:

- Cost reduction;
- Geographic coverage; and
- Increased security.

The reliability and data protection guaranteed by the cloud are key features for a bank. Antivirus, antispam, and secure storage of emails for ten years, in accordance with the Italian banking regulations on data retention, are all features important to the bank.

The bank may use, thanks to the new messaging system, some online collaboration tools. The aim is to achieve a better collaboration among individual business units and with the customers. This should improve the relationships between central departments and branches, opening the way for the innovative potential of mobile services.

The Credicoop Cernusco is joining Banca Popolare di Pistoia and several others in understanding and choosing the benefits of the cloud.

The transformation to a multichannel distribution model is necessary also to improve commercial and relational effectiveness:

- Financial institutions could in this way acquire new customers, especially among the un-banked, as the M-Pesa experience in Kenya demonstrates[16];
- The financial institution's customers are more and more searching for direct channels that offer services at zero cost. The Internet is a great lesson in this direction. Customers love low costs, and to get these they are even willing to give up territoriality (the success of ING Direct with an initial no-branch approach is a typical example);
- Time is the primary asset in nearly everyone's life; it is one of the key factors that leads the customer to seek alternative forms of managing their financial needs; and
- The continued expansion of the Internet and the mobile, involving increasingly large segments of the population, is another major factor.

5.2.2.4 *Experiential marketing*

Customer experience theories point out the centrality of emotions when analyzing customer behavior. They highlight the importance of the whole customer experience as against just the perception of the attributes of the product/service. Experiential marketing aims to involve the customer throughout their experience of consumption, highlighting the importance of symbolic benefits compared to the functional ones[17].

Financial institution managers increasingly use terms such as "experiential marketing" and "customer experience." They indicate new marketing objectives and tools. The concept of experience, which is quite complex and multidimensional, has been the subject of study in various disciplines such as philosophy, sociology, and psychology. It can offer important contributions for better analysis, and improve marketing processes.

Until recently, some skepticism has prevailed toward any approach that would put the customer's emotions at the center in a sector such as financial services. In general terms, this sector does not lend itself naturally to emotional involvement. But in fact the customer lives experiences and feels emotions in their dealings with the financial institutions just as much as in any other context. Financial institutions, particularly retail banks and insurance organizations, have only recently (on respect to other sectors) started to develop a customercentric approach; increasing competitiveness within the sector and the entrance of new players favor a direct approach to the customer. Customers' changing behavior is a factor supporting the evolution toward customercentric models, and this approach is likely to maximize revenue opportunities and optimize operating costs.

Cloud computing moves the center from the specific financial institution to the cloud. Therefore, it facilitates a different type of experience for the customer, putting him or her at the center.

In the next decade, the challenge for financial institutions with respect to their customers will be:

- Building an effective customer loyalty strategy;
- Gaining new market shares by providing a solid customer experience integrated through the deployment of new advanced technologies. Simplicity in use will be at a premium.

Caja Navarra civic bank

One bank that is reinventing relationships with its customers is Caja Navarra in Spain. The bank has committed itself to a concept that it calls "civic banking"[18]. The brand strategy is built around visibility, accountability, and social responsibility. It helps monitor the progress of those projects.

The bank encourages customers to use social media to get involved with the bank and find out how it uses its profits to support socially responsible projects.

5.2.2.5   Analytics

Analytics has always been a differentiator for financial services (especially insurers). It supports the personalization of their interactions with their customers as well as their products or services. But the analytical capabilities of many banking and insurance companies are still rather immature. This is due to one or more of several factors:

- They do not have the appropriate culture;
- They have difficulty sharing, integrating, and storing vast amounts of customer data for analysis; and
- They lack the appropriate processes or tolls.

Cloud computing has the potential to help remove such shortcomings. In fact, analytics is tailor-made for the cloud for several reasons[19]:

- The cloud enables organizations to store a vast amount of data, not necessarily centralized, and put dormant data to work;
- It provides a cost-effective platform for developing analytics models and reports, and driving business intelligence (BI);
- It can enable an organization to work with historical as well as real-time or transaction information from a variety of sources (for instance the agency network in the case of insurance companies);

- It enables organizations to churn through vast amounts of data. It can find patterns and anomalies not only in the past, but also projected into the future fast, efficiently, and cost-effectively; and
- Organizations can also use the cloud to help design their web personalization engines, customer behavior analyzes, and data mining algorithms.

For all these reasons and others, the cloud can enable organizations to transform the quality and speed of their responses to customer requirements, in both their service interactions and their product design and delivery. New developments are in the making through the so-called Big Data initiatives.

5.2.3 Compliance

Due to the financial and economic crisis, many governmental institutions are introducing new regulations and laws. To comply with them in a timely matter is an increasing challenge for the financial institutions. The more this effort is made by joining with other Institutions, the easier and cheaper it will be to comply. This is another factor pushing towards cloud computing.

At the international level, for instance in the European Union, legislative interventions are accelerating convergence towards common standards, tools and infrastructure. They are pushing towards a digital economy and the progressive dematerialization of commercial and financial transactions.

The introduction in 2007 in Europe of the Payment Service Directive (PSD) legislation, together with the project of a Single European Payment Area (SEPA), and subsequent further changes that the regulations will undergo, will affect the financial world significantly. All these elements will open up the markets not only to international competition, but also to competition outside the financial sector itself. The new directive on electronic money[20], and the new requirements to become a payment institution, laid down both at the European level and in each EU country, are examples of such changes.

C-Card payment institution in Italy[21]

In 2010, C-Card, a subsidiary of the Italian Group Cedacri, specializing in financial service processing services, was authorized by the Bank of Italy to operate as the first payment institution in Italy, even though it was not a bank.

Since then, C-Card has started to offer its services in the cloud to both financial and non-financial institutions.

The genesis and objectives of the E-Money Directive (EMD2), as well as issues relating to regulatory compliance, are already signals that show the centrality of this matter in Europe.

Embracing cloud computing implies reviewing many of the cornerstones of financial services controls in applications, regulatory concerns, security, and accountability. They require process re-engineering. By using cloud services, financial institutions can tap into:

- One of today's most promising sources of value, innovation, and competitive advantage in financial services; and
- One solution that in the next few years will become a standard part of the way ICT enables business compliance, innovation, and success.

To get the maximum value out of cloud computing, financial institutions must apply to it the same rigorous, analytical approach as that which they apply across their existing business.

5.2.4 Costs

The financial institutions' choice of ICT solutions and vendors is increasingly dependent on costs. Many types of service already appear to be largely undifferentiated. Entrusting ICT services to the clouds for many financial institutions, especially those of small and medium size, provides an important opportunity for savings and flexibility. The current financial crisis is a major driver for the diffusion of such architecture. According to data from several studies[22], financial institutions have reduced their investments in technology, in some cases in a rather drastic way[23].

The confirmation of the difficulties comes also from the 2011 Assinform report (see also Figure 5.1). The continuing years, with a general decline of profitability and little, if any, growth, have prompted financial institutions to rethink their strategic priorities.

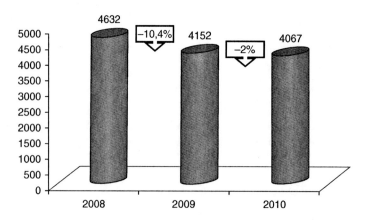

Figure 5.1 Trend of ICT spending in the Italian banking sector (2008–2010) (in millions of Euros and percentage variations)[24]

There are two main reasons:

- The economic crisis is an incentive for financial institutions to pick up the most efficient solution. The crisis has not interrupted the financial institutions' process of marketing, organizational and infrastructure innovation. It has rather pushed towards increasing efficiency while reducing costs ("more with less"); and
- The completion of a process of ICT systems integration, because of acquisitions and mergers of recent years, forms the basis for the generation of significant synergies in costs.

Following the economic crisis, financial institutions need to adopt a new business model. Basel III will require higher capital ratios, and the challenge is to pay for this increase in equity, possibly by reducing costs. The financial institutions need to assess in a holistic way where they can achieve cost savings to fund this new business model. Cloud computing, with its focus on making available a substantial reduction in capital expenditures, provides an interesting opportunity for financial institutions to reduce overall costs and especially investments.

The predicted €183 billion EMEA-wide cloud computing benefits for the financial institution sector constitute a 24 percent share of the total EMEA (Europe, Middle East, and Africa) benefits[25]. This is broadly equivalent to, but slightly less than, the contribution of the sector to EMEA-wide Gross Domestic Product (GDP) (see Table 5.1). The drivers of these forecast benefits are:

- The size and importance of the financial institution sector in the broader macro economy;
- Its future growth prospects; and
- The projected rates of cloud adoption.

In view of the current economic context, the priorities of financial institution executives and managers are cost reduction and liquidity reinforcement strategies. The innovation of the business model comes in second place in the list of most important things to do. In the future, the industry will see a strengthening of the technological platforms according to the logic of integration and new modes of use, such as cloud computing, aimed at reducing costs.

Cloud computing, which leverages the Internet to enhance speed and flexibility, represents a fundamental opportunity for financial institutions to dramatically consolidate and rationalize their ICT costs through the creation of virtual shared ICT utilities. It will be popular initially among smaller and medium-size financial institutions. In fact, it is the only way for them to survive. Cloud computing is indeed a disruptive innovation; it has the potential to redefine the future operating model for all financial institutions. By moving to cloud computing, financial institutions will no longer need to develop and manage their own systems. This will lower costs and investments while improving productivity and helping flexibility.

As regards the outlook for the next few years, technological choices to reduce costs will be directed mainly towards cloud computing, mobile, business intelligence, and Big Data, for both internal users and customer contacts. This trend emerged in the latest survey conducted by CIPA and ABI[26]. In Europe, the financial services industries will be among the most aggressive cloud adopters. Technology and service vendors should accelerate their initiatives aimed at bringing cloud service offerings to their customers in this sector.

La Caixa achieves business/ICT alignment[27]

La Caixa is Spain's largest savings bank and the country's third largest finance organization. La Caixa follows a multichannel management strategy that leverages advanced technologies and skilled employees to provide high quality and comprehensive banking services to its customers.

To power its 5300-plus locations and network of more than 8000 ATMs (the largest in Spain), La Caixa relies upon a complex technology landscape comprising large mainframes, thousands of servers, and more than 1000 network devices.

La Caixa worked with external consultants to define a multigeneration plan to move in the direction of a private cloud. The first phase was the installation of automation tools. In this way, La Caixa was able to enforce compliance in an automated manner.

The project is multiphase:

- In Phase One, the team carefully mapped the written security policies into rules – ensuring strict adherence going forward. The first phase in the transformation project includes virtual and physical server provisioning and server and network device monitoring;
- Phase Two of the project expands the solution to all platforms in La Caixa's infrastructure. It adds further automation and self-service features. This phase also introduces a single, consolidated configuration repository and customized management dashboards. In this way, it sets up the basis for a lower-cost internal cloud computing service delivery model; and
- Phase Three offers support and maintenance services. They will keep the bank's ICT services running at peak performance for years to come.

5.3 Cloud computing in support of the transformation of financial institutions

Cloud computing is a powerful support to the transformation of financial institutions. It is much more than a technology when it is used in support of business transformation.

There are essentially three ways in which cloud computing can be both the catalyst and the support of such a transformation. They are

Table 5.1 Benefits of cloud computing (Source: CEBR)

Benefits	France	Germany	Italy	Spain	UK	EMEA
	€M	€M	€M	€M	€M	€M
Business development opportunities	7.809	10.24	5.362	2.921	9.526	35.858
Business creation	17.696	22.647	12.882	7.403	6.831	67.458
Net total cost savings, of which:	1.688	4.151	1.571	1.279	1.716	10.405
– IT Capex savings	4.262	4.902	2.84	1.39	4.777	18.171
– IT Opex savings	2.795	3.411	1.861	965	3.166	12.198
– IT Opex savings (power and cooling)	2.303	2.809	1.533	795	2.241	9.681
Additional cloud expenditure (PAYG)	–7.671	–6.971	–4.664	–1.871	–8.468	–36.87
Indirect GVA	16.756	21.465	12.259	7.234	12.131	69.844
Total Economic Benefit	43.949	58.503	32.073	18.836	30.204	183.57
Direct and indirect employment (000s)	37.17	55.85	29.98	29.00	54.72	296.73

connected with the three main types of future CIOs[28]. Cloud computing can support:

- Managing ICT systems that effectively, efficiently, and economically support the organization's operating model;
- Bridging boundaries, both internally and externally, to innovate products and services for customers. In this way, the introduction of entirely new products and services can result in a completely different relationship with customers; and
- Ensuring that business processes are re-engineered, coordinated and operated efficiently, efficiently, and economically across business units. Transformation of business processes allow these objectives to be reached.

The following pages analyzes the last two types. The first case is not expanded here, since it is the traditional way that cloud computing has been used, and has already been fully described, in Chapter 3.

5.3.1   Customer innovation

5.3.1.1   New products and services

Service customization will become very important. Financial institutions need to differentiate their offerings. They must become key partners in the overall financial supply chain composed of customers, suppliers, and service vendors. Cloud computing provides a real opportunity to build a solid network to facilitate and boost business and deliver results to all its users. It can become the new desk[29] on which to interact with the customers, the suppliers, and other service vendors.

The financial institutions' potential in using cloud services can leverage their extensive experience in terms of:

- Payment systems and e-commerce;
- Corporate and retail channels of distribution through inter-bank networks and insurance agencies and brokers;
- Infrastructure for the exchange and settlement of payments, for both commercial and retail banking, and the management of insurance; and
- Domestic (for instance, Link or SIAnet) and global (SWIFTNet) switches and networks.

Financial institutions need to develop the ability to go beyond the traditional information services. This might mean, for instance, the redesign, automation and integration of processes for innovative credit, innovative insurance, and risk management. New information can be exchanged via the cloud, acquired throughout the lifetime of the business relationship with customers. Banking in the cloud may be the key to enable retention strategies with customers and, at the same time, increase market penetration.

Some potential cloud-based services allow financial institutions to expand in several fields:

- For both consumers and commercial customers:
  - E-Commerce services will capitalize on cloud computing in the next few years. Customers will have access to e-commerce banking and insurance services to facilitate secure, real-time processing; and
  - A centralized payment infrastructure, such as the bank payment hub derived from the Open Payment Framework (OPF), allows financial institutions to manage payments from origination through instruction management to execution. Financial institutions are already launching electronic payment gateway solutions integrated with the core banking system. In this way, they are facilitating e-commerce and e-procurement services for businesses, consumers, and resellers;

- For commercial customers:
  - Bank and insurance cloud services can make access to cloud services and applications available to Small and Medium Enterprises (SMEs). This opportunity would allow the integration of SMEs and financial institutions in a much shorter time and with much more immediate return[30]. This is important to give agility to the organizations. The SMEs could move more quickly worldwide and have complete visibility of their cash position and availability. The common global implementation framework for ISO 20022 (corporate-to-bank) messaging is paving the way to the use of cloud computing. Cloud solutions will be integrated with the applications of both the financial institutions and the customer/agency organizations. They will remain open to the interfacing of components and services from third parties such as:
    - Payment Institutions cloud services. E-payments and e-invoicing can drastically change the procurement models of the SMEs. By moving SME account management to the cloud, a financial institution could help SMEs manage their businesses and cash flow more economically. Financial services can have a completely different engagement with their customers. The cloud would become increasingly critical for SMEs. Financial institutions have a huge opportunity to become not just a trusted partner for banking and insurance services; they can extend their platform to help SMEs build their business jointly with them[31]; Accounting, cash flow modeling, credit banking services, and use of new and integrated insurance products can allow SMEs to plug in their basic financial statements to get breakeven analyzes, cash flow forecasts, and what-if scenarios. Such tools can integrate with the customer basic account information, forecasts, and invoicing data. In this way, financial institutions can give SMEs a set of very useful tools embedded within banking to start looking at basic overdraft facility, procurement, factoring, inventory financing, and a whole range of additional services. In this way, the cloud would become increasingly critical to SMEs. It would also enable closer connections with partners by integrating shared services, marketing their products, improving payments, and managing their cash flow better; and
    - E-Invoicing services and EIPP (Electronic Invoice Presentment and Payment) Systems will become increasingly important as part of the organization tool set for commercial banking. Several banks have already launched a range of services including e-invoicing and the electronic management of accounts receivable/payable. This service can be coupled with factoring and managing procurement for SMEs, with further benefits to the customers.

- For consumers, cloud services can make available new, advanced products and services such as;
  - E-wallets, a new way to make payments. They transform electronic devices such as a phone into an e-wallet, which would include various integrated features: electronic transactions and the ability to store data on payment cards, choose a method of payment, and pay through the device. E-wallets can be used also as marketing devices to inform on promotions, support loyalty points, and so on;
  - Person to Person payments or P2P payment. Individuals can send one another payments. This practice could fundamentally change the payments business. It could even eventually break the credit card industry's grip on customers and small businesses that pay high fees for accepting credit and debit card purchases or transferring money; and
  - Contactless payment systems (Near Field Communication (NFC) devices). These allow shoppers to use their mobile phones to make purchases, thanks to a contactless payment system. The device can help select a product to buy by reading a bar code or taking into account loyalty points at the retailers. It can also be used as a marketing channel for customized promotion and communication.

Cryptomatic invents cloud wallet[32]

Cryptomatic has invented what it claims as the market's first Cloud Wallet. The Cloud Wallet enables a secure payment application to run off a connected trusted platform that is accessible through a network such as Internet. It securely links the user and all their devices – such as smartphones, tablets, or personal computers – to their wallets.

Visa, the credit-card scheme, used cloud computing to crunch two years of test records, or 73 billion transactions amounting to 36 terabytes of data. The processing time fell from one month with traditional methods to 13 minutes[33].

Cloud services help reach the targets of:

- Simplifying processing;
- Implementing rapid payments;
- Integrating financial services into payments and receivable/payable processes;
- Signing up for insurance from anywhere, at any time, and via any device; and
- Accelerate claim processing for insurance.

See, for instance, the cloud architecture for card processing systems in Figure 5.2.

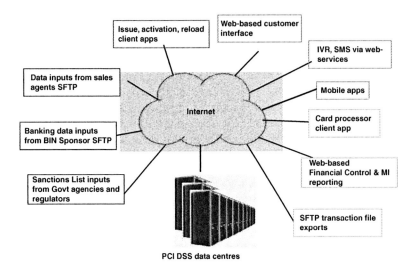

Figure 5.2 A cloud in card processing

Small businesses should adopt the cloud[34]

Small businesses should adopt cloud computing. It would allow them to spend less time managing their ICT and more time to focus on the growth of their businesses.

Furthermore, once this growth has been achieved, cloud systems can easily be scaled up to match the businesses' increased ICT demands.

Many small business owners should consider cloud computing as a very interesting option available to them. They may consider using factoring services to free up the cash needed to make their important investments. Businesses can improve their data security and outsource services like email or storage. This approach would provide organizations with all the benefits of advanced technology without the hassle of having to manage them.

In order to support this opportunity, a certain number of financial institutions are planning to offer and operate cloud services to SMEs. The Italian Post Office has focused on its connections with SMEs and the promotion of cloud computing technologies[35].

The Post Office had long ago put its five centers, processing data from 14.000 post offices, onto a private cloud system. This system allows short transformation times, a high level of security, and more efficient management of infrastructure and data streams that go through it.

The Post Office's cloud system could allow SMEs to share sophisticated business continuity programs and disaster recovery that would otherwise be incompatible with the micro budgets of SMEs. The Post Office will make large computing capacity and storage available on the cloud platform. In addition to that, SMEs can always rely on the technology to guarantee secure communication and identification of the Post Office. Payments between individuals and between business and public administration, and payment platform for the management of basic financial services, complement the potential of the cloud services offered to SMEs by the Post Office.

5.3.1.2   Social networks

Financial institutions are striving to find distinguishing features for successful relationships with customers. Financial institutions need to consider putting online marketing actions at the forefront of their communications strategies; they should simply listen and watch how network users talk about financial products. Then the institutions should use the web and social media as if these were an extended customer care channel and market research tool.

The following development opportunities are emerging:

- Improving Knowledge of Your Customers (KYC) support in order to optimize the marketing of products and services, based on advanced segmentation techniques;
- Improving customer experience to reduce the risk of abandonment and maximize sales opportunities;
- Optimizing contact channels, together with the introduction of innovative channels; and
- Optimizing territorial and display presence.

Some of the tools necessary to implement such strategies already exist, and financial institutions are already exploiting some of them to listen to people's opinions and take action on:

- Brand awareness and engagement;
- Buzz;
- Social media;
- Increased visits and fans;
- interaction;
- Conversation; and
- User actions.

Additional innovations will appear more and more in the future. For instance, Banca Intesa Sanpaolo has already developed and introduced into the market a dialog and helpdesk platform for customer interactions that are totally online/social networking. The application seeks to communicate with the customer to make them feel like an active and integral part of the organization.

Non-traditional channels, particularly web and mobile channels, also referred to as e-Banking and m-Banking, are playing an increasingly strategic role in financial institutions' customer services. These channels shine, both in terms of the importance given to the customer and in terms of number of transactions. As a result, the number of transactions through indirect channels will gradually decrease, becoming a high value-added channel for advice and complex transactions. In this context, the branch or agency will continue to be the customers' favorite contact channels for high value services.

Facebook and Twitter are no longer a mystery for many financial institutions, which are increasingly using social media to make themselves known and to establish direct links with their customers.

It is not so long ago that financial institutions started to place emphasis on customer experience. Financial institutions need to understand how to implement this new category of culture and practice of marketing. Customer involvement appears to be the basic concept on which to build a new strategy for customer experience, and this is a topic already widely present in the most accredited literature in the field. Financial institutions have only recently started to look at these applications from new virtual channels. Some financial services organizations use social media to engage customers in online discussion forums, advertise services, and monitor what is being said about the organization activities (the so-called sentiment).

Susan Feinberg, an analyst with Tower Group's commercial banking practice, summarizes the situation in this way[36]:

> Every financial institution is already involved in social media...it is part of a conscious strategy or not. Customers today are using social media all the time for personal purposes and business.

Financial institutions feel that the need to combine the quantitative measurement of customer satisfaction with a more qualitative approach is becoming more and more important [37]. The latter should be based on free expression with respect to what the customer thinks of his relationship with the financial institution. Customers' opinions and comments can be found in real time and up to date on the Internet, but capitalizing on information contained in a large number of free text comments has always been a major limitation of this approach, as highlighted in an article by Marco Barbato, Manager of Banca Intesa Sanpaolo's customer satisfaction department[38]:

> With new semantic technologies...it becomes possible to analyze and structure this information to make them usable in the analysis and to correlate them with indicators derived from other sources.

Financial institutions compete on the quality of their services. It is essential to assess customer satisfaction and perceived quality properly, in a timely manner, and fully. Automatic text comprehension, enabled by semantic technologies, not only facilitates the financial institutions' dialog with their customers; it also ensures a higher level of precision and accuracy in the analysis of the customers' sentiments. In this way, the monitoring of customer satisfaction becomes more effective, efficient, and economical.

5.3.1.3   Mobile revolution

A trend very much affiliated with cloud computing is mobile technology. The mobile phone is a communication device that links perfectly with cloud-based services, and mobiles have surpassed PCs in terms of users and popularity[39].

Mobile banking is revolutionizing the customer experience. For instance, mobile devices are increasingly versatile, acting as a wallet or security token. Although financial institutions recognize this development, they admit that they are not yet fully acting or investing in accordance with the importance of this trend. The mobile device creates distinct areas of opportunity, and the financial institutions that could gain will be those that act quickly and decisively with these new technologies. Financial institutions should think on the lesson of the medium-size Dutch bank ING, which acted quickly in online banking and spread around the world. In Kenya, M-Pesa is a payment system based on mobile phones, and in a very short period it won millions of customers[40].

The mobile device possesses several distinct characteristics that between them turn it into a unique value proposition:

- It is portable and accessible 24/7;
- It has a unique identifier. This means its use and identification is specific to each customer;
- It is simple to use and entertaining, with its increasingly user-friendly interfaces and capabilities (for instance Apps on IPhones);
- It allows geographical positioning which in turn permits products and services to be tailored to different territories;
- It is the device that customers most frequently have with them and use; and
- With a mobile, customers can interact with their financial institutions anytime and anywhere.

These features, plus a flexible cloud and app-based technology platform, enable more rapid development, and integration with third party products.

Interest in mobile banking is intense and increasing. Smartphones are taking over phones in popularity, and new applications are proliferating. Financial institutions are mobilizing to respond to the growing "mobile" opportunity, as they are already seeing a step change in the number and frequency of interactions they have with their customers via mobiles. The interaction between customer and bank was once a monthly experience, in the branch, whereas now it happens daily, through a mobile.

Mobile banking encourages the evolution of banking services by aligning them to the increasingly strong digital awareness of customers. This shows a growing trend, and relates to the multichannel approach that financial institutions are taking. Cloud computing can represent an evolution in support of a financial institution's interaction with its customers. The opportunity is the design of front-end applications developed specifically for new mobile devices. They will optimize customer experience, thereby expanding two-way communication with their customer. Such a solution is compatible with all major mobile operating systems and with the world of smartphones and tablets.

Cloud computing can bring the benefits of mobile operability to financial institutions. This can be achieved by making the financial institution's processes leaner, by providing mobile applications for internal use, to support banking and insurance operations. New solutions will be available for banking and insurance through mobiles and tablets. An example in this direction would be the approval of a loan by a manager who is not in the office or near a workstation. S/he can use a mobile phone to authorize a loan, or if in insurance, to deal with a claim from a customer that includes pictures of the damage.

Mobile devices and smartphones are the trigger for the next revolution in e-commerce, thanks to the Internet, a ubiquitous real-time channel for contact and interaction with customers. Financial institutions can leverage the low-cost mobile channel. They can develop new business partnerships to access under-served and/or un-banked and un-insured new market segments, in both old and emerging markets. In this new market context, financial institutions must ensure they are part of this revolution; they should try to own the end-to-end value chain and they should develop strong customer digital commerce functions for agencies, traders, and other third parties.

Financial institutions can start to act as the means that drive digital commerce, for instance:

- At pre-purchase, by combining financial institution and non-financial institution data to deliver marketing communications and event-based and location-based promotional offers;
- At the moment of purchase, from making financing services, instant credit, and insurance products available via SMSs and mobile apps, to making transaction processing possible through financial institution-enabled mobile e-wallets; and
- At post-purchase, by producing statements or alerts of suspicious operations, or for accepting claims from customers.

Mobile financial servicing as part of a remote-only business model could prove to be a very competitive strategy in both mature and emerging markets.

The risk of price erosion is real as non-financial institutions start to familiarize themselves with core banking services, competition intensifies, and visibility becomes greater. Telecommunication organizations or vendors' search engines may start to offer free or cheap financial services to enter into profitable initiatives and to retain customers loyalty. The opportunity is massive, with multiple players such as Google, PayPal, Facebook, and Amazon striving to capture customers.

In this context, financial institutions can increase their business opportunities by building partnerships and relationships with telecom organizations, cloud service vendors, and merchants, which are more likely to rapidly establish a winning position in the new financial landscape. Incumbent financial institutions may more easily build a low-cost proposition by forming a strategic partnership with an established telecom organization.

The partnership model will be at premium. In the past, the financial institutions industry has kept pace with technological innovation by turning to external vendors, for example vendors of ICT services, but with mobile banking, successful financial institutions need an even more flexible framework; they should quickly accept external parties as vendors of services and products or joint venture partners.

Some key conclusions are:

- Mobile has the potential to revive and innovate the customer experience in personal financial services. Non-financial institution competitors are already leading the way;
- Mobile banking and insurance will transform the retail financial services market more and more; and
- The unique characteristics of mobile devices together with cloud computing present potential benefits for three distinct areas of marketing innovation:
  - Highly convenient banking and insurance;
  - Digital commerce; and
  - The opening up and expansion of new markets and segments.

5.3.2 Business process management

Cloud computing can support also the improvement in the internal processes of financial institutions. To this end, cloud computing needs to be coupled with a re-engineering of the processes. "Lean and digitize" is the right way to exploit cloud computing for process re-engineering[41].

5.3.2.1 Business process re-engineering

A certain number of financial institutions are dropping their hierarchic and functional organizational models to embrace a process-oriented organization. The redesign and re-engineering of processes and activities is today at center stage of organizational improvement. Business Process Re-engineering (BPR) is the right method to work in this direction; the combination of BPR and ICT allows managers to analyze and transform technology and their organization applying a method based on facts rather than on subjective opinion.

In recent years, BPR has become the basis for observing, measuring, and improving business processes. It represents the main tool for the improvement of service levels and service management control. The target is to use BPR as a cultural background not only for top management but as a useful tool for the entire management structure. The ambitious objective is to move from a functional approach to the management of financial institutions' processes[42]. Process mapping is the formalization of the knowledge on the functioning of the financial institutions through visual models (maps) which depict the logical flow of processes. Mapping is not an end, but a means first to learn and then to improve processes in financial services operations.

Research has shown that the recognition of processes through their mapping is just the beginning of a transformation. BPR needs the following features to support the transformation of organizations:

- It must be driven by the strategic objectives of the organization;
- It should not be bound, in the identification of new solutions, to the existing situation. It should aim at a dramatic change to ensure a significant improvement in the results;
- It should act on one or more service-correlated end-to-end processes;
- It should operate on all components of the process in an integrated way;
- It must see technology as an enabler for overall change; and
- Finally, it should monitor the progress through a system of metrics, and control the advancement of the project.

5.3.2.2 From BPO to BPaaS

One of the re-engineering solutions to support BPR is Business Process Outsourcing (BPO). This means delegating the management, operations, and optimization of an entire business process or one of its sub-processes to an external service vendor that then becomes responsible for executing the task[43]. While the strategic control of the process and the integration with other processes remain within the organization, the operational control of the process or sub-process outsourced is entrusted to the service vendor. The benefits of BPO are:

- Flexibility;
- Cost reduction;
- Risk reduction; and
- Improvement of service levels.

Many financial institutions have already implemented BPO, especially in back office and ICT[44]. At the time of writing, it is forecast that the global core banking BPO market will be worth nearly $7 billion by 2011, and it is expected to grow 45 percent between 2012 and 2017[45].

BPO services are used by, for example:

- Financial institutions of all sizes that require the cooperation of a valid partner to whom to entrust the management and operation of some of their processes;
- Consumer credit institutions;
- Insurance companies;
- Networks of promoters; and
- Online financial institutions.

At present, most of the outsourced financial services processes are in the following fields:

- Support for the channels;
- Middle and back office;
- Collections; and
- Dematerialization and document management.

There are services offered in more relevant processes, such as marketing, risk management, technology scouting, or strategy support. They are called KPO (Knowledge Process Outsourcing).

BPO is an important enabler for the migration of the business processes at the top of the cloud. In this respect, cloud computing should not be seen as a pure technology approach but as a way to move towards Business Process as a Service (BPaaS). In BPaaS, entire processes, or part of them, are outsourced to vendors in the cloud. In this way, the financial services can concentrate on their core activity: the management of funds and of the risks.

There have already been a significant number of moves in this direction. The expectation is that they will increase significantly over time. BPaaS is an emerging model for using BPO. In it, BPO is accessed via web-centered interfaces on multitenant and shared infrastructures.

New BPaaS offerings are emerging; it is the next major layer of cloud computing, and the evolution will be cloud-enabled BPO, as traditional infrastructure, applications, and BPO become cloud-enabled.

Businesses from several industries have for many years leveraged the traditional outsourcing contractual agreements. They are now evaluating dropping the idea of entering into rigid contracts with rigid delivery structures; the pillars that built and supported legacy outsourcing are now under serious pressure. Labor arbitrage, dinosaur technologies and traditional business models represent a limit to business effectiveness[46], and businesses are looking for more flexibility, innovation, and responsiveness from their outsourcers. BPaaS may provide that alternative with all the benefits of cloud computing. They are a variable pricing model, combined with technology and business process excellence that reduce or eliminate resource demands. The current trends are:

- Financial service firms, are already ahead of the curve, compared to other sectors, in adopting the cloud for BPO services;
- BPO service vendors with their traditional offerings are finding it more and more difficult to enlist new customers. The market is mature, and is giving way to new service delivery options such as cloud computing;
- Financial institutions are realizing that BPaaS helps save critical capital expenses and costs by eliminating the acquisition of expensive hardware, software and key talents, and allows them to pay according to their dynamic needs; and
- Thanks to the cloud, BPaaS can in a certain number of cases be provided from low-cost countries.

Some service vendors are now providing robust proprietary platforms and application modules that they have developed for financial institutions' in-house use, as either fully integrated solutions or on a modular basis. Analysts project that half of all BPO engagements by 2015 will involve BPaaS elements in the contracts[47]. The cloud will provide the platform for service vendors of all shapes and sizes, located anywhere in the world. They will contribute to the re-energizing of traditional outsourcing services and to the launching of new services. In time, one key implication is that financial institutions will ask for cloud BPaaS innovations within the re-negotiation of traditional outsourcing contracts.

BPaaS will continue to increase its share of the BPO market. This delivery model provides benefits that go beyond cost savings and hence will meet with widespread acceptability. For capital-starved firms especially, this model offers tangible business benefits.

There are also some concerns around BPaaS. They include:

- Long-term commitment;
- Continuity of service;

- Perceived risks;
- The complexities around technology and BPO service integration; and especially
- Data security and privacy.

Demand will start to increase as soon as it is possible to see increased adoption experiences across many industries. In time, more and more customers will share their implementation experience and especially their return on investment. Financial institutions will start to show more and more interest in such flexible offerings. Cloud computing will be an excellent support to this wider use of BPO.

5.4   Technological innovations

In order to support the realization of the improvements in products and processes described in the previous pages, it is essential for the financial institutions to clearly define a transformation path. This requires three aspects:

- A new financial services architectural framework;
- Standardization; and
- Support from the technologies.

The following pages define the requirements and the possible evolution of cloud services in this direction.

5.4.1   New financial services architectural framework

Until now, business outsourcers have been able to provide a complete and integrated range of services to financial institutions such as full outsourcing, application solutions, facility management, BPO, printing and mailing services, business information processing, and many other services. Over time, however, the provision of ICT services for the financial services sector will follow a plug-and-play approach towards new distribution channels, products, services, and processes delivered through on-demand cloud-integrated solutions. Today, a large part of the software used by financial institutions consists of a range of vertical solutions implemented in ICT systems. In the future, cloud vendors and software vendors will extend their application offerings to SaaS and cloud computing environments, possibly in an integrated way.

5.4.1.1   *Reference architectures*

There are several reference architectures for financial services, most of which are connected with vendors. They are interesting since most of them are also starting to consider the cloud computing model. Some examples are:

- Microsoft Industry Reference Architecture for Banking (MIRA-B)[48];
- IAF and Cap gemini architecture[49];
- SAP for Banking on System z Reference Architecture[50]; and
- Life Insurance Reference Architecture[51].

Three logical levels provide a key to understanding the areas that constitute the benchmark of several architectural references to the financial services sector (see Figure 5.3):

- Front office is the trade side. It is composed of all customercentric services that can be activated directly by the operators in contact with the customer, or by the customers themselves. It is directly linked to the channels;
- Middle office ensures the control and processing of transactions. It represents the point of conjunction between the business side (front office) and the operational side (back office). The middle office includes all those activities that have the common goal of maximizing the match between supply and demand. Its relevance has increased with the widespread use of e-banking, m-banking and online insurance; and
- Back office is the operational side. It is composed of all the services that can be operated without direct contact with the customer.

The terms "front office" and "back office" have been generally used to describe those organization areas dedicated respectively to the direct relationship with the customer and the execution of the operations.

"Middle office" is a term introduced recently. In modern financial institutions, the middle office has a more and more expanded definition and role. In the older financial services model, the transactions would be conducted in the front office and then handed to the back office for settlement and accounting; the middle office came into being with the development of online banking and insurance, risk management functions, and corporate oversight requirements. The term "middle office" commonly refers to risk management and checking functions. It is a great way to speed up the front-office operations. The middle office can free up the front office for

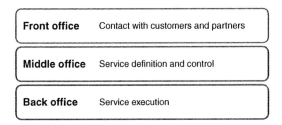

Figure 5.3   Three-level financial institution processes distribution

customer-facing operations, and at the same time, it makes a much cleaner input available to the back office.

Figure 5.4 represents a general financial institution reference model.

In reality, however, the layers of processes and sub-processes are more complex. In this context, the figure shows a generic retail financial institution with its three logical levels:

- Front office: composed of a wide range of traditional and non-traditional delivery channels;
- Middle office: composed of processes which ensure the control and correct processing of transactions; and
- Back office: core banking processes, ancillary processes, accounting and support processes.

The reference architecture shown in Figure 5.4 represents the backbone of the macro processes that characterize and describe the internal functioning of the financial institutions[52]. Starting from such reference architecture and considering actual market trends, it is possible to define which processes should be candidates for migration towards the cloud models.

With reference to this architecture, while deciding on a migration path to the cloud, it is necessary to take into account that the processing of back office applications tends to be rather stable, whereas front office, and in particular channel, applications tend to undergo rapid changes. To reduce integration costs, and increase reuse across the organization, it is important to take a multilayered, modular approach to the ICT architecture, decoupling business services from the front and middle office processes.

From a strategic business perspective, the innovation in the financial institutions that is made possible by cloud computing will be the driver that will lead to:

- A focus on customers rather than products;
- Customer interaction through multichannels, with the concept of everywhere, every time and in every possible way;
- Leaner front, middle and back offices;
- Process management strongly integrated with digitization; and
- Business and ICT alignment.

Another interesting development is the use of cloud computing for collaborative use and ICT management. The ICT market has at the time of writing just passed the stage of early adoption, and is moving towards the beginning of a more mature phase. In considering the ICT industry as a whole and its future development, the role of ICT-as-a-Service will have a fundamental impact.

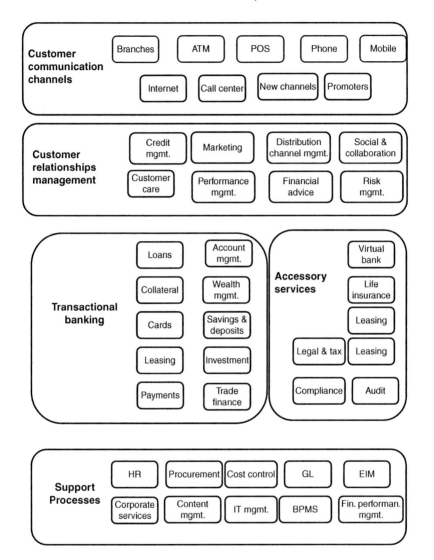

Figure 5.4 Financial institutions components reference model

Today, financial institutions need to redesign their processes and reconsider the way they operate in the market:

• From proprietary technology infrastructure to Infrastructure as a Service;

- From proprietary development, testing and deployment platforms to Platform as a Service;
- From software outsourcing solutions to Software as a Service; and
- From BPO to Business Process as a Service.

The expectation is that in the short term the more likely approach will be based on hybrid clouds, with solutions partially on public clouds and partially on private clouds. This is already a reality for most financial institutions; even if they have applications in house, they already use services in the cloud, be they transaction switches, card acquirers, network vendors (for example SWIFT), credit bureaux, and so on. These services are normally paid per use, and they are often processed in the cloud rather than in specific data centers.

For other applications, such as core banking and core insurance, there are still some concerns about security. In the short term, the private cloud solution seems to be of greater interest for the large financial services institutions. A private cloud could be a first step, through the adoption of an intermediate solution, such as IaaS. This would allow the use of computing capacity, storage, network, and other basic resources from the cloud infrastructure, not providing the delivery of specific services. Most outsourcing vendors will be able to take a financial institution's legacy applications, and deploy and operate them in a cloud in a more cost-effective, flexible, and productive way. In this way, the financial institution would be able to attain:

- Lower costs;
- Advanced services; and
- Continuous development and updating of the solutions.

Cloud-enabled outsourcing solutions include all types of managed services solutions that are developed, bundled, and packaged as components of the offerings.

The ICT service vendors leverage one or more cloud computing technologies within their solution's overall architecture, either in the business process, applications, and platforms or in the infrastructure layers.

The attention of the financial services focuses in particular on areas where today this approach seems able to bring the greatest benefits: high resilience in distributed technological structures through IaaS, and the ability to disengage from the usual logics of acquisition of a service, to converge on a SaaS model. The financial services industry is taking its first steps in the adoption of cloud-based solutions, and the focus is on areas where it is already possible to perceive benefits, as in some IaaS and SaaS models.

Financial institutions should first look at cloud computing as a grid that shows what should be kept in house versus moved to the cloud. In the short and medium term, functions that are kept in house tend to be core business processes to which the organization might add value, security, and privacy, whereas functions ready for moving to the cloud are non-core processes such as: CRM, finance and accounting, HR, procurement, ICT infrastructure, and administration. Non-core services are better suited to outsourcing to public, hybrid, or community clouds, subject to the level of sensitivity of the data and to regulatory constraints. Recently, however, some financial services' core business processes have been evolving towards cloud-based provision, and in time this is likely to result in more cloud-based BPO. Service vendors will be able to offer pay-as-you-process capabilities at a far lower price than ever before. Figure 12 identifies the business processes, functions, and ICT components (Application, Platform, or Infrastructure), candidates to migrate to the cloud; these could be delivered through a "as a service" mode in the short–medium term.

5.4.1.2 Integration challenge

This hybrid solution requires an integration and orchestration layer which would enable the broadest form of integration by providing interfaces and incorporating the exchange of data among any number of SaaS, public cloud, private cloud and ICT components. Moreover, it orchestrates human workflow, traditional systems, and cloud services by automating business rules.

The following scenarios for integration can be distinguished when cloud solutions are implemented as part of the ICT landscape:

• Intra-organization Integration between legacy applications and cloud applications;
• Intra-organization Integration between cloud applications; and
• Inter-organization B2B integration.

In general, it is necessary to take into account that the use of cloud computing requires three functional layers[53]:

• Business Service Factories (be they private or public), which act as service providers;
• Product Composers, which support service assembly; and
• Delivery, which consumes the services. These are typically applications supporting the front and middle office or another service (provider or composer).

The integration of these three layers imposes some additional difficulty.

The relevance of possible brokers to provide this integration is an important aspect. Brokers could perform the same function as they do in real-world markets: they mediate between clients and vendors by buying capacity and functionality from the vendor and sub-leasing these to the clients. A broker can accept requests from many clients, who in turn have a choice of submitting their requirements to different brokers. Clients, brokers and vendors are bound to their requirements and related compensations through SLAs, which specify the details of the services in terms of metrics agreed upon by all parties, and bonuses and penalties for meeting or violating the expectations, respectively[54].

A broker essentially acts in the cloud services procurement process.

Some vendors are also trying to offer their own integration layer with multiple clouds to provide redundancy across clouds. In other words, if a particular cloud goes offline, applications can be rerouted to a different cloud without disruption of service.

Financial institution customers' and transaction data are stored in an in-house data warehouse dedicated to the storage of all sensitive and private data.

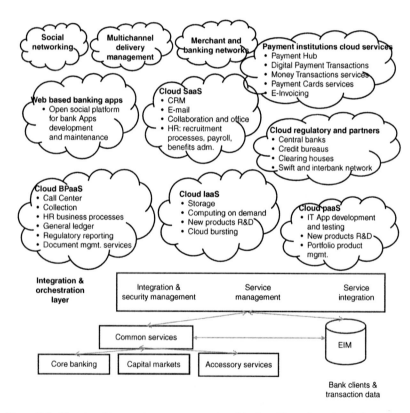

Figure 5.5   New banking system components with cloud-based service delivery

5.4.1.3   Medium and long-term model for cloud computing in the financial institutions

Figure 5.5 shows a model for the medium- and long-term use of cloud computing by financial institutions.

Among the SaaS solutions, cloud vendors can offer:

- Cloud General Ledger (GL), which consists of a SaaS solution tailored to the specific needs of the financial service sector. It enables the complete management of general accounting and operations accounting such as purchasing and inventory, accounts payable, and asset management and maintenance.
- Messaging and collaboration in the cloud, which provides a complete set of collaboration tools. It enables financial institutions to improve communications both internally and with external partners and customers. It combines email, instant messaging, file sharing, project management, shared contacts, communities, social networking, and web conferencing;
- Business Information services in the cloud, which consist of flexible services in the field of business information. They allow financial institutions to fully understand their customers, assess their potential, and prevent and recover insolvencies;
- HR business processes, which are progressively evolving towards cloud-based provision. Over 30 percent of the HR BPO market is effectively delivered as a cloud service, with penetration even higher among the more mature HR sub-processes such as payroll; this is expected to grow to 43 percent by 2014[55]. Highly automated HR processes are being incrementally added, such as benefits administration, lunch tickets, and recruitment process outsourcing in the form of both SaaS and BPaaS;
- Document Management services, which can cover the entire operational process of document management, from design to printing to packaging to storing. It can cover several segments of a process, such as massive financial institution communications, bank checks, bank drafts and money orders, secret codes (debit- and credit-card PINs, and passwords for e-services), claims, and financial services records for internal use. The use of new cloud-based tools and applications for content management requires a redefinition of the ways of managing different stages of the life cycle of a document. The goal is manifold, to:
  - Digitize paper documents, initially ensuring coexistence with the corresponding virtual copies;
  - Define appropriate solutions for the progressive reduction or elimination of paperwork;
  - In time, extend from document management to content management. These services currently support the financial institution with other activities, such as:

- Storage on magnetic media and dematerialization of the paper files;
- Management of communications via email or fax;
- Assistance and monitoring in the production phase and the delivery of communications,
- Web visualization of the progress of batch processing;
- General mailing solutions.
- The new cloud-based document management services will support financial institutions in the improvements of process automation, enabling the exchange of electronic documents, in an end-to-end mode. These services are characterized by flexibility and adaptability to the most common standards. They allow for greater integration and quality of communication.

IaaS solutions may cover areas such as:

- Data storage in the cloud, which is a solution enabling the rapid implementation of a scalable global file storage system on top of virtualized storage resources;
- Computing on demand, which provides access to servers and storage in cloud centers, available on a pay-for-use basis, by the hour, day, week, or year(s) just for heavy computations; and
- Cloud facility management and desktop management, which are cloud-stored desktops or virtual desktops stored in the cloud. Data as a Service (DaaS) is about transforming desktops into a cloud service in order to process transactions in SaaS and cloud computing modes. It is possible to access them from anywhere, anytime, and from any device. These services offer the possibility to entrust to a cloud vendor the complete management of all components within the ICT infrastructure, such as mainframe/servers, middleware, individual workstations, and other devices. It would be a full service, including related services, including helpdesk, security, disaster recovery and business continuity, and many others. The cloud vendor provides the financial institutions with computing power, data storage units, server farm, and all the hardware and software resources necessary to carry out activities within the system partitions, exclusively dedicated and accessible via protected telecommunications networks. No hardware or software investment is required, while all processing and maintenance matters are handled by the cloud services vendor.

Platform as a Service solutions may cover areas such as:

- New product test and development in the cloud, which are activities aimed at the renewal of the financial institution applications. As the pace of change in the market grows, financial institutions will need to move ever faster in the deployment of new products and services. The trend is a focus on value-added services and functionality while leveraging models and approaches such as Platform as a Service to reduce the operating costs of application environments. With a single set of completely virtualized resources accessed via the web, financial institution developers can meet new requirements in line with changing customer needs and with the increasingly articulated regulatory framework; and

- Open social platforms for financial institution service project and development allow financial institutions to take advantage of the potential of social media and crowdsourcing to involve Internet and mobile users in using new financial products and services to be integrated into the financial institution service portfolio. An example of a similar initiative was launched in August 2011 by First Direct, a retail bank controlled by the HSBC Group, that operates solely on telephone and Internet channels.

Other cloud-based industry-specific solutions are:

- Analytics in the cloud; this refers to a cloud solution consisting of a set of products that are tailored to the financial institutions' needs. The solution helps to deploy a shared business intelligence and analytics environment rapidly and at a low cost. With shared analytics in the cloud, the financial institutions can connect new data sources and users more easily, and deliver analysis and insight more rapidly in order to:
  - Improve focus on customers;
  - Achieve operational and internal efficiency;
  - Monitor risk and compliance; and
  - Access distributed data (like the agent's data in the case of insurance companies);
- Cloud-based solutions for financial management planning and control; these consist of an integrated and modular platform. They support the management, at both the financial institution group and the individual financial institution level, of real-time discounting of all cash flows; the management benefits from flexibility in the analysis and allocation of costs. This solution allows the integration of various functions such as: management reporting, business reporting, cost allocation, strategic and operational planning;
- Cloud-based solutions for regulatory reporting management; these provide reports directed to the Supervisory Bodies.
- Cloud-based e-Payment systems, which are a leading-edge payment solution enabling financial institutions to provide value-added services to their corporate and retail customers engaged in e-businesses or to

institutions/ organizations accepting e-payments to facilitate customers. SaaS e-payment solutions enable a secure, real-time, online payment bridge between the trader's customers and the acquiring financial institution's back office systems;

- Card services in the cloud, which offer a fully outsourced service for card issuing and processing activities and related services. These can cover all types of cards, such as credit, debit, prepaid, payment, loyalty, and so on. They specifically offer facilities for the production and management of cards, as well as related account management and card owner management. These solutions can add also other services such as dispute management, fraud investigation, collection, and call centers in a BPaaS mode;
- Cloud-based payment-acquiring services, which support Payment Institutions such as those provided by PayPal to develop a global merchant acquiring market. In this solution, financial institutions can choose external service vendors for their merchant processing; and
- Cloud-based invoice management services, which integrate several technologies and software solutions to make the management cycle of vendor invoices more efficient. This is obtained by dematerializing and optimizing the entire process, from invoice presentment, to receipt, to payment, and to final storage, be it paper-based and/or electronic.

It is very important that the opportunities linked to the cloud services respect the security requirements. They should be evaluated based on a preliminary assessment of their associated costs and benefits. It is necessary to take into account the impact on the existing architectural solutions and the required investments over time.

The Commonwealth Bank of Australia takes a decision[56]

The Commonwealth Bank of Australia (CBA) stated that they would never buy another rack, server, storage, or network device again. It aims not to be locked into proprietary hardware, software, or network solutions.

The Sydney-based Commonwealth Bank of Australia is a member of the TeleManagement Forum's Enterprise Cloud Leadership Council, which evaluates vendors on the use of their cloud services.

CBA's comments encapsulate the two clearest benefits of cloud computing for financial institutions:

- The ability to buy on demand computing capacity, storage, network bandwidth, and so on. In this way, it is possible to pay only for what is used rather than buying hardware or software up front or paying a pre-set annual subscription fee; and
- The speed and ease of provisioning and managing hardware, software, and network services when the institution goes into a private or public cloud.

5.4.2 Interoperability, standards, and automation of banking processes

The world is striving to achieve effective interoperability between ICT products and services, to build a digital society. The Internet is the best example of the power of technical interoperability, its open architecture having given interoperable devices and applications to billions of people around the world. Something similar has happened in the financial services. Industry standards have played a key role in the implementation and definition of payment processes in the financial industry. The payment standards were specifically designed to structure and align collaborative business scenarios between persons, organizations, and financial institutions.

The financial service industry has invested heavily in ICT; financial institutions in general are quite advanced in its use. However, when it comes to standardization and industrialization of systems and processes within financial institutions, they are not always able to integrate systems, adopt new technology, or adapt to business changes as easily as required. In mature markets, the real differentiators are effectiveness, efficiency, economics, ethics (full compliance), and quality of business processes. These characteristics can be obtained through an integrated management approach to applications and standards. The reality is often, however, very complex, and the stratification of standards is a factor generating more complexity in the financial sector. Industry standards have already defined the foundation for business process interoperability in the financial services industry, particularly with respect to the exchange of funds with other financial institutions or financial networks[57]. Standards are always shifting, being adopted by the market at different speeds. Cloud computing should not be considered as an isolated phenomenon; it is a more general trend of radical restructuring of the computing world in a context of convergence between information systems and telecommunication.

Cloud computing will certainly help the financial sector to reach industry standards faster and in a coordinated way. This is a problem not yet fully addressed, and the search for a solution can be delayed no longer.

Today, the number of standards is increasing dramatically as financial organizations start to adopt standards for their internal business processes such as loan processing, cash accounts, treasury, and so on. Financial institutions are preparing to take advantage of these emerging standards to improve collaborative business processes and to increase operational efficiency. Financial services are an industry where execution can be critical to mission success.

In order to reap the full benefits of ICT deployment, interoperability among devices, applications, data repositories, services, and networks must be further enhanced. Many financial institutions have made significant investments in time and resources to deploy shared services and outsourcing solutions for back office functions. But few financial institutions have fully achieved the benefits associated with standardization and transformation leading to an end-to-end global delivery model. Cloud services can be part of the solution to help financial institutions address the technology and process barriers in a more timely and cost-effective manner; for example, a financial institution might look at deploying cloud-based reporting and control tools to improve monitoring across all divisions and areas.

This is the current situation:

- Technology standards provide the underpinnings of openness and inter-operability, such as standards for web services and APIs, like those issued by ISO. An example of these new standards is IFX; it is an open interoperable financial messaging standard for defining financial message payloads[58]. The IFX message specifications and object-oriented design make it well suited to be leveraged in web services. IFX is designed for SOA, but the IFX Forum mission does not focus on defining standardized services;
- Business semantic standards and languages support cross-industry and industry-specific standards such as the Banking Industry Architecture Network[59]. Major global financial institutions, software vendors, and solution integrators are members of BIAN. It works on the iterative process of defining common, industry standard banking services at a business semantics level and provides creative guidance. The objective is the implementation of these services at a business semantics level and the creation of the guidance for the implementation of these services in a banking organization; and
- Common standards are available across some business processes, in some cases dictated by central banks.

Resorting to cloud services allows financial institutions to have the necessary information available in the network through their back office systems, performing well and flexibly, and based on open standards that facilitate interoperability.

The business benefits that can be achieved with cloud services are:

- Acceleration in the achievement of industry standards;
- Reduction of duplication;
- Reduced time-to-market in the introduction of new standards;
- Improved control over operations;
- Solutions scalable to changing market needs;
- Reduction in overall costs; and
- Help with reducing the lock in with cloud services vendors.

In Europe, the Digital Agenda of the European Commission has set standards and interoperability as a priority when it comes to cloud computing.

EU Commissioner Neelie Kroes, at the launch of a cloud computing center in Brussels, said[60]:

Users must be able to change their cloud vendor as fast and easily as changing one's Internet or mobile-phone vendor has become in many places.

International standardization efforts currently being made will have a huge impact on cloud computing. Financial institutions are preparing to take advantage of these emerging standards to:

• Improve collaborative business processes; and
• Increase operational efficiency in the industry.

Various cloud certification programs and benchmarks have been launched[61]. But there is still no *de facto* standard for moving workloads or data among different clouds, and this difficulty can amount to an effective lock in with a vendor, undermining the very flexibility that makes cloud computing so appealing.

It is possible that there will be a strengthening of a collaborative infrastructure that will govern the processes of multiple sectors, thus establishing a scenario for cross-industry cooperation. In this new scenario, standards will be defined supporting processes in an end-to-end perspective and expanding the value chain of products and services offered by financial institutions.

The small Credicoop Banca di Pistoia in Tuscany, Italy, has moved to the cloud for a series of collaboration tools[62]

The Credicoop Banca di Pistoia has moved to a public cloud for:

• Emailing;
• Sharing its calendar in the branches, to offer better services to its customers, and coordinate employees;
• Chatting internally, to improve communication;
• Using a videoconference (for the time being 1:1, but moving to 1:n); and
• Collaborating to write and edit documents.

5.4.3 Support from the vendors

In order to reach the full benefits of cloud computing, vendors must excel. But although this is not easy, when they work well, they start a virtuous cycle of growth. The team's assumption is simple: if they serve customers well, customers will give them more work. That increased demand is more profitable to service. And the cycle begins again. Earl Sasser, Jim Heskett, and Len Schlesinger call this cycle the "service profit chain."[63]

The growth flywheel at Rackspace[64]

Rackspace is a global leader in the hosting and cloud computing industry. It grew from $12 million in revenue to $800 million, and from 100 employees to 4000, in a few years. To obtain this growth Rackspace used this approach.

First, it had to get its service model under control. The organization started by retooling its service offering. A lack of resources forced the organization to realize that its original service model was not working; that model has been designed to rent out server hardware and then to wish customers the best in figuring out how to use it. Now the organization wanted to offer cloud computing and full service.

Having learnt their lesson, Rackspace decided to offer a premium service. The organization began to build a service model and culture to pull it off:

- Higher prices would be needed in exchange for a high touch and a high level of service experience;
- In addition to higher prices, the real key would be higher retention;
- The organization would use a values-based selection of rackers; clear, team-based incentives. Many decisions would in the hands of the front line; and
- Rigorous tracking tools – a pricing tool, a churn tool, and a retention tool – would make the profitability of every customer completely visible, along with the cost of every internal action.

The Rackspace culture is now codified in a series of living values based on whole-hearted support for its customers. To attain this goal, Rackspace relies heavily on the capabilities of its workforce, and Rackspace excels in the way it treats its personnel.

5.4.4   From private to community to public cloud

The case of the financial institutions is somewhat special. There is a clear case for groups or consortia of financial institutions, or entire groups of financial institutions to come together and agree on common requirements. In this way, they can lead the way to a community cloud approach. A community cloud is:

> A cloud infrastructure shared by several organizations, which supports a specific community that has shared concerns (for instance mission, products, market niches, security requirements, policy, and compliance considerations)[65].

Until today in Europe, not many large, dominant, and influential financial services vendors have driven the change toward community clouds. There are cases of financial institutions, such as Banca Intesa Sanpaolo, adopting in-house ICT solutions or a private cloud infrastructure. In certain European countries, the financial service industry is clearly distinguished from the rest of Europe in the methods and procedures it carries out in order to adhere to the new infrastructures and technological systems. In analyzing the context of financial institutions with respect to the use of ICT infrastructures, there is a distinction based on the size of the organizations. The figures show that around 95 percent of small and medium-sized financial institutions entrust their information system to an outsourcer. In Italy, Cedacri, SIA-SSB, or a credit bureau such as CRIF, are a few examples of ICT vendors offering cloud-oriented services to the financial services sector. Most of their customer base is composed of medium and small financial institutions, which are more willing to delegate their ICT functions for several reasons, including the fact that to be constantly compliant working on a stand-alone basis would be very expensive. This finding is particularly interesting. The financial system is characterized by the strong presence of small operators, who are mostly active at territorial level and offer services mainly related to retail banking.

Community cloud vendors offer an ICT system that is multifinancial institution, multisite, multichannel, and multilanguage. The system can be easily tailored to the organizational and operational needs of a single financial institution, thanks to a modular, and highly integrated and parameterized architecture.

Southern California Credit Union alliance endorses compushare's technology management solutions for its credit union members[66]

The Southern California Credit Union Alliance (SCCUA), a forum for collaboration and cooperation for credit unions, has endorsed Compushare's full suite of technology solutions.

Compushare Inc. is a USA leading technology management vendor serving the financial industry. It is one of the few vendors of fully cloud-based solutions for the financial market. Compushare focuses on providing a full suite of technology solutions that satisfies the regulatory needs of Credit Unions across the country. With the technology management and cloud-based solutions from Compushare, SCCUA is able to provide its members with a cost-effective solution using the technology expertise and support from an industry leader.

Through the partnership with SCCUA, Compushare provides a unique set of value-added technology solutions, including fully hosted cloud solutions and cost-effective technology solutions to all SCCUA members. This will allow Credit Unions to focus on their core business and strategic objectives.

A case of cloud-oriented financial institution community[67]

Cedacri's industry community includes retail financial institutions and some non-financial institutions, commercial banks, credit unions, co-operative financial institutions, building societies, smaller commercial financial institutions, and specialized institutions that focus on providing mainly retail financial services. In recent years, it also attracted some major financial institutions that recognize the strategic value of sharing technological infrastructures. With one of the first Community Data Centers operating in Italy on an operational dimension, Cedacri is collaborating and partnering with organizations from both the financial and the industrial environments.

A relevant number of financial institutions, representing in all 10 percent of the Italian market, have migrated most if not all of their ICT components to an external vendor. Cedacri is a good example of such a service shared among financial institutions, and it could well be accessed through a community cloud in the future. By following a SaaS business model, financial barriers are removed and smaller financial institutions can enjoy the benefits of the ICT vendor services at a price they can afford.

Several financial institutions have already migrated to this new platform and are experiencing a transformational improvement in business agility and efficiency. Costs are aligned with revenues, and the burden and risks of a capital investment are transferred to the cloud vendor and its partners.

Community clouds already exist in higher education, pharmaceuticals, and other markets, and they will become popular in central and local government departments. This is another testament to how real the community cloud computing market is, and it demonstrates best practice on how to set up a solution that serves the unique needs of a particular market.

With this type of cloud, the financial institution can use an Internet cloud-based SaaS solution on a pay-per-use basis.

In the future, new public cloud solutions will offer the opportunity to transform the community cloud landscape by empowering many thousands of institutions and millions of customers. Financial organizations of all sizes and in all locations will deploy core banking solutions with the full functional richness of the many community cloud offerings. They will not invest in multiple software licenses, expensive hardware, or infrastructure.

For the time being, for some financial service functions the public cloud appears risky. The reasons range from security and privacy issues to concerns about business continuity and technological maturity. The apparent control and security offered by the community cloud is likely to appeal to financial institutions looking to a more cost-effective way to access core applications. The community cloud is where cloud infrastructure is shared, and it supports a community that has a mutual interest in increasing collaboration and assuring security.

In time, financial institutions are likely to move to a hybrid cloud environment. This approach would combine the private, public, and community cloud approaches with existing systems, and it would provide the correct functionality to meet each institution's specific needs. Then in the more distant future, financial institutions are likely to move more and more applications to the public clouds.

The expectation is that quite a lot of cloud computing usage by financial institutions will come from BPaaS. More and more institutions will delegate

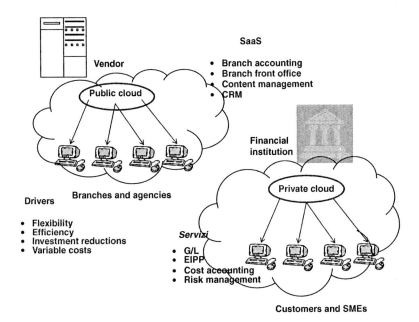

Figure 5.6 A hybrid cloud model for financial institutions

operations externally. They will start by moving back office operations to public clouds, then slowly move the middle and front-office applications (see Figure 5.6). The comparison would be with what manufacturing has already done with operations and back office.

A community cloud at NYSE[68]

NYSE Technologies has built a community cloud. It is called Capital Markets Community Platform. It is offering cloud computing. This effort is a good example for other vertical markets to follow.

For years, financial services firms such as investment banks and hedge funds have been competing on trade execution speed and volume – where milliseconds per trade can translate into billions of dollars in competitive advantage. And in doing so, they have found that you can't beat the speed of light. If one institution needs a very fast connection to the stock market, it will need to be as close as possible to the servers used to process the market transactions. The way to do this was to find out where the data center for an exchange was located. Servers were installed as close as possible to the exchange, possibly on the same network backbone. If the exchange was in a colocation facility, the best was for the financial institution servers to be right next door. This method gave larger investment banks a distinct advantage, as they were able to afford a full server and had priority access.

To help level the playing field a bit more, NYSE Technologies' new IaaS offering let financial firms of any size place themselves on the same infrastructure as the exchange. With the cloud computing solution, NYSE is able to separate financial firms from each other as well as from the exchange itself. It also let NYSE control access that presumably promotes fairness in the market. In this way, financial firms can compete on their trading algorithms, market insights, and knowledge rather than on distance from the exchange servers. This does not mean that a large financial institution cannot still co-locate a massive server farm near the exchange, just that winning is not defined by the financial institution's ability to do so. This effort by NYSE is a classic example of a community cloud. It is designed specifically to meet the needs of a particular market. It is open to all members of that community, leveling off the competition from the point of view of the infrastructure.

5.5   Conclusions

The future of financial institutions does not lie within cloud computing alone. When the car was introduced, the initial expectations were only to have transportation without horses; in fact, early cars were very similar to carriages, made with wood and leather. In time, people discovered that the car was something different. The car started to differentiate. More technologies started to be used in car building: metal-working, electronics, computers, etc. Not only did the car change in form, size, and so on, but it started to impact on the social and economic models of life and of doing business in a powerful way.

We anticipate that something similar will happen with computers. The future is not in cloud computing alone. It will be the merging of cloud computing with social, mobile, web, big data, and business intelligence, and so on to provide a new model to support the three Cs: clients, channels, and collaboration. In time, this will also change the social and economic models. This is the message of this book.

This chapter cannot be completed without including a quote attributed by some to Darwin[69]:

It is not the strongest of the species that survives, nor the most intelligent, but rather the one that is the most adaptable to change.

The managers in any industry (and we would say especially in the financial services) should take into account that at any given moment if they do not move somebody else will.

Cloud computing moves economics from fixed investments to variable costs. This reduces the barrier to entry for new entrants. These technological aspects can combine with new regulations such as that which facilitates entry to the so-called Payment Institutions and with the wider availability of network access. The impact of all these aspects could bring new entrants with advanced functionality into the financial services world[70].

Cloud computing is a disruptive innovation. In the long term, it could bring about a blurring of the roles of financial services with technology providers, processors, payment schemes, and connectivity providers.

Financial services should concentrate in the short term on piloting cloud technology immediately and using it as well as possible, taking into account the plus and deltas for each use. At the same time, they should also evaluate the long-term scenarios; the future will of course bring risks, which the more innovative and brave financial institutions will be able to turn into opportunities[71].

6
Case Study: Gruppo Banca Intesa Sanpaolo

6.1 Introduction

This chapter presents a business case, describing cloud computing for the Gruppo Banca Intesa Sanpaolo. The aims are to address the questions of whether cloud computing is a model suited to financial institutions, and whether it can bring benefits or not; also to present a possible introductory route. Apart from the technology solution, the case is interesting in that it shows a route towards the cloud computing model.

The Gruppo Banca Intesa Sanpaolo is a universal bank, with headquarters in Italy. It operates in several market segments, embracing different business contexts. It offers a full range of banking products and services – retail, commercial, private, and so on.

In the last few years, this group has undergone a process of fundamental change in the management mode of its ICT infrastructure. The goal is an increasing alignment between the business and its technology environment. This renewal process has revolutionized the methods of managing the technology resources.

For the time being, the Gruppo Banca Intesa Sanpaolo has decided to move towards the private cloud model for supporting the Group and its subsidiaries.

6.2 Gruppo Banca Intesa Sanpaolo[1]

Gruppo Banca Intesa Sanpaolo is the largest financial service in Italy, with 10.8 million customers and 5600 branches. It is also one of the largest in Europe. It is the leading Italian organization in financial activities for families and businesses, and it is especially active in banking intermediation, pension funds, bankassurance, asset management, and factoring.

The Group, with its strategic territorial coverage through its local subsidiaries, is one of the largest banking groups in 13 countries in Central and Eastern Europe, the Middle East, and North Africa. In 2011, it was ranked first in Serbia, second in Croatia and Slovakia, third in Albania, fifth in Egypt and Hungary, sixth in Bosnia and Herzegovina, and eighth in Slovenia.

On December 31, 2011, the Gruppo Banca Intesa Sanpaolo had[2]:

- Total assets of €639 billion;
- Receivables from customers of €377 billion; and
- Direct deposits of €357 billion.

The operational structure of the Gruppo Banca Intesa Sanpaolo is divided into six Business Units serving different types of customer. There is a corporate office with the tasks of providing guidance, coordination, and control over the entire Group.

The Business Units are (see Figure 6.1):

- The Banca dei Territori, which includes the Italian subsidiary banks. It is based on a model that supports and strengthens relationships with individuals, families, SMEs, and non-profit entities. Private banking, bankassurance and industrial credit are also part of this division;
- The Corporate and Investment Banking division, which supports customers, with a medium–long-term view, the development of corporate and financial institutions both domestically and internationally. Its main activities include corporate banking, structured finance, and capital markets carried out through the subsidiary Banca IMI, as well as leasing, factoring, and merchant banking;
- The International Subsidiary Banks division, which includes the subsidiaries engaged in retail and commercial banking operations outside Italy; and
- Three other Group subsidiaries:
  - The Public Finance division, which operates through the Group's subsidiary "Banca Infrastrutture Innovazione e Sviluppo" in the public finance sector, and finances infrastructure and services for public utilities;
  - The Eurizon Capital entity, the leading asset manager in Italy, managing approximately €140 billion assets; and
  - The Banca Fideuram, the leader in the financial advisor sector in Italy, with 4779 private bankers and 98 domestic branches.

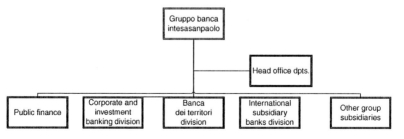

Figure 6.1 Banca Intesa Sanpaolo organizational structure[3]

6.2.1   Banca IMI

The new Banca IMI was formed in October 2007 from the merger between Banca Caboto and Banca IMI, two important financial institutions in Italy. Banca IMI operates in the main domestic and international markets, with offices in Milan, Rome, London, and New York (IMI Securities Corp.).

Banca IMI is part of the Corporate and Investment Banking division of the Gruppo Banca Intesa Sanpaolo. It is the investment bank of the Group, as shown in Figure 6.2.

The Corporate and Investment Banking Division represents an important part of the Group's total operating income: 23.5 percent at December 31, 2010[5].

Banca IMI provides services to banks, companies, institutional investors, governments, and public administrations. It has a strong presence in the equity and debt placements in extraordinary finance and securities trading.

Banca IMI's organizational model reflects its areas of specialization. It is built on three business units:[6]

- Capital Markets;
- Investment Banking; and
- Structured Finance.

Thanks to several domestic and international partners of Gruppo Banca Intesa Sanpaolo, Banca IMI has long-term leadership in structured finance in Italy. It supports the growth of domestic and international corporate clients through mid–long-term financing operations. It has expertise in a financial advisory role, particularly in the real estate sector, and in project and industry specialized lending. It assists client companies in raising

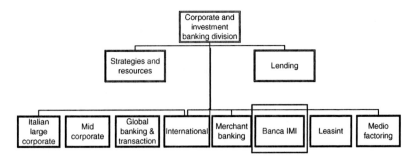

Figure 6.2   Intesa Sanpaolo's corporate and investment banking division and Banca IMI[4]

venture and debt capital. It provides financial consultancy services. It structures risk management products for companies, institutional investors, and local authorities.

Banca IMI leads the structured finance domestic market through:

- Structured financial transactions for corporations;
- Complex financial transactions, in both the domestic and international markets, with the use of project finance, acquisitions and specialized lending;
- Tailor-made solutions for corporations (structured finance for customers of the Banca dei Territori division, securitization and risk transfer, and corporate lending);
- Market risk management through syndication and market placement of syndicated transactions; and
- Financial advisory and structured financing for the Italian and international real estate markets.

As a major capital market player, the main activities it carries out are:

- Brokerage, trading and market making of derivatives and cash instruments, in both domestic and international contexts;
- Structuring and management of innovative products and derivatives;
- Equity financing, securities lending and prime brokerage in Europe;
- Financial products placement; and
- Market and product research.

Banca IMI provides a wide range of products and services to a diversified client base including corporations, financial institutions, and governments. Furthermore, Banca IMI structures and develops retail market products. Most of these products are distributed via Gruppo Banca Intesa Sanpaolo's Banca dei Territori network as well as third party networks.

The assessment process of financial instruments used by Banca IMI is fully centralized within the Risk Management Department of the parent organization, Gruppo Banca Intesa Sanpaolo. The main tasks of this department include the:

1. Identification, certification, and processing of market data and sources for assessments;
2. Certification of pricing models and model risk assessment;
3. Monitoring of the consistency of pricing models over time;
4. Re-pricing of instruments; and
5. Monitoring of benchmarks.

6.3   Background

The increased volatility of financial markets pushed the financial institutions working in asset management to introduce advanced risk control techniques, and procedures for measuring performance. These are critical to maintaining a proper risk/reward profile of a portfolio investment product.

To support these challenges, Banca IMI, along with the Risk Management Department of the Group, adopted grid computing technologies as a first step, and more recently cloud computing. These technologies are based on three different grid-supporting platforms: Murex, Layer and Risk Management services:

- Murex is one of the market leaders in trading and risk management platforms, and is used by investment banks, corporate treasuries, asset managers, and hedge funds. This risk management platform is used to measure current exposure, potential future exposure, credit value-at-risk, credit evaluation adjustments, and incremental changes to these counterparty risk measures[7]. Through the Murex platform, Banca IMI enhanced its structured product trade infrastructure. It was also able to strengthen its Straight Through Processing capabilities and its computing support for its pricing and risk analytics. As of Jan. 2013, Murex was taken over. The expectation is that their product range will continue and further developed.
- The Layer grid refers to the platform where all discrete business applications are deployed; and
- The Risk Management platform refers to the computing infrastructure for central use by the Risk Management Department.

6.4   Initial scenario of the ICT architectural framework

These platforms were required and developed at different times. Therefore, they were operated independently from one another. They had:

- Different hardware architectures;
- Different operating systems; and
- Separate networks.

From a business perspective, Banca IMI faced several growing concerns related to the increase in:

- Demands for computing capacity; and
- Complexities in the control and management of risks.

The separate ICT Infrastructure management did not allow the bank to share the grid platforms. A working group was set up to review the ICT architecture of the Gruppo Banca Intesa Sanpaolo; the task given to the team was the optimization of the ICT infrastructure resources already available in the Group.

Banca IMI also had to face the additional challenge of properly integrating structured products into its organization's risk management infrastructure.

6.5   Goal statement

Gruppo Banca Intesa Sanpaolo decided to deploy a private cloud infrastructure, to be operated and managed by its internal ICT department.

At the time, Banca IMI was facing a heavy merger and acquisition process, joining the Gruppo Banca Intesa Sanpaolo in 2007.

The private cloud project focuses on the consolidation of the ICT facilities, and the final step of the consolidation process is the development and deployment of a private cloud with a model of Infrastructure as a Service.

The goals are:

1. Upgrading and consolidating the Murex and Layer grid;
2. Creation of a Risk Management grid, which did not exist until then; and
3. Consolidation and Federation of Murex, Layer, and Risk Management into a single finance grid, in the form of a private cloud infrastructure.

The outcome was a single federated Finance Area for the management of financial instruments and over the counter derivatives, and for Risk Management operations.

The interventions are designed to ensure the availability of a new services execution platform. This platform should be able to dynamically adjust the supply capacity of the data processing services in support of the Group. The objectives are the improvement of:

- Time to market;
- Performance;
- Agility; and
- Ease of management.

6.6   Transition towards a private cloud and shared services model

There has been a gradual transition towards a private cloud and shared services model. This process has taken place over several years, and it consists of a process of change incorporating the following steps[8]:

1. In 2009, the Risk Management Department (RMD) set up a team to conduct an assessment of the internal technological infrastructure;
2. In 2010, the RMD conducted an initial consolidation and integration of the ICT infrastructure already available; and
3. In 2011, the consolidation and integration process continued, reaching a higher level of consolidation in the form of a private cloud.

The goals of this project were an increased virtualization and the consolidation of the information silos. The latter were geographically dispersed, and poorly or not at all connected.

After the initial assessment, the team scheduled the first interventions into the infrastructure, planning the preparatory activities for the upgrade, which they completed in 2010:

- Upgrade of the Layer grid, through applications streamlining;
- Upgrade of the Murex grid;
- Unification of the two grids (Murex and Layer);
- Setup of a new risk management grid platform for the Risk Management Department;
- Enablement of Scavenging[9]; and
- Final assessment and lessons learnt session.

The private cloud model brought the following benefits:

- A marked reduction in capital expenses by avoiding the need to procure additional ICT resources, through an optimization in the use of resources available. A further extension of the grid will require only licensing software with no additional hardware. Maximizing the reuse of existing resources implies containment of the need for additional infrastructure;
- A larger processing capacity was obtained by sharing computational resources across different divisions and departments, enabling a more extensive use of resources. It is still possible however, if needed, to separate and segregate the needs of each application. In this way, the Group obtained more computing power but in autonomous sections; and
- Thanks to the alignment of the business needs with the performance of the grid platforms, there was an improvement in the time to market.

The team set up a centre of excellence to monitor the application server platforms grids. The goal is to adapt the dynamic processes of the evolution in the application to the new cloud-based configuration of the infrastructure resources.

6.6.1   Murex grid consolidation at Banca IMI

The Murex grid consolidation step of the consolidation project involved an architectural review of Banca IMI's ICT systems. By the end of 2010, the team had achieved the following results:

- Higher Technological Streamlining: Intervention on the Layer grid, obtained by eliminating two applications;
- Savings: made possible by the natural expiration of the contracts;

- Innovation thanks to the alignment of the version of the Layer grid to that of Murex. This evolution was made possible by the interventions on the Layer grid;
- Improved performance of the grid as a result of the upgrade; and
- Increased streamlining of the overall system thanks to the unification and standardization at the Banca IMI infrastructure.

The results of the technical feasibility study, obtained from an internal impact assessment, have given the following positive results:

- No service disruption during the project: no users complained of delays or anomalies on their workstations:
- Increased computing capacity (up to double during night hours) without requiring any investment for the purchase of new hardware, not even base licenses:
- Stable maintenance costs: no additional costs for maintenance operations;
- Virtualization with the option to use two different operating systems;
- Opportunity for Banca IMI to take advantage of increased server capacity, through the sharing of the Risk Management Department servers. Banca IMI can use the Rapid Application Development (RAD) for the execution of its activities (Murex Layer); and
- Dynamic configuration of the existing processing capacity due to the installation and activation of the Federator module for better management of the grid.

6.6.2 Private cloud evolution

The consolidation of the Murex Layer with the Risk Management Layer in 2010 resulted in proven benefits. In the meantime, new fields of action on which to focus effort were identified. The ICT department decided to move to a private cloud model.

From the year 2011 onwards, efforts have focused on:

- Further federation in terms of increased infrastructure sharing. Other server farms (such as those in Turin, Milan, and Parma) are enabled for sharing. They are now part of the cloud infrastructure:
- An increase in the number of cloud-enabled users: new users have been connected to the cloud via Multibroker and Federator;
- Scavenging: This step consists in verifying the presence of machines available, beyond those in the Risk Management Department that are used for a limited time during the day. The goal is to overcome the scavenging limits; the overcoming of current calculation limitations passes through the unused PCs, which represent a reserve of computing power available at peaks. The result will be an extension of the available hardware resources and the

overcoming of scavenging limits. This is made possible by checking for any additional hardware resources available in both Milan and Parma server rooms and elsewhere. Once identified, additional exploitable resources not yet connected can be added to the shared resources in the cloud; and

- Continuous upgrading of the grid and shared resources will increase the number and types of applications shared in the cloud. This is the case, for instance, for office applications, such as MS Office.

6.6.3   Activities planned or evaluated for the future

The team is evaluating the extension of other applications to the private cloud. The first steps are an evaluation of the benefits, the effort required for the implementation, and the running costs.

The following interventions would bring about improvements:

- Grid infrastructure reinforcement in order to leverage the available hardware;
- Establishment of a spare capacity in order to maintain a constant level of performance even at peaks;
- Virtualization for sharing the new unified grid based on different operating systems;
- Better use of the Federators: more dynamic management of the grid; and
- Establishment of a single finance grid. The bank would achieve this result by merging the Banca IMI grid and the DRM grid, orchestrated by Federators, and virtualized to help achieve a sharing of resources.

6.7   Case study results

Cloud computing works on top of virtualization. Banca IMI has deployed virtualization by creating virtual servers on top of its existing networking, storage, and security stacks. The private cloud project has added benefits, thanks to the synergy of all these technologies. The result is greater interoperability among back end systems.

The bank has achieved a model of Infrastructure as a Service. Each internal user accesses a portion of a consolidated pool of federated resources to create and use their own ICT infrastructure as needed, when needed, and in any way it is needed.

The model is a private cloud in the sense that the pooled infrastructure is entirely owned and controlled by the central organization. It was created by joining and federating the private resources of the Group.

The benefits are:

- Consolidation and standardization of ICT components;
- Increased virtualization and sharing of resources;
- Rapid scalability;
- Increased overall computational capacity;

- Increased resource sharing among services;
- Increased speed and efficiency;
- Greater degree of control over available resources; and
- Better risk management activities.

Equity linked and other types of structured products are among the most demanding financial instruments. They must be properly measured and managed, and their complexity requires highly sophisticated and accurate pricing analytics. The development of the new private cloud-enabled Banca IMI to bring complex structured products to the market rapidly while remaining in control of their risks; the new internal cloud gave Banca IMI the ability to rapidly incorporate new structured products into a risk management platform.

6.8   From physical infrastructure to private cloud: the Gruppo Banca Intesa Sanpaolo's route to ICT as a service

The area of application of the paradigm of cloud computing was part of an initiative limited specifically to Banca IMI and the Risk Management Department of the Gruppo Banca Intesa Sanpaolo Services, which has set up a more ambitious project, involving the banking group as a whole. This time, many legal entities, as part of a single banking group, have taken part in the consolidation and federation process. The scope of the project is larger, encompassing more business units, legal entities, and subsidiaries. This case has a different aim: to learn about and test the steps and methods of intervention that a financial institution has to follow in order to develop a cloud-based architectural framework.

The progression from ICT physical resources to a private cloud followed by Gruppo Banca Intesa Sanpaolo included the following steps:

- From physical to virtual resources;
- From virtual resources to service technology; and
- From service technology to ICT as a Service.

The following paragraphs examine each step.

6.8.1   From physical to virtual resources

The consolidation and virtualization of ICT infrastructure are prerequisites to the enabling of the implementation of a cloud ecosystem. At this stage, the virtualization layer provides the basic components:

- Virtual storage;
- Backup infrastructure;
- Network; and
- Random Access Memory.

More resources come from the virtualization of the physical components of each technology domain[10].

6.8.2   From virtual resources to service technology

The Service Delivery Platform enables the automatic delivery of the infrastructure. There may be multiple delivery platforms, each of which displays a catalog of infrastructure configurations. Within each delivery platform, the individual technical elements are appropriately aggregated to form the elements of a service technology.

6.8.3   From service technology to ICT as a service

The cloud service management platform aggregates into services the elements outlined by each delivery platform. In this way, the services are available to the end user through a web portal[11].

6.9   Context and scope of the private cloud project

Gruppo Banca Intesa Sanpaolo Services has started to move towards a private cloud computing model aimed at creating services within the bank and its subsidiaries.

This evolution implies a process of business transformation that requires a focus on enabling technologies and at the same time adjusting the operation, management, and organization models.

The first project on the private cloud deals with two topics simultaneously:

1. Defining the cloud roadmap: The objective is to define and structure the course of evolution of the ICT services of the Gruppo Banca Intesa Sanpaolo Services private cloud, with respect to a medium–long-term plan; and
2. Private cloud Release 1.0: The first private cloud platform will be created based on the architectural model of reference identified during the definition phase of the roadmap. This cloud platform addresses the initial and most urgent needs.

Once the first project has been completed, the Group would launch new projects that include:

1. Private cloud release 2.0, an evolution of Release 1.0, encompassing more ICT components, business functions, and processes; and
2. Technical architecture vision: After the results achieved with the first and second releases, the bank is planning to develop a model that is more and more "as a Service." This represents an advanced stage of the transformation process, with the bank adopting global industrial and

technology standards as well as an advanced degree of automation across the complete financial value chain.

6.9.1 Method followed by the bank

In order to implement this vision, the Gruppo Banca Intesa Sanpaolo developed a medium–long-term plan. The method used includes:

- Defining a functional framework of reference that will cover current and future needs;
- Identifying different paths to move to cloud computing. For each of these, evaluating different alternatives, their benefits, their technical feasibility, and their costs;
- For each path, evaluating the technologies and tools aligned both to the functional reference framework and to the ecosystem;
- Among the different possible options, identifying the most appropriate path of transformation, taking into account impact, costs, and time; and
- Planning a roadmap for the development of Infrastructure as a Service and Platform as a Service.

6.9.2 Private cloud release 1.0

According to one of the paths of transformation identified during the definition phase of the roadmap, the bank started the implementation of Release 1.0[12].

The aim of Release 1.0 was to test the robustness and manageability of the selected cloud computing solution and to define guidelines for its structured introduction.

Business areas of applications are:

- Point of Contact;
- Application Test;
- Prototyping ICT Infrastructure as a Service; and
- Test Platform.

6.9.3 Private cloud release 2.0

A second release[13] is an evolution of the first one. New cloud services are added. The platform offers services such as:

- Infrastructure as a Service;
- Platform as a Service;
- Storage as a Service; and
- Software as a Service

Other possible business areas of application, beside those already covered by the first release, are under consideration.

6.10   Benefits from the private cloud in the Gruppo Banca Intesa Sanpaolo

From these efforts, the bank gained benefits in terms of greater efficiency, scalability, and flexibility, as shown in Figure 6.3.

Today the bank has reached a high level of consolidation, standardization, and virtualization. Due to such interventions, resources are pooled.

As shown in Figure 6.3, the first releases are projecting the bank towards a higher level of the cloud wave, to a point well up in the curve, pushing towards a sourcing model of cloud services. The greater the investments, the more the internal ICT architecture approaches the private cloud model, and the lower the overall operating costs for running the Group's activities.

The points from 1 to 4 in Figure 6.3 indicate times and types of investment. The items refer to different stages of intervention:

1. Consolidation and standardization;
2. Virtualization and resource pooling;
3. Industrialization;
4. Automation; and
5. Sourcing model of cloud services.

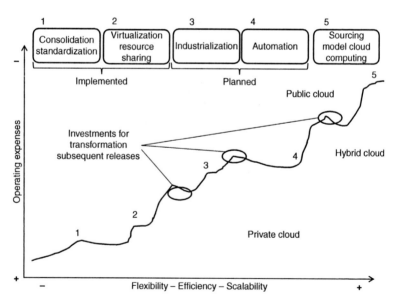

Figure 6.3   Benefits of the introduction of private cloud[14]

During this transition, there is a temporary increase in operating costs (short-run). However, the costs, having reached their peak, begin to fall because of the corrective actions initiated (medium–long-term).

Circles in the graph in Figure 6.3 indicate the points where operating costs start to fall owing to:

- Consolidation efforts;
- Improvements in efficiency;
- Moving through the learning curve; and
- Sharing of resources.

The system becomes more efficient and streamlined overall. The level of control is greater, especially after Steps 1 and 2, when the Group reaches a level of automation such that the ICT services can be orchestrated with great precision.

6.11 Conclusions

The financial and economic crisis has provided a great opportunity to pause and rethink traditional approaches. Financial institutions, seeing it as essential to get "more with less," are transitioning to next-generation models of ICT applications and infrastructure delivery.

In this scenario, characterized by investment and cost constraints, financial institutions must become more flexible and agile to adapt rapidly to the new market challenges. They should also adopt a new approach to Information Technology and Communication.

One of the best ways to move in this direction is to become leaner and use more digitization. Methods and technologies, if used in the right way, are powerful aids to improving effectiveness, efficiency, transparency, and economics, and can deliver more advanced services to not just customers but also the organization itself.

Financial institutions are starting to explore the cloud computing model as one of these transformational approaches; it can increase efficiency and flexibility, and yield substantial savings in costs that can be reallocated to client-oriented programs and services. In the words of a Gruppo Banca Intesa Sanpaolo executive, the future lies in the "cloud of services."[15]

The case study presented in this chapter confirms how cloud computing is a model both suitable for, and deployable to, the financial institution environment. Cloud computing can certainly bring benefits. The Gruppo Banca Intesa Sanpaolo has begun a process of fundamental change in the management mode of its ICT systems, aiming for increased alignment within the organization, processes, and technology. This change has revolutionized the Group's management of technology resources and will continue to do so. The aim is to increase value to the customers, be they external or internal.

It is not by chance that the Gruppo Banca Intesa Sanpaolo has changed the formal name of the division serving the customers to Division Valore (value).

The case of Gruppo Banca Intesa Sanpaolo proves the validity of the thesis in this book. Cloud computing represents a fundamental opportunity for innovation in financial institutions. This can be achieved by dramatically consolidating and rationalizing ICT projects and costs through the creation of virtual shared ICT utilities. Cloud computing is a "disruptive innovation" with the potential to redefine the financial system's future operating model.

ICT as a Service will have a fundamental impact in the near future. Today, financial institutions need to redesign their processes and reconsider the way they operate in the markets. In light of these findings, it is foreseeable that in the years to come the use of cloud services will grow substantially.

Notes

Introduction

1. NIST (2011) *Final Version of NIST Cloud Computing Definition*, Published October 25, http://www.nist.gov/itl/csd/cloud-102511.cfm, Retrieved August 12, 2012.
2. Mell, P. and Grance, T. (2011) "The NIST definition of cloud computing (Draft). recommendations of the National Institute of Standards and Technology," *NIST Special Publication* 800–145, January.
3. Nicoletti, B. (2010) *La metodologia del Lean and Digitize*, FrancoAngeli, Milano, Italy.
4. Wikipedia defines a "disruptive innovation" as an innovation that helps create a new market and value network, and eventually goes on to disrupt an existing market and value network (over a few years or decades), displacing an earlier technology. The term is used in business and technology literature to describe innovations that improve a product or service in ways that the market does not expect, typically first by designing for a different set of consumers in the new market and later by lowering prices in the existing market.

1 Financial Institutions and Information and Communication Technology

1. Saunders, A. and Cornett, M. (2004) *Financial Markets and Institutions*, McGraw-Hill, New York, NY, USA.
2. Bucur, A. (2011) *Banking 2.0: Developing a Reference Architecture for Financial Services in The Cloud*, Master Thesis at Delft University of Technology, June.
3. Pohl, M. and Freitag, S. (1994) *Handbook on the History of European Banks*, European Association for Banking History, Edward Elgar Pub, Cheltenham Glos, UK.
4. Bucur, A., *op. cit.*
5. Legislative Decree of September 1, 1993, N. 385.
6. White, W. R. (1998) *The Coming Transformation of Continental European Banking?* Bis Working Papers No. 54, June, Basle, Switzerland.
7. Directive 89/646/EEC of December 15, 1989 – *EC Official Journal* N. 386 of December 30, 1989.
8. Directive 77/80 of December 12, 1977.
9. Directive N. 646 of December 15, 1989.
10. Legislative Decree 385/1993 (Consolidated Law on Banking), Legislative Decree 58/1998 (Consolidated Law on Finance), *Bank of Italy*, Rome, Italy.
11. Website, interactive methods of payment and so on.
12. Onado, M. (2010) *In Banca Torni L'efficienza*, Il Sole 24 Ore, Milano, Italy,19 Dic, http://en.wikipedia.org/wiki/Basel_III, Retrieved March 10, 2012.
13. Buchman, D., Wahl, J., and Rose, S. (2010) *Executive's Guide to Solvency II*, John Wiley and Sons, Hoboken, NJ., USA.
14. Nicoletti, B. (2011) "Applicare il Lean and Digitize nei servizi finanziari," *Bancamatica*, January/february, pp. 12–14.
15. Nicoletti, B. (2010) *La Metodologia del Lean and Digitize*, FrancoAngeli, Milano.

16. Nicoletti, B. (2012) *Lean and Digitize*, Gower Publishing, Abingdon, UK.
17. Nicoletti, B. (2010) "Lean and digitize project management," *IPMA World Congress*, November 1–3, Istanbul, Turkey.
18. Evans, P. and Wurster, T. (2000) *Blown to Bits: How the New Economics of Information Transforms Strategy*, Harvard Business School Press, Boston, MA, USA.
19. Locatelli, R., Morpurgo, C., and Zanette A. (1999) "Verso Un Sistema Bancario E Finanziario Europeo?" Ente Per Gli Studi Monetari, Bancari e Finanziari Luigi Einaudi, *Quaderni di Ricerche*, No. 33.
20. De Angeli, S. (care of) (1990) *Evoluzione Dei Rapporti Tra Attività Bancaria e Assicurativa in Italia e Nei Principali Paesi Della Cee*, FrancoAngeli, Milano, Italy.
21. Miklos Dietz, N., Walter, C., and Reibestein, R. (2008) "What's in store for global banking," *The McKinsey Quarterly*, January 17.
22. European Central Bank (2000) *Mergers and Acquisitions Involving the EU Banking Industry: Facts and implications*. Nicoletti, B. (2008) *Alliances and Co-Evolution: Insights from the Banking Sector*, www.academici.com, June 27.
23. Galbraith, J. R. (2006) "Designing the customer centric organization," Center for Effective Organizations, University of Southern California, *CEO Telecon*, Febraury 22.
24. Nicoletti, B. (2011) "Tra smartphone e prepagate: le opportunità per i pagamenti," *Bancamatica*, Nov.–Dic., pp. 16–18.
25. Miklos Dietz, N., Walter, C., and Reibestein R. (2008) "What's in store for global banking," *The McKinsey Quarterly*, January 17.
26. Nicoletti, B. (2011) *Appunti Dalla Visita a CARTES2010 di Parigi*, http://www.bancamatica.it/approfondimenti.aspx?id=75574.
27. —— (2012) "Mobile payments in Italy: if not now, when?" *Conference of the School of Management of Politecnico di Milano*, Italy, http://en.wikipedia.org/wiki/Single_euro_Payments_Area, Retrieved March 10, 2012.
28. —— (2011) *ABILab Forum*, Milan, Italy March 24–25.
29. —— (2011) *ABILab Forum*, Milan, Italy March 24–25.
30. Brett, K. (2010) "Bank 2.0: how customer behavior and technology will change the future of financial services," *Marshall Cavendish Reference*, Tarrytown, NY, USA.
31. http://www.insurancenetworking.com/issues/2008_85/cloud-applications-crm-employers-insurance-30786–1.html, Retrieved ! August 7, 2012.
32. http://www.bis.org/publ/bcbsca.htm, Retrieved March 6, 2012.
33. http://ec.europa.eu/internal_market/insurance/solvency/index_en.htm, Retrieved August 19, 2012.

2   Cloud Computing

1. Carr, N. C. (2004) *Does IT Matter? Information Technology and the Corrosion of Competitive Advantage*, 1st edition, Harvard Business Review Press, Boston, MA, USA, April.
2. Etro, F. (2009) *The Economic Impact of Cloud Computing on Business Creation, Employment and Output in Europe*, University of Milano-Bicocca, Department of Economics publication, Milano, Italy.
3. Rappa, M. (2004) *Business Models on the Web: Managing the Digital Enterprise*, http://www.startupjunkies.org/business_models.pdf. Retrieved May 1, 2012.
4. O'Reilly, T. (2005) *What Is Web 2.0. Design Patterns and Business Models for the Next Generation of Software*, O'Reilly, Sebastopol, CA, USA.
5. Zittrain, J. (2009) *The Future of the Internet – And How to Stop It*, Caravan Books, Alexandria, MN, USA:

6. Moschella, D. et al. (2004) *Consumerization of Information Technology.* Leading Edge Forum, Falls Church, VA, USA.
7. Carr, N. (2008) *The Big Switch*, W.W. Northon and Co, New York, NY, USA.
8. McCarthy, J. (1960) "Recursive functions of symbolic expressions and their computation by machine," *Communications of the ACM*, 3 (4):184–195.
9. —— (2011) "Simplify your journey to the cloud," *Capgemini and Sogeti*, Paris, France, pp. 1–8.
10. http://www.gartner.com/it-glossary/cloud-computing/, Retrieved August 16, 2012.
11. Mell, P. and Grance, T. (2011) "The NIST definition of cloud computing: recommendations of the National Institute of Standards and Technology," *NIST Special Publication 800–145*, January.
12. http://en.wikipedia.org/wiki/Cloud_computing/, Retrieved August 16, 2012.
13. Vaquero, L. M. et al. (2012) *Open Source Cloud Computing Systems: Practices and Paradigms*, IGI Global, Hershey, PA, USA.
14. —— (2011) "Fulfilling the Cloud," *Easynet Whitepaper.*
15. http://www.proformative.com/ December 9, 2011, Retrieved April 12, 2012.
16. Mell, P. and Grance, T. (2011) *op. cit.*
17. —— (2010) "The NIST definition of cloud computing," *NIST* http://www.nist.gov/it/cloud/upload/cloud=def=v15'.df. Retrieved May 2, 2012.
18. Catteddu, D. and Hogben, G. (2009) "An SME perspective on cloud computing," *An Enisa Survey*, November.
19. Hall, R. (2012) *Radical IT as a service*, Richmond Events, The IT Directors' Forum, May 17.
20. Alexander, S. (2011) *Bank Bets Big On Cloud Computing*, December 1, http://technorati.com/technology/cloud-computing/article/bank-bets-big-on-cloud-computing/ Retrieved May 1, 2012; Lazzarin, D. (2012) "Il caso ing: legacy, private e 'community' Cloud," *ZeroUno*, May, p. 24.
21. Craig-Wood, K. (2011) "Definition of cloud computing- nist cloud," http://www.katescomment.com/definition-of-cloud-computing-nist-g-cloud/, Retrieved August 14, 2012.
22. Bussler, C. (2003) *B2B Integration*, Springer Verlag, Berlin, Germany.
23. Hatch, M. (2011) *Cloud Computing and B2B*, Microsoft Corporation.
24. Viswanathan, N. (2011) "B2B integration and collaboration," *Aberdeen Group Research Brief*, June.
25. Buyya, R., Yeo, C. S., and Venugopal, S. (2008) "Market-oriented cloud computing, vision, hype, and reality for delivering IT services as computing utilities," *High Performance Computing and Communications, 2008.* HPCC '08. 10th IEEE International Conference, September 25–27.
26. Kerravala, Z. and Hamilton, G. (2004) "Unified collaborative communications for the real time enterprise," *Yankee report*, February
27. Porter, M. (2001) "Strategy and the internet," *Harvard Business Review*, 79(3), pp. 62–72.
28. Smith, A. (2011) *Cloud Computing: A Briefing For The Business Analyst*, Black Circle, Canberra, Australia.
29. Alpern, P (2011) "Debunking 5 myths on cloud computing," *Business Finance*, June 22, http://businessfinancemag.com/article/debunking=5=myths=cloud=computing=0 622. Retrieved May 1, 2012.
30. Hugos, M. H. (2009) *Business Agility: Sustainable Prosperity in a Relentlessly Competitive World*, Wiley, Hoboken, NJ, USA; Poppendieck, M. and Poppendieck, T. (2003) *Lean Software Development: An Agile Toolkit*, Addison Wesley, Boston, MA, USA.

31. Harris, J. and Nunn, S. (2010) "Agile ICT reinventing the enterprise," *Outlook*, Accenture, June.
32. Armbrust, M. et al. (2010) "Above the clouds: a view of cloud computing," *Communications of the ACM*, April.
33. Owens, D. (2010) "Securing elasticity in the cloud," *ACMqueue*, http://queue.acm.org/detail.cfm?id=1794516. Retrieved August 8, 2012.
34. —— (2008) "The data center 'Implosion Explosion'," *Cabbly Analytics*, February.
35. Smith, A. (2011) *op. cit.*
36. https://www.cdproject.net/en-US/WhatWeDo/Pages/Cloud-Computing.aspx. Retrieved May 1, 2012.
37. Kroes, N. (2010) "Openness at the heart of the EU Digital Agenda," *Open Forum Europe 2010 Summit*, Brussels, June 10.
38. Mahapatra, B. et al. (2012) "Five important cloud contract considerations for IandO leaders," *Gartner Report*, April 5.
39. —— (2012) *Cloud Computing Changes the Game*, Accenture paper. http://www.accenture.com/SiteCollectionDocuments/PDF/Accenture-New-Era-Banking-Cloud-Computing-Changes-Game.pdf. Retrieved August 17, 2012.
40. King, L. (2011) "Deutsche bank completes cloud computing overhaul," http://www.cio.co.uk/news/3322358/deutsche-bank-completes-cloud-computing-overhaul/ Retrieved May 1, 2012.
41. —— (2011) "Fulfilling the cloud," *Easynet White Paper*, http://www.easynet.com/ch/de/solutions/hosting/cloud.aspx?TertiaryNavID=874, Retrieved January 15, 2013.
42. Proposed law is available at: http://democrats.senate.gov/pdfs/WH-cyber-breach-notice.pdf, Retrieved May 17, 2012.
43. http://www.insurancenetworking.com/issues/2008_85/cloud-applications-crm-employers-insurance-30786-1.html?pg=1, Retrieved August 17, 2012.
44. Smith, A. (2011) *op. cit.*
45. Vouk, M. A. (2008) "Cloud computing – issues, research and implementations," *Journal of Computing and Information Technology*, December, 16 (4): 235–246.
46. Grossman, R. L. and Gu, Y. (2009) "On the varieties of clouds for data intensive computing," *Bulletin of the IEEE Computer Society Technical Committee on Data Engineering*, 32(1), pp. 44–51. Grossman, R. L. (2009) "The case for cloud computing," *IT Professional*, March–April, 11 (2): 23–27.
47. Gray, P. (2006) *Manager's Guide to Making Decisions about Information Systems*, Wiley, Hoboken, NJ, USA.
48. Alpern, P. (2011) "Debunking 5 myths on cloud computing," *Business Finance*, June 22, http://businessfinancemag.com/article/debunking=5=myths=cloud=computing=0 622, Retrieved May 1, 2012.
49. —— (2011) "Fulfilling the cloud," *Easynet White Paper*, http://www.easynet.com/ch/de/solutions/hosting/cloud.aspx?TertiaryNavID=874, Retrieved January 15, 2013.
50. Tha, P. (2012) "Yamamay experience," *CIONET meeting*, Milan, May 8.
51. As also mentioned in 'Introduction to cloud computing architecture', June 2009, *White Paper* 1st Edition, Sun Microsystems
52. Smith, A. (2011) *op. cit.*
53. —— (2012) *From Virtualization to Private Cloud; Cut through the cloud clutter*, IT Process Institute.
54. Nicoletti, B. (2011) "Case history: L'esperienza cloud dell'Istituto per il Credito Sportivo," *ZeroUno PMI, cloud computing e competitività*, Roma, October 6.

55. A third of European Enterprise IT budgets to go on cloud computing this year, *VMware survey* http://www.vmwareemeablog.com/enterprise-uk/a-third-of-european-enterprise-it-budgets-to-go-on-cloud-computing-this-year-vmware-survey. Retrieved May 28, 2012.

3 Cloud Computing in Financial Institutions

1. —— (2009) "Analisi KPMG su bilanci 2009," *KPMG*.
2. —— (2012) "Financial institution of Italy and ANIA, NetConsulting elaboration of ISTAT data." Internal Document.
3. —— (2011) *Rilevazione dello stato dell'automazione del sistema creditizio, anno* 2010, Cipa, Frascati, Roma.
4. —— (2011) "Differences in cloud adoption across global industries," *The TCS Cloud Study*, http://sites.tcs.com/cloudstudy/differences-in-cloud-adoption-across-global-industries#.T6F9ELPt_pc, Retrieved May 20, 2012.
5. Gunning, M. (2011) "New Year, New Trends," *Mobile Marketing*, December, http://www.mobilemarketingmagazine.co.uk/content/new-year-new-trends, Retrieved August 11, 2012.
6. —— (2010) "How cloud computing will transform insurance," *Accenture* paper, http://www.accenture.com/SiteCollectionDocuments/PDF/Accenture_Banking_Cloud_Computing.pdf, Retrieved August 17, 2012.
7. Suresh, M. C (2010) "Cloud computing strategic considerations for banking and financial services Institutions," *TCS White Paper*, http://www.tcs.com/SiteCollectionDocuments/White%20Papers/Bfs_whitepaper_Cloud-Computing-Strategic-Considerations-for-Banking-and-Financial-Institutions-03_2010.pdf, Retrieved January 15, 2013.
8. ATM, Kiosk, Call center, Branch, Online functions, Mobile based functions, Content management, and Business partner delivered functions.
9. Thews, C. (2008) *Unified Communication and Collaboration*, http://www.dfn.de/fileadmin/3Beratung/Betriebstagungen/bt48/forum-voip-cthews.pdf, Retrieved August 9, 2012.
10. For instance, functions such as originations, transaction processing, customer servicing, collections, reconciliations, analytics, collaboration, and reporting.
11. Mehta, O. (2011) "Finance in the Cloud," *Profit*, February.
12. Multiple Enterprise Service Bus (ESB) implementations are common within the portfolio, leveraging the maturity of technologies like Websphere, TIBCO, WebMethods, XML, and Java. See for instance —— (2006) *Enterprise Service Bus and SOA Middleware*, Aberdeen Group, June.
13. http://www.cio.in/case-study/bajaj-auto-finance-adopts-cloud-based-crm-and-increases-general-staff-productivity-50-per, Retrieved August 6, 2012.
14. —— (2010) *Rilevazione sullo stato dell'Automazione del sistema creditizio*, Convenzione Interbancaria sui problemi dell'automazione (CIPA) e Associazione Bancaria Italiana (ABI).
15. Baumann, N. et al. (2012) *Insurance Tech Trends 2012*, Deloitte paper, http://www.deloitte.com/assets/Dcom-UnitedStates/Local%20Assets/Documents/us_consulting_2012Insurance_Technology_trends_05312012.pdf, Retrieved August 17, 2012.
16. http://press.bbva.com/latest-contents/press-releases/spain/bbva-banks-on-the-google-cloud(9882–22–101-c-92220).html, Retrieved April 11, 2012.

17. Howarth, B. (2010) "Commonwealth bank CIO talks cloud computing: an indepth interview with CBA chief information officer and group executive for enterprise services," Michael Harte, CIO, July 21.
18. ——— (2011) "IBM teams up with Nawanagar cooperative bank to implement core banking solutions on cloud," *Information Week*, October 11.
19. SAP cloud solution has been developed in Switzerland and complies with the highest Swiss Quality standards. "SAP Business Suite applications as PaaS" is offered within a public cloud, as an on demand SAP cloud platforms (www.sapcloudcomputing.com). Oracle is also already offering a broad portfolio of software and hardware products and services to enable public, private and hybrid clouds. Other vendors are active in this space.
20. ——— (2012) *AWS Case Study: Bankinter*, http://aws.amazon.com/solutions/case-studies/bankinter/ Retrieved August 17, 2012.
21. http://www.procurementleaders.com/news-archive/news-archive/ambank-deposits-sourcing-function-in-the-cloud?highlight=cloud%20banking, Retrieved June 4, 2012.
22. ——— (2010) *Indagine sull'utilizzo dell'ICT in gruppi bancari europei con articolazione internazionale*, CIPA and ABI, October.
23. Crosman, P. (2010) "BSandT survey: banks take to cloud computing," *BSandT*, August 16.
24. Fregi, F.(2011) "Ride the technology and social trends to innovate your way of doing business," *The Innovation Group Banking Summit*, September 29, Milano, Italy.
25. Arora, P. (2011) *To the Cloud: Cloud Powering an Enterprise*, McGraw-Hill, New York, NY, USA.
26. Fregi, F. (2011) *op. cit.*
27. Henschen, D. (2010) "Bank Of America executive maps out cloud puzzle," *InformationWeek*, April 12.

4   Governance of Cloud Computing

1. Nicoletti, B. (2010) *La Metodologia del Lean and Digitize*, FrancoAngeli. Milano, Italy.
2. http://www.iso.org/iso/iso_catalogue/management_and_leadership_standards/quality_management/iso_9000_selection_and_use/iso_9000_family_core_standards.htm, Retrieved 5 May 2012).
3. Deming, W. E. (1986) *Out of the Crisis*. MIT Center for Advanced Engineering Study, Boston, MA, USA.
4. In this book, the Data Controller is the Financial Institution. Under the Italian legal system the Data Processor is called "Responsabile del trattamento dei dati" defined as "a natural person, legal person, public administration or any other body, association or body appointed to the processing of personal data by the holder" (ai sensi dell'art. 4, comma 1, lett. g) del decreto legislativo 30 giugno 2003, N. 196, Codice in Materia di Protezione dei Dati Personali). In this book, the Data Processor could be the cloud computing vendor.
5. Mell, P. and Grance, T. (2011) The NIST Definition of Cloud Computing (Draft), *Recommendations of the National Institute of Standards and Technology*, Special Publication 800–145, January.
6. Compliance Risk Management is a discipline that supports the organization in the definition, management and compliance monitoring of the organization's

conduct with respect to the legal provisions, regulations and business rules. There are many people dealing with this subject within an organization. They include: – Managers and employees who work in the Compliance Department – Employees who operate in different business functions (Legal, Organization, Risk Management, Internal Audit, and so on) involved in the management or supervision of the stages of compliance risk management.

7. Officially "Directive 95/46/EC on the protection of individuals with regard to the processing of personal data and on the free movement of such data." It has been implemented in many Member States.

8. Transposed in Italy through the "Decreto Legislativo 17 Settembre 2007, N. 164 sul 'Recepimento della direttiva 2004/39/CE relativa ai mercati degli strumenti finanziari, che modifica le direttive 85/611/CEE e 93/6/CEE del Consiglio e la direttiva 2000/12/CE del Parlamento europeo e del Consiglio e che abroga la direttiva 93/22/CEE del Consiglio'" or Legislative Decree of 17 September 2007, No 164 on the "Implementation of Directive 2004/39/EC on markets in financial instruments".

9. De Luca, A. (2008) Mifid, l'Italia e il resto del mondo, *Computerworld*, July 10.

10. The Sarbanes-Oxley Act of 2002 (often shortened to SOX) is legislation enacted in response to the high-profile Enron and WorldCom financial scandals, to protect shareholders and the general public from accounting errors and fraudulent practices in an enterprise.

11. The aim of the SEPA project is the harmonization within EU and EFTA of the conditions for the execution of payments, through the provision of a single set of rules, access on a non-restrictive and equitable basis, transparency and interoperability, encouraging competition and enabling financial institutions to negotiate better terms with their vendors.

12. Furthermore, the German Authority – with a ruling on June 18, 2010, clearly indicated that ICT considers such a principle as not suitable to offer sufficient guarantees on data protection in the context of cloud services.

13. The "Council of Europe Convention for the Protection of Individuals with regard to Automatic Processing of Personal Data" (ETS Convention No.108) is the only international treaty dealing specifically with data protection. Its adoption was a significant achievement, and the Convention is still considered the blueprint for a minimum standard of protection in national law. The Convention entered into force on October 1, 1985. All EU Member States are parties to this Convention.

14. According to Article 7 of the same Convention, "Appropriate security measures shall be taken for the protection of personal data stored in automated data files against accidental or unauthorized destruction or accidental loss as well as against unauthorized access, alteration or dissemination."

15. Communication from the Commission to the European Parliament, the Council, the Economic and Social Committee and the Committee of the Regions, Brussels, November 4, 2010, "A comprehensive approach on personal data protection in the European Union," European Commission.

16. See the Study on the economic benefits of privacy enhancing technologies, *London Economics*, July 2010 (http://ec.europa.eu/justice/policies/privacy/docs/studies/final_report_pets_16_07_10_en.pdf), p.14, Retrieved August 11, 2012.

17. *EU Directive 95/46* of October 25, 1995 of the European Parliament and of the Council on the protection of individuals with regard to the processing of personal data and on the free movement of such data, transposed in Italy by the Law No 675 December 31, 1996. The Directive applies to both public and private sectors.

18. Bucci, P. (2010) Processi Direzionali e Risk Management, *Data Manager*, February, pp. 92–99.
19. —— (2011) "Understanding the New SOC Reports," *ISACA Journal*, http://www.isaca.org/Journal/Past-Issues/2011/Volume-2/Pages/Understanding-the-New-SOC-Reports.aspx, Retrieved January 15, 2013.
20. Smith, A. (2011) *Cloud Computing: A Briefing For The Business Analyst*, Black Circle, Canberra, Australia.
21. —— (2011) *Cloud UK. Paper Three. Contracting Cloud Services. A Guide to Best Practice*, Cloud Industry Forum, High Wycombe, UK.
22. It is important to state clearly in the contract that the vendor is "responsible for the treatment of data".
23. Dettori, S. and Passante, E. (2011) "I contratti di outsourcing," *Strategies and Procurement*, pp. 25–26; Smith, A. (2011) *op. cit.*
24. IBM (2011) Tips for embracing cloud computing, *Help Net Security*, June 9.
25. NIST: FISMA Overview, *Csrc.nist.gov*. Retrieved April 27, 2012.
26. http://www.rtbot.net/Federal_Information_Systems_Management_Act;(FISMA), Retrieved August 10, 2012.
27. http://www.itil-officialsite.com/
28. Senft, S. and Gallegos, F. (2009) *Information Technology Control and Audit*, 3rd Edition, Auerbach Boca Raton, FL, USA.
29. www.tmforum.org/EnterpriseCloudLeadership/8009/home.html, Retrieved August 6, 2012.
30. CSA, Cloud Control Matrix, https://cloudsecurityalliance.org/, Retrieved May 20, 2012.

5   The Future of ICT in Financial Institutions

1. Redshaw, P. (2011) "Five ways to drive creative destruction with cloud banking," *Gartner report*, September 13.
2. As emerged also from the Assinform Report 2011 on the Finance sector.
3. —— (2010) Rapporto Assinform, Assinform, Milan, Italy.
4. —— (2010) *Project Europe 2030: Challenges and Opportunities*, The Reflection Group on the Future of EU 2030, May.
5. Mariotti, S. and Piscitello, L. (2002) "Le Banche multinazionali Italiane," *Economia e Politica Industriale*, 13, pp. 151–166.
6. Saccomanni, F. (2008) "Il processo di Internazionalizzazione del sistema bancario: la presenza delle Banche Estere in Italia," *Associazione fra le banche estere in Italia*. February 19, Milano, Italy.
7. Tarantola, A. M. (2009) "Intervention of the Vice Director of Bank Italia," *Associazione fra le banche estere in Italia* on November 20.
8. According to last annual report of the EU Commission, the annual expenditure for a bank account in Italy is around €292, a record figure in Europe. The use of cards is particularly expensive, but so are the counter operations and commissions on financial services. Critiques were also recently forwarded to the Italian banking system by two Italian consumer associations, Federconsumatori and Adusbef: the two groups go so far as to speak of savers as victims of an actual robbery at the time of cash withdrawal at the counter.
9. "Il processo di Internazionalizzazione del sistema bancario: la presenza delle Banche Estere in Italia. Intervento del Direttore Generale della Banca d'Italia Fabrizio Saccomanni," *Associazione Fra le Banche Estere in Italia*, February 19, 2008, Milan, Italy.

10. De Nicolò, G. et al. (2004) "Bank Consolidation, Internationalization, and Conglomeration: Trends and Implications for Financial Risk," *Financial Markets, Institutions and Instruments*, 13 (4), November, pp. 173–217.
11. Gruppo Banca Intesa Sanpaolo is an example in Italy.
12. As much as 78 percent according to Nielsen (2009) "Trust in advertising: October 2007 investigation," *A Global Nielsen Consumer Report*, New York, July 7.
13. From July 1, 2011 Banca Intesa Sanpaolo made a new customer service available: Intesa Sanpaolo on Facebook. The aim is to provide quick answers and support the development of new forms of relationship,and it is addressed especially to young people who use innovative channels of interaction. The Facebook page is titled IntesaSanpaolo Customer Service.
14. Bolton, R. N. and Tarasi, C. O. (2006) "Managing customer relationships, in Naresh K. Malhotra (ed.) *Review of Marketing Research*, Volume 3, M.E. Sharpe, Inc., New York, NY, USA, pp. 3–38.
15. —— (2011) "Sicurezza, innovazione e riduzione dei costi: Credicoop Cernusco sceglie Google per la posta elettronica," http://www.credicoop.it/news/dettaglio_news.asp?I_menuID=12317andhNewsID=70525, Retrieved May 13, 2012.
16. http://en.wikipedia.org/wiki/M-Pesa, Retrieved May 13, 2012.
17. Perasso, C. (2011) "Totally immersive experiential marketing, Financial Services Club Blog by Chris Skinner," July 27, http://thefinanser.co.uk/fsclub/2011/07/totally-immersive-experiential-marketing.html, Retrieved May 13, 2012.
18. http://www.cajanavarra.es/en/, Retrieved April 12, 2012.
19. —— (2010) "How cloud computing will transform insurers," *Accenture Document*, http://www.accenture.com/SiteCollectionDocuments/PDF/Accenture_Banking_Cloud_Computing.pdf, Retrieved August 17, 2012.
20. Directive 2009/110/EC of the European Parliament and of the Council, September 16, 2009 on the taking up, pursuit and prudential supervision of the business of electronic money institutions amending Directives 2005/60/EC and 2006/48/EC and repealing Directive 2000/46/EC.
21. http://www.cedacri.it/wps/wcm/connect/Public/cedacri/inglese/financial+information/ Retrieved May 13, 2012.
22. —— (2010) "Rilevazione dello stato dell'automazione del sistema creditizio," *CIPA*, Ago.
23. —— (2011) "Scenario e trend del mercato ICT per il settore bancario," *ABILab's 2011 Forum*.
24. —— (2011) "Rapporto," *Assinform NetConsulting*. Assinform, Milan, Italy.
25. —— (2011) "The cloud dividend: part two," *CEBR Report for EMC²*, London, UK, February.
26. —— (2011) "Indagine sull'utilizzo dell'ICT in gruppi bancari europei con articolazione internazionale," *CIPA and ABI*, October.
27. —— (2011) "La caixa achieves business/IT alignment," *Unisys case study*, http://www.unisys.com/unisys/inc/pdf/casestudies/11–0055.pdf, Retrieved May 13, 2012.
28. Weill, P. and Woermer, S. L. (2009) *The Future of the CIO*, MIT Sloan CISR Research Briefing, 9 (1), January.
29. The word bank comes from the Italian word *banco*, meaning desk. The first banks were formed in around the 15th century. The relationship with the customers took place on a desk in a public place.
30. Different, however, is the situation for large enterprise customers who need to examine more carefully and comply with policies and regulations which are much more stringent.

31. —— (2010) "Bank 2.0: SME banking in the cloud," http://bank2book.com/2010/06/24/bank-2-0-sme-banking-in-the-cloud/#comments, Retrieved May 15, 2012.
32. —— (2012) "Cryptomatic invents cloud wallet," *Payments Cards/Mobile*, March–April.
33. http://www.economist.com/node/15557465 Retrieved August 6, 2012.
34. http://www.ltsbcf.co.uk/news/2011/August/small-businesses-should-adopt-th e-cloud-says-expert/, 03/08/2011, Retrieved April 12, 2012.
35. Orioli, A. (2012) "Poste vola sulle «nuvole» per le Pmi," *Il Sole 24 Ore*, May 3.
36. —— (2011) "L'occasione sociale è anche per le banche tra collaborazione, promozioni e clienti," Computerworld, July 7.
37. —— (2012) "Osservatorio ABI della customer satisfaction della clientela privata – Sistema di analisi del posizionamento competitivo e di benchmarking – Edizione 2012–2013, *ABI document*, Rome, Italy.
38. —— (2011) "Stakeholder engagement, IntesaSanpaolo Report con stakeholder engagement 2010," May.
39. —— (2011) "Il domani supera anche il computer," *Sole24Ore*, Milan, Italy, January 2.
40. Hughes, N. and Lonie, S. (2007) "M-PESA: mobile money for the Un-banked turning cellphones into 24-hour tellers in Kenya," *Innovations*, Winter/Spring, 2 (1–2): 63–81.
41. Nicoletti, B. (2010) *La Metodologia del Lean and Digitize*, FrancoAngeli, Milano.
42. —— (2007) "Dalla mappatura dei processi al business process re-engineering," Document *ABI*, Rome, Italy.
43. —— (2009) "L'attualità dell' outsourcing: le promesse del BPO," *Azienda Banca*, March, pp. 74–79.
44. Rachel (2012) "UniCredit and HP to optimize payroll production, human resources processes," May 8, http://www8.hp.com/us/en/hp-news/press-release.html?id=1233868#.T7AYb-jt_pc. Retrieved June 4, 2012.
45. —— (2012) "Core banking BPO industry assessment and forecast," NelsonHall, http://www.procurementleaders.com/news-archive/news-archive/global-banking-bpo-to-soar-by-2011-research-claims?highlight=cloud%20banking, Retrieved June 4, 2012.
46. The global labor arbitrage phenomenon has been described by economist Stephen S. Roach (Roach, S. (2010) *The Next Asia: Opportunities and Challenges for a New Globalization*, J. Wiley and Sons, Hoboken, NJ; 1st edition, October 5, 5). It is an economic phenomenon where, as a result of the removal of or disintegration of barriers to international trade, jobs move to nations where labor and the cost of doing business (such as environmental regulations) is inexpensive and/or impoverished labor moves to nations with higher paying jobs.
47. McCracken, B. (2011) "Business process as a service – the next wave of BPO delivery," http://www.outsourcing-center.com/2011–02-business-process-as-a-service-the-next-wave-of-bpo-delivery-article-42948.html, Retrieved May 13, 2012.
48. —— (2012) "Microsoft industry reference architecture for banking (MIRA-B)," *Microsoft Document*, May.
49. IAF and Capgemini (2007) "Enterprise, business and IT architectures and the integrated architecture framework", http://www.capgemini.com/m/en/tl/Enterprise__Business_and_IT_Architecture_and_the_Integrated_Architecture_Framework.pdf, Retrieved January 15, 2013.

50. Gerwens, H. (2008) "SAP for banking on system z reference architecture," *SAP Community Network*, http://www.sdn.sap.com/irj/scn/go/portal/prtroot/docs/library/uuid/a00e4718-314f-2b10-19a6-a76f257addaf?QuickLink=index&overrid elayout=true, Retrieved January 15, 2013.

51. http://lifeinsurance.codeplex.com/, Retrieved August 19, 2012.

52. Modification by the Author of an original illustration in Bokur, A. (2011) *op. cit.*

53. —— (2012) *Microsoft Industry Reference Architecture for Banking (MIRA-B)*, Microsoft document, May.

54. Buyya, R., Yeo, C. and Venugopal, S. (2008) "Market-oriented cloud computing vision, hype, and reality for delivering IT services as computing utilities," *Proc. 10th IEEE Int. Conference on High Performance Computing and Communications*, HPCC 2008, Dalian, China, September.

55. —— (2011) "The cloud dividend: part two. The economic benefits of cloud computing to business and the wider EMEA economy. Comparative analysis of the impact on aggregated industry sectors," *CEBR for EMC2*, London, UK.

56. Crosman, P. (2010) "BSandT survey: banks take to cloud computing," *BSandT*, August 16.

57. With the introduction of standards such as UNIFI or ISO 20022, SWIFT, XBRL and so on.

58. www.ifxforum.org, Retrieved August 14, 2012.

59. BIAN (2009) "Banking industry architecture network, BIAN's relationship to other standards initiatives," *BIAN Positioning White Paper*, Version: 1.0, September 10; http://bian.org/, Retrieved August 11, 2012.

60. David, M. (2011) "The EU calls For cloud support standardization," http://siliconangle.com/blog/2011/03/24/the-eu-calls-for-cloud-support-standardization/. Retrieved June 1, 2011.

61. http://cloud-standards.org/wiki/index.php?title=Main_Page, Retrieved May 14, 2012.

62. http://www.pmi.it/tecnologia/software-e-web/articolo/51503/le-aziende-italiane-hanno-scoperto-google-apps-for-business.html, Retrieved May 14, 2012.

63. Heskett, J. L., Sasser, Jr. W. E. and Schlesinger, L. A. (1997) *The Service Profit Chain*, Free Press, New York, NY, USA

64. Information presented in this case is derived from Sasser, Jr W. E., Heskett, J. L. and Ryder, T. (2010) "Rackspace hosting (2000)," *Video product number 9–811–701*, Harvard Business School, Boston, MA, USA.

65. Di Maio A. (2010) "Community clouds from governments to banks will challenge vendors," http://blogs.gartner.com/andrea_dimaio/2010/04/27/community-clouds-from-governments-to-banks/, Retrieved May 14, 2012.

66. —— (2011) "Southern California credit union alliance endorses Compushare's technology management solutions for its credit union members," *Marketwire*, August 18,

67. Bevilacqua, E. (2012) "Cedacri: una piattaforma per mettere il cliente al centro di tutto," *ZeroUno*, Mag.

68. Adapted from Staten, J. (2011) "Are banks using cloud computing? A definitive Yes," *Forrester*, June 1. http://blogs.forrester.com/james_staten/11-06-01-are_banks_using_cloud_computing_a_definitive_yes, Retrieved March 15, 2012.

69. Megginson, L. C. (1963) "Lessons from Europe for American Business," *Southwestern Social Science Quarterly*, 44 (1): 3–13, at p. 4.

70. Cowan, C. et al. (2012) *Finance in the Cloud*, A report published by Value Partners Management Consulting Ltd., London, UK.
71. Cowan, C. et al. (2012) *op. cit.*

6 Case Study: Gruppo Banca Intesa Sanpaolo

This chapter is derived mainly from the 2011 thesis by Steven Michael Lanzi Mazzocchini "Cloud Computing and Financial Institutions: opportunities and challenges" at the Master in Procurement at the Università degli Studi di Roma "Tor Vergata" and from presentations of executives of Gruppo Banca Intesa Sanpaolo at events such as the Cloud Computing Summit 2011 in Milano, Italy. The case reports what happened until mid-2011.

1. www.intesasanpaolo.com, the website of the Gruppo Banca Intesa Sanpaolo.
2. http://www.group.intesasanpaolo.com/scriptIsir0/si09/governance/eng_assemblea_azionisti.jsp?tabId=2012#/governance/eng_assemblea_azionisti.jsp%3FtabId%3D2012, Retrieved June 2, 2012.
3. Source: Institutional website, www.intesasanpaolo.com, Retrieved August 11, 2012.
4. Source: Institutional website, www.intesasanpaolo.com, Retrieved June 2, 2012.
5. Source: Institutional website www.intesasanpaolo.com. Retrieved June 2, 2012.
6. Source: Banca IMI Institutional Presentation.
7. The Murex platform, developed by the French company Murex Ltd., is in use with investment banks, corporate treasuries, asset managers and hedge funds. The Murex platform MXG2000 was customized for the Gruppo Banca Intesa Sanpaolo. It enables the bank to bring complex structured products (for instance financial instruments) to the market rapidly while staying in control of their risk. Thank to Murex, Banca IMI has in the past year introduced new functionalities, including a real-time credit risk engine and the ability to quickly incorporate new structured products into a risk framework.
8. Author's adaptation of a Gruppo Banca Intesa Sanpaolo presentation.
9. *Resource scavenging techniques* attempt to meet transient resource shortfalls in one part of the system by reassigning resources from other parts of the system.
10. Author's adaptation of chart extrapolated from a Banca Intesa Group Services presentation.
11. Author's adaptation of a chart extrapolated from a Banca Intesa Group Services presentation.
12. Author's adaptation of a chart extrapolated from a bank's presentation.
13. Author's adaptation of a chart extrapolated from a bank's presentation.
14. Author's adaptation of a chart extrapolated from a bank's presentation. To retain confidentiality, the actual numbers are not included.
15. Curcuruto, P. L. (2012) "Cloud e Sistema Bancario," *Cloud Summit 2012*, The Innovation Group, Milan, Italy, March 23, http://www.youtube.com/watch?v=JiOuygqLTeI Retrieved May 6, 2012.

Glossary*

Access management The ability to manage access to systems, either directly or through the cloud.

Advertising-based pricing model A pricing model featuring customer services at low or no cost. The vendor gets most of its revenues from advertisers whose ads are delivered to the customer along with the service.

Agility Referring to a business, agility means its ability to adapt rapidly and cost-effectively in response to changes in the business environment. Referring to cloud computing, agility means how quickly a vendor responds to the client's load variations by allocating additional resources to the cloud.

Amazon EC2 Amazon's Elastic Compute Cloud Web service. This provides resizable computing capacity in the cloud to provide developers with scalability for building applications.

Amazon S3 Amazon Simple Storage Services. Amazon's cloud storage service.

Amazon web services (AWS) Amazon's suite of cloud services (now includes EC2, RDS, S3, SQS, and VPC). Together they make up Amazon's current cloud services platform.

Analytics See Business Intelligence.

Apache Hadoop See Hadoop.

Application programming interfaces (API) A specification for the interfaces used by software components to communicate with each other. An API may include specifications for routines, data structures, object classes, and variables.

Application virtualization A type of client virtualization. The technology allows applications to run as virtual services isolated both from each other and from the underlying operating system.

Audit and compliance The ability to collect audit and compliance data.

Automated broker An automated cloud broker that can dynamically select the most appropriate cloud for a certain service within those contracted.

Automation The automating handling of services. Also the percentage of requests to a party or a system handled without any human intervention.

---

* These definitions are summarized, so they will not necessarily be precise. Please consult the text for a more complete presentation of the terms. Only some terms used in the text are included in this Glossary; we have given priority to terms where there is the need to find a quick reference while reading this book. The source of most of the definitions in this list are websites giving definitions of cloud computing, to which we refer you for more information; most of these sites are included in the sitography at the end of this book.

Banking 2.0 or Bank 2.0   A generic (and vague) term that refers to financial institutions using advanced ICT technologies, such as:

1. Rich Internet applications;.
2. Web-oriented architecture;
3. Social networking.

Benchmarking   Comparison of processes and/or measures related to others implemented by well-organized entities.

Big data   A collection of datasets so large and complex that it becomes awkward to work with when using traditional database management software.

Billing and service usage metering   The client can be billed for resources used. This pay-as-you-go model implies that usage is metered. The client pays only for what it uses.

Broad network access   An essential cloud characteristic, broad network access facilitates network capabilities and their access through standard devices such as PCs, notebooks, tablets, PDAs, and smartphones. Heterogeneous thin or thick client platforms promote the use of the platform.

Broker   In this book, refers to a Cloud Broker (see definition below).

Business intelligence (BI)   A broad category of applications and technologies for collecting, storing, analyzing, retrieving, and providing access to data to help users make better decisions. BI applications include the activities of decision support systems, querying and reporting, online analytical processing, statistical analysis, forecasting, and data mining. In some cases, it is termed Analytics.

Business-oriented architecture (BOA)   Set of computer systems modules to support business process management (BPM). Refers to the SOA computer architecture combined with BPM Business Process Management.

Business process analysis (BPA)   Analysis of organization processes.

Business process as a service (BPaaS)   The provision of a complete organization process, or part of it, as a service – such as accounting, billing, payroll, advertising.

Business process management (BPM)   Management of processes in order to dramatically improve them.

Business process management system (BPMS)   Software supporting Business Process Management.

Business process modeling notation (BPMN)   Documentation of process modeling.

Business process outsourcing or Business process optimization (BPO)   Process optimization obtained through outsourcing.

Business process platform (BPP)   A platform for processes.

Business process re-engineering (BPR)   Process re-engineering to provide dramatic improvements.

Business productivity online standard suite (BPOS)   Online versions of Microsoft's messaging and collaboration solutions. At the time of writing, it includes Exchange

Online, SharePoint Online, Office Live Meeting, and Office Communications Online.

Business rule engine (BRE)   Component of a BPMS for managing the rules of an organization process.

Business to business (B2B)   Refers to organizations that do business with other organizations rather than consumers.

Capability maturity model integration (CMMI)   A process improvement approach that provides organizations with the essential elements of effective processes in order to improve their performance.

Client   In this book, refers to the customer of cloud services. The person who pays for the product, service, or activity. In some cases in this book, the word "client" may also be used to indicate the access device; in this case, we always include a qualification (such as a "thin client").

Also Citizen (the latter in the case of a government organization).   The client is not necessarily the user of the product, the process, or the activity. They can be external or internal with regard to the organization. In the latter case, unless there is an in-house "transfer pricing" system, the internal client does not pay for the product, service, or activity, but only uses it. Clients must be regarded as a reason for the process to exist, rather than just as the recipient of the outputs of the process.

Client self-service   Features that allow clients to provision, manage, modify, and terminate services themselves, via a web interface or programmatic calls to service APIs, without involving the vendor.

Cloud   A metaphor for a global network. It was initially used to refer to the telephone network. It is now commonly used to refer to cloud services or to the Internet as a whole.

Cloud app   Short for Cloud Application. Cloud App is the phrase used to describe a software application that is not installed on a local computer. It is accessed via the network (normally the Internet). It represents the top layer of the Cloud Pyramid. An app is run and interacted with via a web browser or similar; it is tightly controlled, leaving only limited possibilities for modifications. It can be usually parameterized. Examples are Gmail or SalesForce.com.

Cloud arcs   Short for cloud architectures. They are the designs for systems that can be accessed and used over the cloud.

Cloud as a service (CaaS)   A cloud service that has been opened up into a platform that others can build upon.

Cloud bridge   Running an application in such a way that its components are integrated within multiple cloud environments, which could be any combination of private and public clouds.

Cloud broker (also cloud service broker or cloud computing broker)   A broker matches clients requirements and multiple vendors of cloud services. He is supposed to select the best vendor for each client and monitor its services.

Cloud burst   This refers to what happens when a cloud has an outage or security breach and the systems become unavailable. The term "cloudburst" can be used in two ways: – Positive The dynamic deployment of a software application that runs on internal organizational computer resources to a public cloud to address a spike in demand; – Negative The failure of a cloud computing environment as a result of its inability to handle a spike in demand.

Cloud bursting   Cloud bursting is a technique used by hybrid clouds to provide additional resources to private clouds on an as-needed basis. If the private cloud has the resources to handle its workloads, the hybrid cloud is not used. When workloads in the private cloud exceed a certain threshold, the public cloud provides the additional resources needed.

Cloud center   A data center in the cloud using standards-based virtualized components as a data center-like infrastructure. An example would be a large organization, such as Amazon, that provides the infrastructure.

Cloud client   Computing device for accessing cloud services. Updated version of a thin client.

Cloud computing   A computing capability that provides an abstraction between the computing resource and its underlying technical architecture (for instance, servers, storage, networks). It enables convenient, on-demand network access to a shared pool of configurable computing resources. These resources can be rapidly provisioned and released with minimal management effort or vendor interaction. Cloud computing has six essential characteristics: pay-per-use, self service, broad network access, resource pooling, rapid elasticity, and measured service. In general, cloud computing enables Infrastructure as a Service (IaaS), Platform as a Service (PaaS), Software as a Service (SaaS), and Business Process as a Service (BPaaS). Cloud computing means that the infrastructure, platforms, applications, and organization processes can be delivered to an (internal or external) client as a service, over the Internet (or in general over a telecommunication network).

Cloud computing maturity model (CCMM)   Defines five stages by which an organization system can migrate to cloud computing: consolidation, virtualization, automation, utility, and cloud.

Cloud computing reseller   An organization that purchases cloud services from a vendor and then re-sells them to its own clients.

Cloud enablement   The process of making available one or more of the services and infrastructures to create a public cloud computing environment, consisting of a cloud vendor, services, and clients.

Cloud enabler   Refers to organizations that are not cloud vendors *per se*, but make available technology that enables cloud computing. Refers also to a vendor that provides technology, infrastructure, or services that enable a client or another vendor to use cloud computing.

Cloud envy   Describes a vendor that offers cloud services by re-branding existing services.

Cloud governance and compliance   Governance defines who is responsible for what, and the policies, processes, and procedures that an organization needs to follow. Cloud governance requires governing the organization's own infrastructure and/or infrastructure that the organization does not totally control. Cloud governance has three key components: understanding compliance and risk, organization performance goals, and related controls.

Cloud hosting A type of internet hosting where the client leases virtualized, dynamically scalable infrastructure on an as-needed basis. Users frequently have the choice of operating systems and other infrastructure components. Normally cloud hosting is self-service, billed hourly or monthly, and interfaced and controlled via a web interface or API.

Cloud infrastructure The bottom layer – or foundation – of the Cloud Pyramid is the delivery of computer infrastructure through virtualization. It includes servers, storage, networks, and other hardware appliances delivered as either Infrastructure Web Services or "cloud centers". At this level, full control of the infrastructure is available. Examples include GoGrid or Amazon Web Services.

Cloud manageability The provision of a consistent view across both on-premises and cloud-based environments. It includes managing the asset provisioning as well as the quality of service (QOS) that the vendor provides to its client.

Cloud management Software, technologies and methods aimed at operating and monitoring the applications, data, and services residing in the cloud. From the vendor perspective, these are the cloud management tools that help ensure that the cloud services provided by a vendor are working optimally, interacting properly, and correctly measuring the usage with the clients, the users, and other services, applications, or systems.

Cloud migration The process of transitioning all or part of an organization's data, applications and services from on-site premises behind the firewall to the cloud. Once this process has been completed, the data, application, or services can be provided over the Internet or a network on an on-demand basis.

Cloud network See Cloud Storm.

Cloud operating system A computer operating system that is specially designed to run in a vendor's data center and be delivered to the client over the Internet or another network. Windows Azure is an example of a cloud operating system or "cloud layer" that runs on Windows Server. The term is also used to refer to cloud-based client operating systems such as Google's Chrome OS.

Cloud-oriented architecture A term coined by Jeff Barr at Amazon Web Services. to describe an architecture where applications act as services in the cloud and serve other applications in the cloud environment.

Cloud platform The middle layer of the Cloud Pyramid. It provides a computing platform or framework (for instance .NET, Ruby on Rails, or Python) as a service or stack.

Cloud portability The capability to move platforms, applications, and/or their associated data across cloud computing environments to and from different cloud vendors, as well as across private clouds or internal systems and public clouds. It is the opposite of vendor lock in.

Cloud provisioning The deployment of an organization's cloud computing strategy. It typically involves first the selection of which applications and services will reside in the public cloud and which will remain in house behind the firewall or in the private cloud. Cloud provisioning also includes developing the processes for interfacing with the cloud systems, applications, and services as well as auditing, monitoring, and measuring who accesses and utilizes the cloud resources.

Cloud pyramid   A visual representation of cloud computing tiers where differing segments are broken down by functionality. A simplified version includes three tiers: Infrastructure, Platform, and Application.

Cloud security   The same security principles that apply to on-site computing apply to cloud computing security. In a certain number of cases, it is necessary to take into account the network connection, multi-tenancy, and the absence of an internal firewall.

Cloud server hosting   Hosting services are made available to clients on demand via the Internet. Rather than being provided by a single server or virtual server, cloud server hosting services are provided by multiple connected servers in the cloud.

Cloud servers   Virtualized servers that can run diverse operating systems. They are instantiated via a web interface or API. Cloud servers behave in the same manner as physical ones. They can be controlled at an administrator or root level, depending on the system type and cloud vendor.

Cloud service   A service in the cloud sold by a vendor with the model of cloud computing.

Cloud service architecture   The term describes an architecture in which applications and application components act as services on the cloud, serving other applications within the same cloud environment.

Cloud sourcing   Procuring some types of cloud services.

Cloud standards   A standard is an agreed approach for doing something. Cloud standards ensure interoperability. They make it possible to take tools, applications, resources and more, and use them in another cloud environment without having to carry out substantial rework. They are also important for the interfacing of different systems.

Cloud storage   This service allows clients to save data by transferring it via the Internet or another network to a remote storage system(s).

Cloud storm   The connection of multiple cloud computing environments. It is also called a "cloud network".

Cloud vendors   Vendors whose products/services are based on virtualization of computing resources and a utility-based payment model within a cloud computing framework. They can be either external or internal to the organization.

Cloudware   Refers to a variety of software, normally at the infrastructure or platform level, that enables building, deploying, running, or managing applications in a cloud computing environment.

Cloud washing   The use of "cloud" to describe an organization's existing products and services which are not really in a cloud computing model.

Cluster   In this book, a group of linked computers that work together as if they were a single computer, for high availability and/or load balancing.

Community cloud   A cloud shared by several organizations. It supports a specific community with shared concerns (similar sector, mission, security requirements, policy, or compliance considerations). It may be managed by the organization or by a third party. It may exist on or off premises.

Compliance   Respect for, and abiding by, the internal and external rules of the organization.

Compliance risk management   A discipline that supports the organization in the definition, management and compliance monitoring of the organization's conduct with respect to legal provisions and regulations and business rules. There are many people dealing with this subject within an organization. They include:– Managers and employees who work in the Compliance Department.– Employees who operate in different business functions (Legal, Organization, Risk Management, Internal Audit, and so on) involved in the management or supervision of the stages of compliance risk management.

Computer-aided software engineering (CASE)   A way of building software using scientific methods, with the aim of producing a high quality product.

Computer-assisted audit techniques (CAAT)   An auditing method assisted by computer applications. It includes analysis and tests performed with generic software to facilitate auditing.

Configuration management (CM)   A process to establish and maintain consistency of a product's performance and functional and physical parameters or attributes with its requirements, design, and operational information throughout its life. In the case of cloud computing, it is also the ability to federate configuration data for services.

Consumption-based pricing model   A pricing model whose vendor charges its clients based on the amount of the services the client uses, rather than a fee based on time and materials or a fixed price. For example, a cloud storage vendor might charge per gigabyte of information stored on average or at the peak of a specific period. See also subscription-based pricing model.

Content delivery network (CDN)   A system consisting of multiple computers that contain copies of data. They are in different locations within the network so that clients can access the copy closest to them.

Control objectives for information and related technology (COBIT)   A method of ICT governance.

Customer relationship management (CRM)   An information system for managing customer relationships. This is a tool to manage the whole customer life cycle, from the acquisition of new customers to the growing of the relationships with the most relevant ones, to building loyalty with the customers who have stronger relations, whether actual or potential, with the organization. It allows relationships with customers to be optimized by increasing loyalty, selling more products and services, and so on.

Data as a service (DaaS)   Used to make external data available on a pay-per-use basis.

Database   A set of computer files organized in such a way to be rapidly accessible.

Data in the cloud   Managing data in the cloud requires data security and privacy, including controls for moving data from one point to another. It also includes managing data storage and the resources for large-scale data processing (now called Big Data).

Detection and forensics   Separating legitimate from illegitimate activity, before or after a break in security.

Disruptive innovation   An innovation that improves products or services in significant ways and changes both the way things are done and the market itself. Cloud computing has been called a disruptive innovation; it has the potential to completely change the way ICT services are procured, deployed, used, and maintained. In fact, cloud computing can also support the fundamental changes of products and processes of the organization.

Durability   A measure of how likely the data is to be lost.

Dynamic resource pooling   Allows a vendor's computing resources to be pooled to serve multiple clients using a multitenant model with different physical and virtual resources (such as storage, processing, or memory). The resources can be dynamically assigned and re-assigned according to the organization's requirements.

Elastic computing   The ability to dynamically provision and de-provision processing, memory, and storage resources to meet demands of peak usage without worrying about capacity planning and engineering for peak usage.

Elasticity   The ability for a given resource to grow. Resource allocation can get bigger or smaller depending on demand.

EN 9000   The European norms for ISO 9000.

Encryption   Coding to protect information assets.

Enterprise application   Applications or software that a business would use to support the activities, functions, or processes of an organization. When "enterprise" is juxtaposed with "application," this usually refers to a software platform that is large and complex.

Enterprise content management (ECM)   The management of all content (data, unstructured documents, email, voice, video, and so on).

Enterprise information management (EIM)   The management of all information of an organization. It includes Extraction Loading Transformation (ETL) tools, Data Warehouse and Business Intelligence.

Enterprise resource planning (ERP)   The extension of MRP II to the remaining functions in the organization, such as engineering, finance, and personnel administration and management. It consists of a software package with a single data model that facilitates the horizontal and vertical integration of all inter-organizational processes, improves process efficiency and monitors processes through special KPI (Key Performance Indicators) according to quality, service levels, and timeliness. Some components of ERP are accounting, industrial accounting, payrolls, sourcing, warehouse management, production, project control, sales, distribution, and facility maintenance

E-procurement   A tool to manage the procurement cycle with the integration of B2B (Business -to-business) vendors. It integrates the acquisition process and minimizes transaction costs to the client, simplifying the flows for the client and for the vendor, thanks to access to a larger, possibly open, market.

Extended enterprise resource planning (EERP) An ERP evolution, adding tools to control connected third parties (such as controlled companies, resellers, clients, agencies, suppliers, and so on).

External cloud Public, community or virtual private cloud services provided by a third party external to the organization. It is a cloud computing environment external to the boundaries of the organization.

Federal risk and Authorization management program (FedRAMP) A US government-wide program that provides a standardized approach to security assessment, authorization, and continuous monitoring for cloud products and services.

Federation The act of combining data or identities across multiple systems. Federation can be carried out by a cloud vendor or by a cloud broker.

Force.com Force.com is the Platform as a Service (PaaS) offered by Salesforce.com.

Funnel cloud Discussion about cloud computing that goes round and round but never turns into action.

Google app engine A service that enables developers to create and run web applications on Google's infrastructure and share their applications via a pay-per-use plan with no setup costs or recurring fees.

Google apps Google's SaaS offering. It currently includes an office productivity suite, email, and document sharing, as well as Google Talk for instant messaging, Google Calendar and Google Docs. It can also include storage, security, and backup services (see Google websites for a description of these modules).

Governance Governance refers to the controls and processes that ensure the effectiveness, efficiency, economics and ethics (compliance) of a sector.

Hadoop An open-source, software framework that supports the processing of large datasets in a distributed computing environment. It enables applications to work with thousands of nodes and petabytes of data.

Hardware as a service (HaaS) See Infrastructure as a Service.

Hosted Application A network-based application software program that runs on a remote server. It can be accessed via a network-connected PC or thin client. See also SaaS.

Hybrid cloud Combines aspects of both public and private clouds. It enables data and application portability (such as cloud bursting for load balancing between clouds).

Hybrid cloud storage A combination of public and private cloud storage where critical data resides in the organization's own private cloud while other data is stored by and is accessible from a public cloud storage vendor.

IBM cloud Refers to a collection of enterprise class technologies and services developed to help clients assess their cloud readiness, develop adoption strategies, and identify organization entry points for a cloud environment. IBM's cloud computing strategy is based on a hybrid cloud model that focuses on integrating the private cloud services of an organization with public clouds.

IBM smart business IBM's cloud solutions, which currently include IBM Smart Business Test Cloud, IBM Smart Analytics Cloud, IBM Smart Business Storage Cloud, IBM Information Archive, IBM Lotus Live, and IBM LotusLive iNotes (see IBM website for a description of these modules).

Identity management Managing personal identity information so that access to computer resources, applications, data, and services is controlled properly.

Information technology infrastructure library (ITIL) A globally recognized collection of best practices for ICT service management.

Information technology and telecommunication The combination of computers, storage, network, applications, and so on to provide integrated services.

Infrastructure as a service (IaaS) Cloud infrastructure services or Infrastructure as a Service delivers computer infrastructure, typically virtualized, as a service. Rather than purchasing servers, software, storage, data center space, or network equipment, clients rent those resources as a fully outsourced service. The service is typically billed on a utility computing basis and according to the amount of resources consumed. It is an evolution of web hosting and virtual private server offerings.

Integration The process of combining components or systems into an integrated combined entity.

Intercloud A global cloud of clouds, similar in concept to the Internet being a global network of networks. See also Intracloud.

Internal cloud A type of private cloud whose services are provided by an ICT department of its own organization.

Internet protocol (IP) A mechanism by which packets may be routed between devices on a network of networks. IP allows computers to be connected using various physical media ranging from modems to Ethernet cabling, fiber optic cables and even satellite and radio links.

Internet protocol security (IPsec) A framework for a set of protocols for security at the network or packet-processing layer of network communication.

Interoperability The ability of systems to operate in multiple environments.

Intracloud A cloud of clouds consisting of only private clouds.

ISO 9000 A set of standards for quality, quality assurance, and continuous quality improvement. It is managed by the International Organization for Standardization (ISO).

ISO 9001 ISO quality standards terminology: This standard includes criteria for the assurance of quality regarding design, development, implementation, installation, and assistance.

ISO 9002 ISO quality standards terminology: This standard includes criteria for the assurance of quality regarding development, implementation, installation, and assistance.

ISO 9003 ISO quality standards terminology: This standard includes criteria for the assurance of quality in final controls and tests.

ISO 9004 ISO standard terminology: This standard includes criteria related to organization management for quality and the organization quality systems.

IT service management (ITSM) A discipline for managing ICT systems that is in principle centered on the organization's perspective of ICT's contribution to the entity.

Know your customer (KYC) Applications used to know the customer better, using data available internally or externally to the organization.

LAMP A solution stack of free open-source software for web-based applications: Linux, Apache, MySQL and PHP. See also: Open Source Software.

Lean and digitize Make the process simultaneously lean and automated. This is the method suggested in this book to approach cloud computing, based on re-engineering the process to make it lean, and at the same time to automate wherever and whenever it is necessary.

Linearity How a system performs as the load increases.

Linux An open source operating system. In its many and varied distributions, it is one of the predominant operating systems for cloud computing.

Load balancing Balancing the load between different entities (which could be servers, storage, network, or applications).

Mashup A web-based application that combines data and/or functionality from multiple sources.

Measured service Cloud systems leverage a metering capability appropriate to the type of cloud service provided (storage, processing, bandwidth, active user accounts, and so on). Resource usage can be monitored, controlled and reported, providing visibility for both the vendor and the client of the services used.

Middleware Software located between applications and operating systems. It consists of a set of services that enable interoperability in support of distributed architectures by moving data between applications. For example, the data in a certain database can be accessed through another database.

Milestone The end of one of more activities, marking the completion of a work package or phase.

Mission The mission is the way to proceed towards the Vision.

Mobile cloud storage A form of cloud storage that applies to storing an individual's mobile device data in the cloud and providing the individual with access to the data from anywhere.

Multitenancy Multitenancy is the property of multiple systems, applications or data from different organizations hosted on the same physical hardware. Multitenancy is common to most cloud-based systems.

Multitenant In cloud computing, multitenant is the expression used to describe multiple clients using the same cloud.

MySQL   Open source SQL database software.

National institute of standards and technology (NIST)   NIST is a USA Department of Commerce agency that among other stated responsibilities promotes effective and secure use of cloud computing within organizations.

Network virtualization   A method that combines the available resources in a network by dividing the available bandwidth into channels. Each channel is independent of the others. Each one can be assigned (or reassigned) to a particular server or device in real time.

Norms   Legal principles accepted by the community from which no derogation is permitted. In this book, it is also an alternative to the word "standardization".

On-demand self-service   This feature is an essential cloud characteristic that allows a client to unilaterally and automatically provision computing capabilities such as server time and network storage as needed, without requiring human interaction by the vendor. IBM initially introduced the expression "on demand".

On-demand service   A model by which a client can purchase cloud services as needed. For example, if clients need to use additional resources for the duration of a project, they can do so and then drop back to the previous level after the project is completed.

OpenNebula   An open source toolkit for building public, private, and hybrid clouds.

Open source software   Open source software (as an alternative to commercial software whose code is kept secret), is software whose source code is published and made available to the public, enabling anyone to copy, modify, use, and improve the software.

Organization   In this book, this term indicates an institution, a company, a public institution, either central or local, or a non-profit entity.

Output   The result produced by a system or process. The final output is a product or a service.

Pareto principle   This principle states that 20% of the few "vital" elements justify the 80% of the consequences regarding the many "trivial" elements. It was introduced by Vilfredo Pareto, an Italian economist, in the 19th century and popularized by Juran.

Pay-as-you-go   See Pay-per-use.

Pay-per-use   A pricing model for cloud services that encompasses both subscription-based and consumption-based models, whereas the traditional ICT cost model requires up-front capital expenditure for hardware and software and payment of a maintenance fee.

Personal cloud   Synonymous with MiFi, a personal wireless router; it takes a mobile wireless data signal and translates it into Wi-Fi. Apple introduced a service called iCloud.

Personal cloud storage   A form of cloud storage that applies to storing an individual's data in the cloud. It provides the individual with access to the data from anywhere. Personal cloud storage also often enables synchronizing and sharing stored data across multiple devices such as mobile phones and tablets.

Plan-do-check-act (PDCA) An improvement cycle introduced by Deming. It is based on the sequence of actions stated.

Platform as a service (PaaS) Cloud platform services, where the computing platform (operating system and associated resources) is delivered as a service over the network (usually the Internet) by a vendor.

Policy Typically, a principle or rule to guide decisions and achieve rational outcomes. In large organizations, policies are codified and published.

Portability The ability to run applications, components, or systems on one implementation and then deploy it on another implementation, for instance that of another vendor.

Private cloud This is operated solely for an organization or a legal group of organizations (such as a holding). It may be managed by the organization or a third party. It may exist on or off premises. A private cloud can also be hosted on a public cloud infrastructure; in this case, it is also called a Virtual Private Cloud.

Private cloud storage A form of cloud storage where both the organization data and cloud storage resources reside within the organization's data center and behind its firewall.

Process A set of connected activities that transforms a set of inputs into one or more results. Sometimes a process is identified with a system, but in fact it would be more correct to consider it as a system component.

Process control The action of making and keeping a process consistent with its specifications.

Process improvement A continuous effort to learn from the causes and effects in a process, aiming at reducing the complexity, the variation, and the cycle time. It is obtained by improving and eliminating wrong causes and then by redesigning the process in order to reduce the root causes of the most common variations.

Process management A method used to optimize the organization as a system, determine which processes need to be improved and/or controlled, define priorities, and encourage leadership to initiate and sustain process improvement efforts. It manages the information obtained from these processes.

Program A computer program (also software, or just a program) is a sequence of instructions written to perform a specified task with a computer.

Project charter Describes the problem, defines the objectives, outlines the organization, and plans the project's main activities.

Project teams Groups of people coming from the same sector or, ideally, from different sectors, who work on defined activities during a defined period and normally within a limited budget.

Public cloud This service is made available to the general community or a large industry group. A vendor selling cloud services owns and/or manages a public cloud.

Public cloud storage   A form of cloud storage. In it, the organization and storage vendor are separate and the data is stored outside the organization's data center.

Quality   This concept is not easily defined because there are many variations, sometimes determined by an adjective or specifications. In general, quality relates to the client's satisfaction in a way that is profitable for the organization.

Quality assurance   The set of planned systematic actions required to appropriately assure that a product or a service complies with the predefined quality requirements.

Quality control   The operative tools and activities used to monitor and satisfy quality requirements.

Rapid application development (RAD)   A software development methodology that uses minimal planning in favor of rapid prototyping.

Rapid elasticity   This feature allows capabilities to be provisioned rapidly and elastically, in some cases automatically, to quickly scale up and scale down as needed.

Really simple syndication (RSS)   A family of web feed formats used to publish frequently updated information, such as blog entries, news headlines, audio, and video, in a standardized format.

Reliability   Measures the percentage of time the service is available.

Roaming workloads   The backend product of cloud centers.

Salesforce.com   An online cloud computing organization that is best known for delivering Customer Relationship Management (CRM) software to companies over the Internet.

Scalability   This means that the cloud can scale upward for peak demand and downward for lighter demand. Scalability also means that an application can scale when changing the number of users and when application requirements change.

Self-service provisioning   Using this system, cloud clients can provision cloud services without going through a lengthy process. They can automatically request an amount of computing, storage, software, process, or more from the vendor's resources. After they have used these resources, they can be automatically de-provisioned. The client is charged only for the use of the resources.

Server virtualization   This form of virtualization facilitates the masking of server resources, including the number and identity of individual physical servers, processors, and operating systems, from the resource users. A similar technology can be potentially applied to any physical component.

Service level agreement (SLA)   A contractual agreement by which a vendor and a client agree the level of service, responsibilities, priorities, penalties, and guarantees regarding availability, performance, and other aspects of the service(s).

Service migration   The act of moving from one cloud service or vendor to another.

Service-oriented architecture (SOA)   An ICT architecture based on the use of "services", components of information systems reusable in different applications and platforms.

Single sign-on   The ability to federate logins based on credentials. It allows a user to login once and access multiple applications/systems based on his/her profile.

Six sigma   A philosophy and a performance objective. As a method, it is a structured team approach for the continuous improvement of processes. The objective is a measure of process performance defined in terms of defects, with 3.4 defective parts per million.

Society for worldwide interbank financial telecommunications (SWIFT)   Global communication network that facilitates continuous and secure international exchange of payment instructions between banks, central banks, multinational corporations, and major securities firms.

Software as a service (SaaS)   Cloud application services where applications are delivered over the network (normally Internet) by the vendor. With SaaS, the applications do not need to be purchased, installed, and run on the client's computers. Examples of SaaS include customer relationship management as a service as offered by, for example, Salesforce.com, or email services as offered by, for instance, Google.

Sponsor   This term is used to define the role of a member of the top management in charge of supervising and supporting an event, a program, or a project.

Stakeholder   This term indicates a party or person interested in the project.

Standardized interfaces   Standardization of interfaces between cloud services; instructions are provided on how two or more applications or data sources can communicate among themselves. A standardized interface lets the client link cloud services together more easily and rapidly.

Steering committee   Includes the representatives of the top management, the project leader, and the facilitators. Its main responsibilities are to manage the efforts for process improvement, assess needs, supervise, support, educate and train, communicate progress to stakeholders, and guide the efforts made to improve the process.

Storage area network (SAN)   A dedicated network providing access to consolidated, block level data storage. SANs are primarily used to make storage devices, such as disk arrays, tape libraries, optical jukeboxes, and other devices, accessible to servers so that the possible remote or in-the-cloud devices appear as though they are locally attached to the operating system.

Storage cloud   Refers to the collection of multiple distributed and connected resources responsible for storing data online in the cloud.

Storage virtualization   This form of virtualization allows the pooling of physical storage from multiple network storage devices into what appears to be a single storage device. It can be managed from a central console. Storage virtualization is commonly used in a Storage Area Network (SAN).

Straight through processing (STP)   The process that enables the entire trade process for capital markets and payment transactions to be conducted electronically, without the need for re-keying or manual interventions, subject to legal and regulatory restrictions. This concept has also been transferred into other sectors, including insurance, banking, and financial services.

Subscription-based pricing model Lets clients pay a fee to use the service for a specific period. It is mainly used for SaaS services. See also Consumption-based pricing model.

System According to Deming: "A network of interacting components which cooperates for achieving the goals of the system." It could also represent the organizations as a set of clients, or vendors or as a flow of materials and information.

System to system (S2S) A computer to computer interface.

Technical rules Compulsory indications for technical standardization or compliance.

Telematics Synergy of telecommunications and informatics. In this book, it is synonymous with ICT.

Throughput The measure of how quickly the service responds.

Total cost of ownership (TCO) A metric taking into account the cost throughout the life cycle of the solution it refers to.

Trust The ability of two parties to define a trust relationship with a formal authentication of the two parties.

Unified collaboration and communication systems or Unified Collaborative Communication (UCC) Solutions based initially on voice. They focus on embedding different types of communication and collaboration into business processes. UCC solutions should be software-based, open, and extensible, and support customer choice of services.

Universal product code (UPC) A standard used to name products in a unique way.

Utility computing Online computing or storage sold as a metered, commercial or otherwise, service in a way similar to a public utility.

Value Value is defined by the end client. Conceptually, it is the relationship between benefits and cost/risks of a product or service. It is expressed in terms of a product/service that can meet the client's demands at a given price and at a given moment. It is also possible to refer to value as perceived by client, seeing all the product/service characteristics that the client considers as necessary and valuable. Any activity that consumes resources (including time) and does not bring value to the client or to the organization is waste (*muda* in Japanese).

Value analysis An organizational technique that allows alternative solutions to be reached at the lowest cost.

Value engineering Value analysis applied to design.

Value flow The set of activities required to design, order, produce and deliver a given product or supply a given service. These activities cover the total product/service throughput time in the organization up to the delivery to the end client. The objective of value flow analysis is to categorize the activities.

Vendor A person or organization that provides goods, systems or services for use in a process such as public clouds. In the case of the private cloud, the "vendor" is part of the organization.

Vendor lock in   Dependency on a specific public cloud vendor, and difficulty moving from one cloud vendor to another due to lack of standardized protocols, APIs, data structures (schema), service models, or contractual clauses.

Vertical cloud   A cloud computing environment optimized for use in a particular industry, such as financial services, health care, or logistics.

Virtual machine (VM)   A file (typically called an image) that when executed looks to the user like an actual machine. Infrastructure as a Service is often provided as a VM image that can be started or terminated as needed.

Virtual private cloud (VPC)   A term coined by Reuven Cohen, CEO and founder of Enomaly. The term describes a concept similar to, and derived from, the concept of a Virtual Private Network (VPN). It is applied to cloud computing, and it refers to turning a public cloud into a virtual private cloud. It allows a secure VPC to be created across components that are both within the cloud and external to it. For instance, the Amazon VPC allows Amazon EC2 to connect to legacy infrastructure on an IPsec VPN.

Virtual private data center   A data center in which system resources are grouped according to the objectives of the specific organization.

Virtual security   Refers to the proper use of virtualization technologies in the cloud. It makes it possible to develop a security infrastructure secure from access by unauthorized users.

Virtualized desktop infrastructure (VDI)   Refers to the separation of a user's desktop – operating system, applications and associated data – from a specific physical machine. It runs as a virtualized desktop on central servers. Users can access their virtualized desktops from any number of devices, including any PC connected to the network, smartphone, tablet, or, in most cases, a thin client.

Vision   An expression of what would represent success for an organization. The objective is to produce a mental image to aim at, generating creative tensions between the current reality and the vision in the organization. In order to be valuable, the vision must be shared by the whole organization; this can require great effort and much patience. The mission is the way to proceed towards the vision.

Voice of the customer (VoC)   The voice of the client, or of the citizen in the case of public organizations.

Windows azure   Microsoft cloud services that provide the platform as a service (see PaaS). It allows developers to create cloud applications and services.

Windows live services   Microsoft's cloud-based client applications, which currently include Windows Live Mail, Windows Live Photo Gallery, Windows Live Calendar, Windows Live Events, Windows Live SkyDrive, Windows Live Spaces, Windows Live Messenger, Windows Live Writer, and Windows Live for Mobile (see Microsoft website for a description of these modules).

Work.com   The HR application offered by Salesforce.com.

Bibliography

Books and Articles

—— (2009) "Cloud computing: clash of the clouds," *The Economist*, October 15, http://www.economist.com/node/14637206, Retrieved January 15, 2013.

—— (2011) "Il mercato dei pagamenti italiano e le opportunità offerte dal nuovo decennio," *BancaMatica*, April, pp. 50–51.

——(2011) "IT transformation con l'outsourcing," *Executive.it*, Febraury, pp. 84–85.

——(2011) "L'attualità dell'outsourcing," *Aziendabanca*, March, pp. 74–79.

——(2011) "Ripensare il modello di gestione," *Banca Finanza*, March, pp. 64–66.

"Amazon gets SAS 70 Type II audit stamp, but analysts not satisfied." SearchCloudComputing.com. 2009–11–17, Retrieved August 22, 2010.

"FISMA compliance for federal cloud computing on the horizon in 2010." SearchCompliance.com, Retrieved August 22, 2010.

—— (2002) "NIST: FISMA Overview." Csrc.nist.gov, Retrieved April 27, 2012.

—— (2011) "I nuovi servizi bancari? Li sviluppa il cliente," *BancaForte*, August, http://www.BancaForte.it/articolo/i-nuovi-servizi-bancari-l i-sviluppa-il-cliente-RB45856k, Retrieved August 11, 2012.

—— (2011) "Digital Agenda Italia," *e-Gov 2010 Report Italy*.

—— (2011) "Adoption, approaches and attitudes: the future of cloud computing in the public and private sectors," *Redschift Research*, http://www.amd.com/us/ Documents/Cloud-Adoption-Approaches-and-Attitudes-Research-Report.pdf, Retrieved January 15, 2013.

A. G. (2010) "In partnership con il fornitore," *AziendaBanca*, August, pp. 38–55.

A. G. (2011) "Il core banking: un rinnovamento strategico," *AziendaBanca*, March, pp. 34–43.

A.G. (2011) "Un nuovo workflow per il cliente 2.0," *AziendaBanca*, August, pp. 50.

Anderson, J. Q. and Rainie, L. (2010) *The future of cloud computing*, Washington, Pew Research Center's, http://pewinternet.org/Reports/2010/The-future-of-cloud-computing.aspx, Retrieved August 12, 2012.

Armbrust, M. (2009) "Above the clouds: a Berkeley view of cloud computing, February 10, http://www.eecs.berkeley.edu/Pubs/TechRpts/2009/EECS-2009-28. html, Retrieved August 12, 2012.

Arora, P. et al. (2011) *To the Cloud: Cloud Powering an Enterprise*, McGraw-Hill, New York, NY. USA.

Attanasio, S. (2010) "ICT spendere," *BancaForte*, July/August, p. 36.

Aymerich, F. M., Fenu, G., and Surcis, S. (2008) "An approach to a cloud computing network," *First International Conference on the Applications of Digital Information and Web Technologies*, August 4–6, pp. 113–118.

Bentlon, D. and Negm, W. (2010) *Banking on the Cloud*, Accenture http://www.accenture.com/us-en/Pages/insight-cloud-computing-banking-summary.aspx, Retrieved May 26, 2011.

Bonaretti, M. (2011) *Governare la rete: dalle parole ai fatti*, Edizioni Forum PA – Collana Materiali, Giu.

Bucci, P. (2010) "La spesa ICT nelle Banche," *Data Manager*, October, pp. 150–158.

Buyya, R., Broberg, J., and Goschinki, M. (2011) *Cloud Computing: Principles and Paradigms*, Wiley, Hoboken, NJ, USA, p. 664.

Buyya, R., Yeo, C. S., Venugopal, S., Broberg, J., and Brandic, I. (2009) "Cloud computing and emerging IT platforms: Vision, hype, and reality for delivering computing as the fifth utility," *Future Generation Computer Systems*, June, 25 (6).

Campidoglio, E. (2011) "Una firma garantita dall'identità biometrica," *BancaMatica*, April, pp. 88–90.

Cavallini, M. (2011) "II [2011] cloud security: una sfida per il futuro," *Quaderni Consip*, Ministero Economia e Finanze, Roma, Italy.

Cerruti, C., Pacini, V., and Piga, G. (2008) "L'esternalizzazione dei processi gestionali," *Il Sole24Ore*, Milano, Italy.

Chiacchierini, E. (2003) *Tecnologia and Produzione*, Edizioni Kappa, Roma, Italy.

Choo, K. R. (2011) "Cloud computing risks," *Information Age*, January–Feabraury.

Chorafas, D. N. (2011) *Cloud Computing Strategies*, CRC Press Taylor and Francis Group.

Chou, T. (2010) *Introduction to Cloud Computing: Business and Technology*, Kindle Edition.

Chrissis, M. B., Konrad, M. D., and Shrum, S. (2011) "CMMI for development: guidelines for process integration and product improvement," 3rd Edition, Addison-Wesley Professional, Boston, MA, USA.

CIPA and ABI (2010) *Indagine sull'utilizzo dell'ICT in gruppi bancari europei con articolazione internazionale*, http://www.abi.it/doc/129225836259095_g__servizi_1.pdf, Retrieved August 25, 2011.

CIPA e ABI (2011) *Rilevazione dello stato dell'automazione del sistema creditizio*, May, Roma, Italy,http://www.cipa.it/docs/rileva/eser10/Pubblicazione_Rilevazione_economica_2010.pdf, Retrieved July 25, 2011.

CIPA, Segreteria della Convenzione Interbancaria per i Problemi dell'Automazione (2011) *Piano delle attività in materia di automazione interbancaria e sistema dei pagamenti. Periodo 1.1.2011–30.6.2012*, http://www.cipa.it/attivita/piano2011.pdf, Retrieved August 25, 2011.

Cloud Computing. Strategic considerations for banking and financial institutions (2010) "White paper, Tata Consulting Services," http://www.tcs.com/resources/white_papers/Pages/Cloud-Computing-Strategic-Considerations-for-Banking-and-Financial-Institutions.aspx, Retrieved July 13, 2011.

De Ferrari, F. (2010) *Outsourcing Strategico. Flessibilizzare l'IT Senza Perdere il Controllo*, ZeroUno, Milano, Italy, 2 December, http://www.zerounoweb.it/index.php?option=com_contentandtask=viewandid=4574andItemid=192 Retrieved July 7, 2011.

De Piano, L. (2010) "L'evoluzione dell'outsourcing," *Data Manager*, May, pp.114–124.

EMC2, *The Cloud Dividend: Part Two. The economic benefits of cloud computing to business and the wider EMEA economy. Comparative analysis of the impact on aggregated industry sectors*, February 2011, Centre for Economics and Business Research, http://www.globbtv.com/microsite/35/Adjuntos/CLOUD-DIVIDEND-REPORT.PDF, Retrieved August 12, 2012.

ENISA (2009) *Cloud Computing Risk Assessment,* http://www.enisa.europa.eu/activities/risk-management/files/deliverables/cloud-computing-risk-assessment, Retrieved January 15, 2013.

ENISA (2011) *Security and Resilience in Governmental Cloud*, http://www.enisa.europa.eu/activities/risk-management/emerging-and-future-risk/deliverables/security-and-resilience-in-governmental-clouds, Retrieved January 15, 2013.

Europe's Digital Competitiveness Report (Annual Report 2009).

Fingar, P. (2009) *Dot Cloud: The 21st Century Business Platform Built on Cloud Computing*, Meghan-Kiffer Press, Tampa, Fl, USA.

Fondati, P. (2011) "Tecnologie in banca: ecco le priorità per il 2011," *Il Sole 24 Ore*, March 24, http://www.ilsole24ore.com/art/tecnologie/2011-03-24/tecnologie-banca-ecco-priorita-175832.shtml?uuid=AaBunEJD, Retrieved August 21, 2011.

Fountain, J. E. (2001) *Building the Virtual State: Information Technology and Institutional Change*, The Brookings Institute, Washington, DC, USA.

G. R. (2011) "Il risk management e la sfida di Basilea 3," *Azienda Banca*, May, pp.62–67.

Gray, P. (2006) *Manager's Guide to Making Decisions about Information Systems*, Wiley, Hoboken, NJ, USA.

Harms, R. and Yamartino, M. (2010) *L'economia della Cloud*, November, White paper Microsoft, http://download.microsoft.com/download/1/F/6/.../Economia_Cloud.pdf.

Henderson, J. C. and Venkatraman, N. (1999) "Strategic alignment: leveraging information technology for transforming organisations, *IBM Systems Journal*, 38 (2–3), pp. 472–484.

Hume, D. et al. (2012) *Report of the Cloud Computing Working Group*, The Law Society of British Columbia.

IBM (2011) *The Essential CIO. Banking Industry highlights*, white paper, May, http://www-935.ibm.com/services/c-suite/cio/study.html, Retrieved May 1, 2012.

Jaeger, P., Lin, J., and Grimes, J. (2008) "Cloud computing and information policy: computing in a policy cloud?" *Journal of Information Technology and Politics*, 5 (3).

Johnston, E. (2010) *Governance infrastructure in 2020*, December.

Koulopoulos, T. H. (2012) *Cloud Surfing*, Bibliomotion, Brookline, MA, USA.

Kundra, V. (2010) *State of Public Sector Cloud Computing*, May 20.

Kundra, V. (2011) *Federal Cloud Computing Strategy*, Febraury 8.

Linthicum, D. S. (2009) *Cloud Computing and SOA Convergence in Your Enterprise: A Step-by-Step Guide*, Addison-Wesley, Boston, MA, USA.

M. S. (2011) "Obbligati ad innovare," *Azienda Banca*, May, pp. 50–51.

McKinsey and Co., (2011) "The state of global banking – in search of a sustainable model," *McKinsey Annual Review on the banking industry*, http://www.mckinsey.com/clientservice/Financial_Services/Knowledge_Highlights/Recent_Reports/~/media/Reports/Financial_Services/McKGlobalBanking.ashx, September.

Menken, I. (2008) *Cloud Computing – The Complete Cornerstone Guide to Cloud Computing Best Practices Concepts, Terms, and Techniques for Successfully Planning, Implementing ... Enterprise IT Cloud Computing Technology*. Emereo Pty Ltd., Newstead, Australia.

Mille, M. (2008) *Cloud Computing: Web-Based Applications That Change the Way You Work and Collaborate Online*, Que, Indianapolis, IN, USA.

Mulholland, A., Pyke, J., and Fingar, P. (2010) *Enterprise Cloud Computing: A strategy Guide for Business and Technology Leaders*, Meghan-Kiffer Press, Tampa, FL, USA.

Nicoletti, B. (2009) "Review of "Building a Global Bank," Edited by Mauro F. Guillén and Adrian Tschoegl, *www.academici.com*, January 11.

Nicoletti, B. (2009) "Review of "Global Networks," Edited by R. J. Holton, *www.academici.com*, July 21.

Nicoletti, B. (2010) *Gli strumenti del Lean and Digitize*, FrancoAngeli, Milano, Italy.

Nicoletti, B. (2010) *La metodologia del Lean and Digitize*, FrancoAngeli, Milano, Italy.

Nicoletti, B. (2010) "Lean and digitize project management," *24th IPMA World Congress*, Istanbul, Turkey, November.

Nicoletti, B. (2011) "Applicare il Lean and Digitize nei servizi finanziari," *Bancamatica*, January/February, pp. 12–14.

Nicoletti, B. (2011) "E-Procurement e aziende di servizi," *Procurement Channel*, Gen.

Nicoletti, B. (2011) "E-Collaboration e Procurement," *Procurement Channel*, Giu., anno 9, 2: 13.

NIST (2009) *The Nist Definition of Cloud Computing*, October, http://csrc.nist.gov/ groups/SNS/cloud-computing/

Obama, B. (2009) *Memorandum for the Heads of Executive Departments and Agencies on Transparency and Open Government* http://www.whitehouse.gov/the_press_office/ Transparency_and_Open_Government/, Retrieved August 11, 2012.

O'Donovan, G. (2011) *Solvency II*, Gower Publishing, Abingdon, UK.

Open Cloud Manifesto (2009) www.opencloudmanifesto.org, Retrieved August 11, 2012.

Overby, E. (2008) "Process virtualization theory and the impact of information technology," *Organization Science*, 19 (2): 277–291, March–April.

Pajetta, G. (2011) "Cedacri 2.0," *Data Manager*, May, pp. 26–38.

Peruggini, G. (2010) "Cloud computing: la prospettiva della Banca d'Italia," *e-Government e Cloud Computing*, October 5, http://www.digitpa.gov.it/ cloud-computing-banca-d%E2%80%99italia, Retrieved August 22, 2011.

Petri, G. (2010) *Shedding Light on Cloud Computing*, October, CA Technologies, http:// www.ca.com/files/whitepapers/mpe_cloud_primer_0110_226890.pdf Retrieved July 16, 2011.

PWC (2009) *The Future of Banks. Returning stability to the banks and the banking system*, July, PricewaterhouseCoopers paper http://www.pwc.com/gx/en/ banking-capital-markets/ future-of-banking.jhtml, Retrieved August 11, 2012.

Rhoton, J. and Haukioja, R. (2011) *Cloud Computing Architected: Solution Design Handbook*, Recursive Press, p. 384.

Ristenpart, T. et al. (2009) "Hey, you, get off of my cloud: exploring information leakage in third=party computing clouds," *Proceedings of the 6th ACM conference on Computer and communications security*— CCS '09, November 9–13, Association for Computing Machinery, Chicago, IL, USA.

Salvatori, M. (2010) "La Banca al fianco degli assicuratori," *Azienda Banca*, September, pp. 28–32.

Salvi, V. (2011) *ATM and Self-Service. Tra customer experience e integrazione di canali*, BancaMatica Digital Books, Rome, Italy, http://www.bancamatica.it/digitalbooks. aspx, Retrieved August 11, 2012.

Saunders, A. et al. (2001) *Financial Markets and Institutions, a Modern Perspective*, McGraw-Hill, New York, NY, USA.

Scott Morrison, K. (2011) "Power of the people, how cloud management will transform IT," March/April, *Information Management SourceMedia Inc.*

Scotti, E. (2010) "Le soluzioni Cedacri per la Multicanalità," *Bancamatica*, March, p. 75

Smith, A. (2011) *Cloud Computing: A Briefing for the Business Analyst*, Black Circle, Canberra, Australia.

Sotola, R. (2010) "Billing in the cloud: The missing link for cloud providers," Henry Stewart Publications, *Journal of Telecommunications Management*, September 6, 3 (4): 313–320.

Sterling, D. and Kumar, P. (2011) "Dancing on a cloud: a framework for increasing business agility," *Xlibris Corp.*, Bloomington, IN, USA.

Sun Microsystems (2009) *Introduction to Cloud Computing architecture*, White Paper 1st Edition, June, http://sun.systemnews.com/membersonly?pt=%2Farticles%2F137% 2F1%2FCloudComputing%2F21938, Retrieved August 11, 2012.

Tapscott, D. (1999) "Creating value in the network economy," *A Harvard Business School Review*, Boston, MA, USA.

Trivedi, K. and Pasley, K. (2012) *Cloud Computing Security*, Cisco Press, Indianapolis, IN, USA, p. 400.

Vaquero, L. M. (2009) "A break in the clouds: towards a cloud definition," *Newsletter ACM SIGCOMM Computer Communication Review*, 39 (1), January, pp. 50–55.

Wang, L. and Von Laszewski, G. (2010) "Cloud computing: a perspective study," *New Generation Computing*, April, 28 (2), pp. 137–146.

Weinman, J. (2012) *Cloudnomics*, Wiley, Hoboken, NJ, USA, p. 400.

White Paper from Thought Leadership (2010) *Definire un framework per l'adozione del cloud*, IBM Global Technology Services, http://www05.ibm.com/it/services/cloud/definire_un_framework_per_l_adozione_del_cloud.pdf Retrieved 9/08/2011, Retrieved August 11, 2012.

Williams, B. (2012) *The Economics of Cloud Computing*, Cisco Press, Indinapolis, IN, USA.

Winkler, V. (2011) *Securing the Cloud: Cloud Computer Security Techniques and Tactics*. *Elsevier*, Waltham, MA, USA, p. 60.

Some Legal Texts

Basel International Agreements

Convention for the Protection of Individuals with regard to Automatic Processing of Personal Data, Strasbourg, January 28, 1981 (also known as ETS Convention No.108).

Directive 2004/39/EC of the European Parliament and of the Council (Markets in Financial Instruments Directive or MiFID).

Directive 2007/64/EC (Payment Services Directive or PSD).

Directive 95/46/EC, October 24, 1995 (EU Data Protection Directive).

E-Money Directive (2009/110/EC) (EMD).

International Financial Reporting Standards (IFRS).

Pub. L. 107–204, 116 Stat.745, USA, July 30, 2002 (also known as USA Sarbanes–Oxley Act).

Regulation (EC) No 1606/2002, September 14, 2002, OJ L 243 of September 11, 2002 and Regulation (EC) No 297/2008, April 10, 2008, OJ L 97 of April 9, 2008 (also called International Accounting Standard or IAS).

Solvency International Agreements.

USA Sarbanes-Oxley Act of 2002.

Websites

cloud.gigaom.com
cloudglossary.com/
cloudsecurityalliance.org/
cloudtimes.org/glossary/
ec.europa.eu/europe2020/index_it.htm
ec.europa.eu/information_society/eeurope/i2010/key_documents/index_en.htm
eur-lex.europa.eu
http://www.constellationrg.com
it.wikipedia.org/wiki/
thecloudtutorial.com
wefollow.com

www.cio.com/3024/Cloud_Computing
www.cloud.it
www.cloudave.com
www.cloudcomputeinfo.com
cloudcomputingexpo.com
cloudcomputing.sys-con
www.cloudsecurityalliance.org
www.cloudweaks.com
www.dummies.com/how-to/content/cloud-computing-glossary.html
www.forrester.com/search?N=10003&range=504001&tmtxt=cloud+computing
www.nuvola italiana.it
www.redmonk.com
www.salesforce.com
www.tothecloudguide.com
www.xaas.com
www.whitehouse.gov/omb/inforeg_agency_info_quality_links
www.whitehouse.gov/open

Blogs

Randy Bias on cloudscaling.com
Bernard Golden on cio.com
Read Write Cloud http://www.readwriteweb.com/cloud/
Guy Rosen on Jack of All Clouds
John Treadway on cloudbzz.com
James Urquhart on wisdom of clouds at cnet.com
Joe Weinmann on gigaom.com

Index